A
Loving Gentleman

THE LOVE STORY OF
WILLIAM FAULKNER
AND
META CARPENTER

by

Meta Carpenter Wilde and
Orin Borsten

Simon and Schuster · New York

All photographs not otherwise credited are part of Ms. Wilde's collection.

PUBLISHED BY SIMON AND SCHUSTER
A GULF+WESTERN COMPANY
ROCKEFELLER CENTER, 630 FIFTH AVENUE
NEW YORK, NEW YORK 10020

DESIGNED BY EVE METZ
MANUFACTURED IN THE UNITED STATES OF AMERICA

2 3 4 5 6 7 8 9 10

LIBRARY OF CONGRESS CATALOGING IN PUBLICATION DATA
WILDE, META CARPENTER.
A LOVING GENTLEMAN.
1. FAULKNER, WILLIAM, 1897–1962—RELATIONSHIP WITH
WOMEN—META CARPENTER WILDE. 2. WILDE, META CARPENTER.
I. BORSTEN, ORIN, JOINT AUTHOR. II. TITLE.
PS3511.A86Z98568   813'.5'2   [B]   76-21878

ISBN 0-671-22323-2

ACKNOWLEDGMENTS

TO NELDA DAVIS, VICTOR KILIAN, JO PAGANO, EDGAR
REBNER AND ELLA STEWART FOR FILLING IN SOME MISS-
ING PIECES; JEAN REED FOR TYPING THE MANUSCRIPT, AND
LAURA G. BORSTEN AND ARTHUR WILDE FOR THEIR PA-
TIENCE AND ENCOURAGEMENT.

*For Beulah Ussery Doherty
and Minnie Borsten—
two Southern mothers*

FOREWORD

Why this book? Above everyone, I know that William Faulkner was the most private of men and that he suffered from invasions of his fortressed self as from jagged, festering wounds of his very flesh. In these years since his death, I had never thought of writing about this gifted man whose life was so tightly laced with mine. Now it appears that I must do whatever I can while I'm alive to protect the truth and beauty of our relationship from those who stand ready to exploit it immediately upon my demise.

The comfortable delusion that my romance with Faulkner was known by only a handful of people was summarily shattered a few years ago. What had been inconsequential on the gossip scale, without the juice and tang of a bona fide Hollywood scandal in the 1930's and 1940's (Bill was hardly a celebrity in those years and I was a lowly movie-studio script girl), was becoming a genuine Hollywood folk myth as interest in Faulkner mounted throughout the world and as I continued to work on movie sets. Unknown to me, the legendry that William Faulkner was my lover had spread throughout Hollywood; actors and production crew members whispered about it from the darkened areas of sound stages on which I worked. A relatively new star could barely speak in my presence, so awed was he to be within touching distance of the woman who had known William Faulkner intimately.

Some time later, I was given evidence that a number of

film-studio writers, one or two from the group who knew us forty years ago, were only waiting until I died to turn out books about William Faulkner and his Hollywood script girl. When I recovered from numbing shock, I made the decision that there was no option left to me but to write in collaboration with a close friend my own account of my years with Bill. One cannot prevent distortions of the truth from the grave.

I can only hope that the image in these pages of William Faulkner in love, spirited and happy and fulfilled for part of the time at least, will correct the prevalent notion that he was a chill, arrogant man; and also that what I knew of him, which was more than his biographers and his family members and friends will ever know of him in that period of his life, may illuminate some small area in the splendid and matchless body of his work.

When Bill was alive, he was the great joy of my life—my lover, my friend, my spar in a raging sea, my guide from what might have been a perpetual stage of childishness to full maturity—and I am thrice blessed in the knowledge that he loved me deeply.

Because memory is cruelly sieved, a leaky business, as I have discovered, and because Bill in his letters to me rarely noted day, month, and year, some of the dates mentioned herein may not be accurate. Also, what follows may at times be out of sequence, but it is all as I remember it and as it affected me, and if I have made errors here and there in names, addresses, the titles of the film scripts on which Bill worked, the length of our separations and reunions, I comfort myself in the conviction that he would have called them "piddling."

Meta Carpenter Wilde

A singing fire that spun
The gusty tree of his desire
Till tree and gale were one; . . .

—*William Faulkner,*
A Green Bough

Part One

Chapter 1

He walked into the outer office at Twentieth Century-Fox
Studios, a small, quick man in a tweed suit that had never
fitted him, and looked at me for a long, surprised moment, as
if he had forgotten a carefully rehearsed speech or had expected to see someone else behind the desk, before he said
that he was William Faulkner and that Mr. Hawks was "kind
of expecting me."

"*The* William Faulkner?"

I had not meant to say it that way. The awe was a lapse
from the cool professionalism I tried, not always successfully,
to affect. Celebrities were literally underfoot. In the studio
commissary at lunch on any given day, one could glimpse the
likes of Will Rogers, Madeleine Carroll, Spencer Tracy,
Janet Gaynor, John Boles, Charles Farrell, Loretta Young,
Victor McLaglen and Edmund Lowe. High-salaried writers,
many of them from the New York theater, passed my desk on
their way to Howard Hawks' inner office, and only the other
day he had been paid a visit by Zoe Akins. My reaction to his
name had little enough to do with William Faulkner as a
man of letters—at that time he was chiefly known in Hollywood as the author of *Sanctuary*—but with the materializa-
tion of a girlhood image: at thirteen, trembling with excitement in my long taffeta dress, wobbling on baby Louis heels,
I had arrived in Oxford at the invitation of my aunt, Lottie

White, and my cousin, Lottie Vernon, a year older than I, to attend the 1922 Easter Ball. Someone—a relative, another excited young girl in a party dress or a stammering youth with whom I had danced to the music of the Magic City Syncopators—had spoken of William Faulkner, the town scapegrace, who wrote stories hardly suitable for the scrutiny of decent folk, rode horseback recklessly, hunted with riffraff and darkies, and didn't give one hoot for Oxford's opinion of him.

I had imagined him then to be tall, darkly handsome, with a scowling visage, and now he stood before me, an unimpressive, almost diminutive, man, whose nose was curved and pointed over a neatly trimmed moustache and whose glowing brown eyes never left my face.

"I reckon I'm the one, ma'am," Faulkner admitted. "Leastways, I don't know of any other." He cocked his head to one side to study me, then pulled back so that his chin rested magisterially on his throat. "You're from the South; I can tell by your voice."

"Mr. Faulkner, I'm not only from the South," I said, "I grew up in Mississippi."

"I declare."

"Tunica, Mississippi. In the Delta. Though I was born in Memphis."

"Well, I never." He put out his hand to me and pressed gently on my own. "I take it as an augury of something good that on my first day of reporting to a Hollywood studio I meet a fellow Southerner."

In possession of my hand and my executive manner once more, I left him long enough to announce to a mildly surprised Howard Hawks that William Faulkner was outside, and then ushered the man from Oxford into his office.

The meeting over, Faulkner stopped at my desk to say goodbye. How long had I been in Hollywood? Did I miss home? We would have to have ourselves a good, long talk "right soon." Another burning look and he was gone, walking like elderly Southern gentlemen I remembered from childhood—the lower torso thrust forward, the upper part of him leaning backward, so that he was slanted in motion, almost tilted.

I mused for a while on the improbability of two Southerners meeting in the office of a famous Hollywood film director, then went back to my typewriter. During the afternoon, Hawks advised me that William Faulkner would be working with Joel Sayre on the screenplay of *The Road to Glory*. I did not know it at the time, but it would be a second association for Hawks and Faulkner, both aviators in World War I. Faulkner had first come to Hollywood for Hawks in 1932 to work on the script of *Today We Live*, a successful film starring Joan Crawford and Gary Cooper. Although he had written the dialogue, the only screen credit extended to him was for his *Saturday Evening Post* short story, "Turn About," on which the film was based. He had also worked on a number of other screenplays, most of them originals that were ultimately consigned to the shelf of properties that would never, short of a miracle, be produced, and that would be charged off as losses. He had returned to Oxford on the expiration of his Metro-Goldwyn-Mayer contract; now, faced with crop failure on his farm and with payments due on Rowan Oak, the ante-bellum house he had bought in the first flush of book royalties, he was back. A letter to Hawks had worked. It was not an appeal but a simple declaration that his royalties were down to a trickle and that if there was any work around that he could do he would be interested in a Hollywood assignment. Because Hawks knew him to be imaginative and conscientious, and ideally suited to the project at hand by reason of his war experience, a contract was drawn.

Although I loved to dance, I passed up a chance to go to the Cocoanut Grove that evening with some of the Studio Club girls I was friendly with and the young lawyers, doctors, and other professional men who played attendance on them. There was always an extra man in need of a date and I was usually happy to fill in, hoping I had drawn a graceful partner. Instead, after dinner, I went up to my small room to write to my parents in Arizona. Would it reassure them that I had met William Faulkner, of Oxford, in the course of a day's work and that he would be writing a screenplay for my boss? My mother and father had never become wholly reconciled to my involvement with moving pictures. Moreover, they were still in shock over my divorce from Billy Carpenter, a young Southerner I had married almost as soon as I graduated and with whom I had arrived in California in the early 1930's; our separation, dictated by his aeronautical studies in Santa Maria and the necessity that I support myself with a meager-paying job at the Platt Music Company in Los Angeles, brought us sharply to the realization that we were happier apart from each other and that our marriage was a youthful mistake. Even their trip to Hollywood the year before had not allayed my parents' worries. They had suffered themselves to be taken on a tour of movie sound stages and had expressed polite interest. The Studio Club, into which I had been brought by Katherine Strueby, Preston Sturges' secretary, impressed them as a proper ambience and they found Marjorie Williams, our chaperon, a lady in the truest sense. But then I introduced them to a group of actresses and dancers, and they were concerned about me all over again. On their return to Kingman, they urged me to come home, reminding me that I would not have to work at all; that a depression was raging and that I would have been a burden did not occur to them.

I next saw William Faulkner at the studio two days later. Unsteady on his legs, maneuvering toward my desk with a rolling gait, he made a courtly bow in my direction.

"Mornin', Miss Carpenter," he said with an effort. His speech was slurred as he remarked on the beautiful weather we were having and on his pleasure to have run into someone from home, but he was not thick-tongued. Even four sheets to the wind, he was a figure of great dignity, threatened as that dignity was by imminent disruption.

Personal Secretary smiled weakly and busied herself checking off the day's duties on a memo pad.

"You do remember me, ma'am?"

"Oh, yes, Mr. Faulkner."

He leaned dangerously forward, like a circus performer whose shoes are nailed to the floor. "Miss Carpenter, will you have dinner with me tonight?"

I looked up in disbelief. He was glassy-eyed and the strong smell of alcohol was on his breath. Any moment, I thought to myself, he will fall to the floor.

"I'd be obliged," he managed to say, "if you'd pick a nice place, long as it's not fancy. I don't know restaurants in Los Angeles very well."

Stammering an excuse and flourishing papers at hand as if they were documents of the highest priority, I rushed into Howard Hawks' office, closing the door behind me and leaving William Faulkner staring bemusedly at the space I had suddenly vacated. Hawks' toneless "Miss Carpenter?" brought me to the realization of what I had done. Never before had I entered his office without knocking first or being summoned by the intercom. All in one breath, I apologized and announced that Mr. Faulkner was outside, inebriated if you please, and that he had asked me to have dinner with him. I could not possibly go out with Mr. Faulkner. Not only had he had far too much to drink, he was, I was sure I had read somewhere, a married man.

"What do you want me to do, Meta?" my employer asked patiently. He had for the most part been highly considerate toward his Southern-born secretary, naïveté intact after her four years in Hollywood, her shock threshold no higher.

"I want you to tell him, please, that I will not go out with him."

"Very well."

"It's not that I don't think he's a nice man. It's just the condition he's in. I'm not used to men who drink to excess."

"I'll tell him for you, Meta." He rose from his chair, a tall, austere man who threw out charm as though it were film in a high-powered movie projector, and who was never unaware of its potency in business or in his personal life.

"Please don't hurt his feelings, Mr. Hawks."

"The situation will be taken care of," Hawks said with a sigh for those people in the world who are unable to handle the smallest crisis. He returned a few minutes later and told me that I could safely return to my desk; Mr. Faulkner was being sent back to his hotel in a taxi by a studio guard. The incident was worth no more than an impatient sweep of his hand as he applied himself once more to working out the bets that he would place that afternoon with one of the race-track bookies to whom he gave almost as much time as to actors and writers.

Faulkner turned up the next day, bright-faced and sober. He was a little early for his appointment, he noted, and did I have any objections if he just waited here quietly until it was closer to the time for him to see Howard Hawks. No sign was given that he had been stung by yesterday's rejection or, for that matter, that he even remembered anything of his visit to the office. After commenting again on the fine weather—"though it's hotter by a good deal than what we have down home at this time of the year"—he removed a fresh white handkerchief from his left sleeve cuff, patted his forehead with it, then restored the handkerchief once more to his sleeve. Might he smoke in my presence? His hands, small but strong, packed the pipe bowl, then struck a kitchen match that ignited the tobacco. He settled back to puff happily, as though nourished by the smoke, and to regard me with a pleased detachment.

As conscious as I was of his interest in me, I still felt nothing toward William Faulkner beyond a vague sense of kinship with him as a Mississippian and sheer delight in his speech, soft and pleasant and comforting to my ears. Even his harsh pronunciation of certain words, notably those with an "ur" sound—bird, learn, urge—conjured up visions for me of judges and politicians I remembered from my parents' circle of friends as a child. My own voice must have been equally pleasing to Faulkner. He would lead me into a dialogue, then suddenly fail to respond to a question or to agree with an observation; unthinkingly, I would leap in to fill the silence, as though there were no letters to type, no calls to make to Hawks' wife, Athol, who was Norma Shearer's sister, no checks to fill in for signature. If I turned my attention back to work, Faulkner would lead me into more bursts of chatter until I found myself carrying the full burden of communication once again, his contribution having diminished to an occasional "Mmmm" of concurrence or a "Yes'm" spoken from between clenched teeth as he smoked.

Over the intercom, Hawks announced that he could see Mr. Faulkner now. My visitor hastily emptied his pipe of its contents and left me with a lingering mooncalf look. He was back, clearing his throat to announce himself, a half-hour later.

"I'd be very honored, Miss Meta, if you'd have dinner with me tonight."

If he had been anyone but William Faulkner, I would have pleaded a prior engagement. A concert for which I had tickets. A dancing date. Dinner with an old lady. But I could not bring myself to lie to this agreeable, small man whose presence was a reminder to me of my own way of life until only a few years ago.

"I'm sorry," I said, meeting his earnest brown eyes.

"Another night?"

"I'm sorry, Mr. Faulkner."

With a jaunty smile that seemed to say "So be it—for now," he bowed his head in gallant acceptance of my refusal and left the office. Well, I told myself, I've met the situation head-on. I've been forthright, no excuses, no evasions, and this should end it. There were other young women at the studio, I was certain, who would not refuse William Faulkner or any other married man. I had seen for myself at Columbia and Universal studios, where I first worked after leaving Platt's, the complete willingness of secretaries on the lot to enter into relationships with married men. Some of the Studio Club girls, too, were involved with men who were not free to marry them. More often than not, the affairs were of short duration, but I was aware that there were some arrangements that lasted for many years. The scales in a city in which women outnumbered men and in an industry that attracted a large percentage of homosexuals—there were even men who in their passion for the film art became oddly neutered by it and lost interest in sex completely—were tipped in favor of the aggressive and virile male. Obviously, William Faulkner, away from his wife, out of sight of the all-knowing burghers of Oxford, intended to have a holiday, not enforced monogamy. This was Hollywood, where it was whispered that movie queens took bartenders and headwaiters and agents as lovers, in such short supply were "studs" of their caste. But I was not yet ready to become involved with another woman's husband. What I had seen of married men on the prowl collided with a Southern puritanism that I wore like a fender.

My assessment of Faulkner was completely wrong. How was I to know—as he was later to tell me many times—that "When I stood in that door and saw you, I said to myself, 'There she is!' " What did I, newly stripped of the cotton batting in which I had been wrapped like an Egyptian mummy, know of men who read Swinburne and Keats and secretly dream of the one fair woman? What did I know of men who grow old without finding her and who, almost at the grave, still look searchingly into the eyes of passing women?

Chapter 2

A letter arrived from a Mississippi relative who had heard from my mother that I was working with William Faulkner out in Hollywood. She had met Mr. Faulkner and his wife, the former Estelle Oldham, a few years before. They had been childhood sweethearts, did I know that? Estelle had married one Cornell Franklin and had left with him to live in the Orient. Wasn't it always the way that young boys and girls fell in love during the high-school days but always married others? Why Estelle's marriage went bad, nobody seemed to know, but one day she came back to Oxford with her two children by Franklin. And wouldn't you know, William Faulkner began to court her all over again and they were married. Their first daughter, Alabama, had died shortly after she was born. To hear tell it, William Faulkner took it very hard. Now they had a darling little daughter named Jill.

The next time my fellow Mississippian reminded me that his dinner invitation was still open, I was unable to hide my irritation.

"I don't want to go out with you, Mr. Faulkner, and you know why. Please don't keep asking me."

"I'm sorry, ma'am." His face was slightly flushed but expressionless, almost as though he had prepared himself for an even stronger rebuff, but he did not drop his eyes from my steady gaze.

"As well you should be, sir." I was sounding like my own mother and suddenly not at all sure of the outrage from which I was operating.

"The very last thing I want is for you, of all people, to be put out with me."

"Just let's not discuss it, Mr. Faulkner." I broke the eye connection, unable to look a second longer into the worried brown eyes. "Let's just pretend none of this ever happened."

Bill stood there a few minutes as I typed away furiously. "Well, good day, ma'am." I continued to concentrate on the letter in the typewriter until I was certain he had gone. Now, I thought, I've wounded him, unbillowed those arrogant masculine sails, and he won't speak to me again except as a writer arriving for a conference with Howard Hawks. I was wrong. Having found me, William Faulkner had no intention of letting my unresponsiveness deter him. As he was to tell me many times, I was the girl he would surely have married if our paths had only crossed before 1929, when he had taken Estelle as his wife. He was as sure of that as he was of his hand before his face and the fingers attached to it. Wherever it might have been—Oxford, Memphis, New Orleans—he would have known instantly that I was the one for him. What an irony that he had had to come all the way from Oxford to Hollywood, where he had never been happy, to find the Southern girl with whom he would fall in love on sight. And to think that in Memphis there might have been times when we passed within a few yards of each other without meeting.

When Sally Richards dropped by to see me at the Studio Club the following Sunday, I told her of my encounters with William Faulkner. Another refugee from Memphis, she was aware of the Faulkners of Oxford and amused by the persistence of Oxford's most famous son. Sally had come to Hollywood to make a new life for herself and had fallen in love with John Crown, a brilliant pianist, who was equally in love with her. I counted them both among my closest friends and was grateful to Sally for inviting me to go with them to recitals. With them, I could talk music endlessly and feel, with sixteen years of training behind me, something of a musician myself, though not in John's virtuoso league and admittedly less accomplished than Sally.

"You don't blame me for not going out with him?" I asked.

"Oh, no, Meta," Sally assured me. "It's just that I would love to meet William Faulkner. So would John. He's read all his books, I'm sure."

"I don't see how I could arrange that without seeming to give the man encouragement."

"You stick to your guns," Sally said. "You just keep telling him no!"

On Monday, Howard Hawks called me into his office, handed me Faulkner's first pages for the screenplay of *The Road to Glory,* and asked if I could decipher the writing.

I looked at the sheets of ink-stroke script, each letter meticulously formed, like Chinese calligraphy.

"Not very well," I finally said, wondering at the erratic style of penmanship, letters sometimes connected, sometimes not, each downward stroke perfect in itself, but the whole difficult to fathom.

"If you have trouble transcribing it," Hawks said, "ask him to come in and help you get the hang of it."

"I don't think I'll have to bother Mr. Faulkner," I said, all efficiency and dispatch, and returned to my desk to puzzle out the strange handwriting, at once private and cryptic, now graspable, now unyielding. Where had he learned to write like that? By the end of the day, I had become familiar with Faulkner's difficult handwriting—the beautifully made *g*'s, the open *y*'s, the crossed *f*'s—but I could not type from the pages. Exasperated, I finally telephoned him at the Knickerbocker Hotel, where he was being allowed to work part of the time instead of in one of the small offices in the writers' building.

"Miss Carpenter?" The voice that had first sounded faltering and weary became infused with vitality. "Is it really you?"

I apologized for interrupting him at work. "But I'm having great trouble with your handwriting, Mr. Faulkner."

"Bill." The tone was insistent. "Please call me Bill."

"Bill, then."

"And may I call you Meta, which, by the way, is a very beautiful name?"

"If you wish." What was I getting into?

"Meta, everybody has trouble making out my hand. Now don't you feel bad about it, please."

I went over sentences but he was not able to fill in the words I couldn't decipher. Would he drop by the office and help me with the copy?

"Yes, ma'am, you tell me the time and I'll be there."

He sat close to me as I typed, looking over my shoulder when I came to words in which the letters were so closely positioned that they seemed to be in a foreign alphabet. "Miss Meta," Bill Faulkner said, "you'll get the sense of it by and by. Don't fret about not being able to read it."

Part of that day and the next he was at my side, helping me through work that was extremely difficult. I was not at the time a first-rate typist and I was still taking dictation from Hawks in a shorthand of my own invention. When I came to another of those maddeningly unclear words, Faulkner would come to my aid. The fault was his, not mine, he would insist. What in God's name had caused him to write that particular word that way, so that he, who had perpetrated the hickory nut of a word in the first place, couldn't himself read it right off? When I came to sections that gave me no trouble, Faulkner would solemnly turn toward the blank wall until I needed him again; it was a small, well-considered act of courtesy, an almost instinctive movement, to make himself unobtrusive as I typed away.

My response to William Faulkner began to change. Whether I wished it or not, he saw to it that a relationship was being established as we worked together. Corrections were made by glances, hearty Southernisms, the accidental touching of hands fumbling for sheets of paper, and his reminders to me that we were both from Mississippi and therefore different by upbringing and outlook from anyone else for miles around. It had been a long time since I had experienced a sense of support from another person. My need of it was great in those early years in Hollywood, when I had learned that even the attraction to the industry of its lesser members—electricians, carpenters, grips, all manner of craft workers—was voyeuristic.

That I was pretty enough, with blond hair that fell in a straight sweep to my shoulders, with a ninety-two-pound body as lean and as lithe as a ballerina's, and with a waist that was a handspan around, I knew without undue vanity. But Bill during those first days of work together made me feel uncommonly prepossessing. His intelligent brown eyes glittered in a kind of wonder and worship as he looked at me. In turn, I caught myself stealing covert glances at him. The bones in his face were fine, the cheekbones high and prominent, the chin strong and thrusting. His moustache concealed a small, sensitive mouth somewhat out of keeping with the strong facial planes. The brown springy hair was freshly barbered and the smell of the barber's talcum was still faint on the nape of his neck. Nothing in his likeness at thirty-eight suggested the face that was to overtake his young visage as he grew older—proud, hawklike, forceful, austerely handsome.

As the screenplay took shape, I realized that while he did not like the scenario form, he was, nevertheless, a writer who was incapable of doing less than his best; unlike other novelists and some playwrights who had been brought to Hollywood, he did not write down to the medium or hold with the take-the-money-and-run cynicism that was prevalent in that era. His dialogue tended to run to greater length than was the norm, but it was well-observed speech and carried the story forward with the tension required. For a novelist primarily concerned with the interior man, he had a visual sense that few of the Hollywood imports from *belles-lettres* possessed. Hawks could not photograph thoughts, Faulkner well knew, and what he gave his director was—for him—remarkably cinematic and fluid.

Between lines to be spoken—his unerring ear for human speech did not desert him in Hollywood—came descriptions and indications that he had labored over as painstakingly as he had passages in his published work. Even in the concision that was mandatory in the screen form, his facility for word portraiture was uncanny. I began to feel the presence, within touching distance, of a being in whose skull was implanted a powerful, awesome mind. Every now and then, struck by his imagery, I would look up, startled, as overwhelmed by his absolute command of language as by a Brahms theme first heard, then stare for a second, almost as if I might see behind that thoughtful forehead a faint luminosity.

Bill Faulkner continued to ask me to go out with him and I continued to refuse him, but now with a quiet "No." It became a game that could give neither of us hurt and we played our assigned parts with a leavening of humor. Had the possibility of love occurred to me, I would have summarily rejected it. Like every young woman in the 1930's, I had been conditioned by romantic novels and fantasy movies; in my case, there was also the soaring music of the classic composers, stirring visions of tall, white-clad, garlanded heroes and swooning maidens. There was yet no physical attraction for me to this soft-spoken man. I talked to Sally about him in our nightly telephone conversations—talked of little else, I expect—but even she, who knew me better than anyone, failed to guess the extent of my involuntary preoccupation with William Faulkner. I am certain that when I spoke of him to a few friends at the Studio Club, it was with an ill-concealed boastfulness, for who among them was being importuned for a few hours of her time by a novelist of great, if undeserved, notoriety? Since little was private within those walls for very long, girls who had read *Sanctuary* or had seen the screen version, titled *The Story of Temple Drake,* approached me with sly questions about him. What was he like? Did I think he was normal? Had I not better be careful with a man who had written about such a terrible sexual aberration? Did I notice a funny glint in his eye?

Then suddenly our sessions at the office came to an end. I had learned to unscramble Faulkner's handwriting and Howard Hawks decided there was no longer any need to impede the flow of his writer's daily output of dialogue. When I came to a rare word locked into the mystery of its letters, I could then call Mr. Faulkner at his hotel and he would, by its contextual place in the script, enlighten me.

Without clearly knowing it, I began at once to miss him. Afternoons seemed to stretch on interminably. Superstars came in for their appointments with Hawks, trailing effluvia of power and glamour behind them, but it was no more to me than if someone plucked from the streets had arrived. I made more than my usual percentage of typing errors in letters and reports, but not in Faulkner's pages for *The Road to Glory;* they were the Talmud, the Bible, the Koran to me, and I rarely had to erase. After lunch, I would find it difficult to attack the dictation pad and would stare longer than was my wont at motes of sunlight shafting through the window. Unaccountably restless, I began to leave the office frequently to take care of Howard Hawks' personal affairs (in most cases a telephone call would have sufficed), thinking that driving my tiny car and moving about would help me; it didn't. My state of mind persisted during an evening on the town with Studio Club girls and their young men. Although my date was young and polite and danced well enough, I was curiously abstracted, and apologized as we said good night for my inattention.

One day on the way to shop for Hawks at I. Magnin's on Hollywood Boulevard, I was hailed with "Hi, Meta" by at least five men whose recognition I could gratefully have done without. I clenched my teeth and reflected on the turn of events in my life that made me instantly known to every racetrack bookie and tout who did business with my employer.

Chapter 3

When Bill Faulkner next asked me to go out with him, his voice flat and devoid of expectation, almost as if he were an actor running lines with the first person at hand, I pushed back the demurrer that rose in my throat and answered "Yes, thank you, I would be pleased to." Drifting off to sleep a few nights before, I had revised my initial judgments. Clearly, he was no womanizer to be lumped with the common garden variety of Hollywood lecher or he would have given up on me weeks before to chase the next pretty girl. No, William Faulkner was a gentleman of incontestable probity who found himself among a breed of people with whom he could never be completely at ease. His invitations to me were no more than the reaching out of a stranger to one of his own kind, like the visitor from Rome who seeks out the Italian quarter of a city. As for my reservations about going out with a married man, Estelle Faulkner need have no qualms about me; I liked her husband, but I had no intention of taking him away from her. Perhaps I would write her a brief note: "Dear Mrs. Faulkner, I hope you won't mind that I had dinner with Mr. Faulkner last night. It was a very pleasant hour or so for me, and he seemed to enjoy talking to someone from Mississippi. If you should come to Hollywood with him in the near future, I hope that we may all get together for a quiet evening of talk. . . ."

Bill Faulkner's eyes were shining. "You would, ma'am?" he stammered. "Tonight?"

"Why, yes." Straight-faced. Composed. Sweet-tongued. As if I had not doused whole buckets of water on him every time he had asked. "It just happens that I'm free tonight."

For a moment, the man of letters was as rattled by female perversity as a gangling boy at a high-school prom. Then belief flooded his face and he smiled in purest joy, the sun-incised lines at the edges of his eyes spreading like a fan, his skin alive with a rush of blood. He was a newly handsome William Faulkner.

He called for me that night like any other hat-in-hand male with a girl friend at the Studio Club—seven dollars a week if you didn't mind sharing space with others in a dormitory arrangement, or nine if, like me, privacy was more important than clothes and cosmetics. He entered through the Spanish arches that fronted the building at the corner of Lodi and Lexington and gave his name to the telephone operator who presided at the message center at the right; at her buzz, so many shorts, so many longs, I dashed to the hallway telephone.

"Thank you," I said. "Please ask Mr. Faulkner to take a seat in the drawing room and I'll be right down."

With much younger men, he waited self-consciously, wetting his lips, crossing and recrossing his legs, liberating his neck from his shirt collar in a twisting upward movement, in the vast high-ceilinged room with its high windows, proud old chandeliers, a shallow stage where we presented plays to Mary Pickford and other movie stars who contributed to the club's upkeep, a huge fireplace where logs burned and popped shards of fire onto the worn rug in the winter, enough couches, chairs, and tables for three hotel lobbies, and a Steinway grand piano. The girls ran down the stairway one by one, laughing, pulling on their gloves, holding on to floppy hats, and claimed their dates. Bill was looking at old volumes in the glass-covered bookcase when I called his name; he spun around, stammering "Meta," and held out a single gardenia to me. I pinned it to my dress, slipped a gloved hand under his arm, and our first evening together began.

"Miss Meta," Bill explained, "I walked over here from the hotel thinking we could get a taxi from here. I wonder if your switchboard lady would . . ."

"Bill, we can use my car," I insisted. "It's a ramshackle one, but it will get us where we want to go."

He manfully took the driver's seat and fumbled with choke, stick shift and gears.

"I hate driving," he confessed. "Hate it worse than poison."

"But you fly planes!" I was genuinely puzzled.

"Up there it's all sky and no fool drivers in a hurry."

"If you like, I'll drive us."

"That would ease my mind some this first time. I don't want to kill us both in the traffic we'll be getting into."

We changed seats and I drove to Musso & Frank's restaurant on Hollywood Boulevard, where Bill had made reservations. Most of the money he earned for his work on *The Road to Glory* was deposited every week in a bank in Oxford, but tonight, he told me, the sky was the limit. Knowledgeable about wines, he ordered a white wine of good vintage and recommended that I try a glass. Today, forty years later, I still drink white wine at dinner. We looked around the restaurant with its parquetry and murals, we smiled at each other shyly in the way of a man and a woman who know too little of each other, and clinked our glasses together.

Bill had been light-hearted and boyishly engaging on the drive from the Studio Club, but now, as the waiter hovered over us, an uncommon solemnity came over him. The smile he gave me was polite but strained. He had little to say. I was to see him slip abruptly into that paralyzing gloom again and again during the period when he was working on *The Road to Glory,* and I was not to understand it until he finally confided that he had lost his younger brother in November. Dean Faulkner was piloting Bill's own Waco plane when he crashed.

"I grounded Dean," Bill said bitterly. "I told him not to fly."

In his imagination, he had reconstructed the death scene down to the last graphic detail, and it would leap into his mind at odd times during the day with the force of guilt.

But on our first night together, I did not know that he was haunted by the death of his brother and concerned for the young widow, who was in her seventh month of pregnancy, and his silence made me uneasy. Years before, I had been taught that the well-brought-up Southern girl, finding herself in the company of a noncommunicative gentleman, should gaze at him with an interest so compelling that anything short of his recitation of all the facts of his fascinating existence, nothing omitted, would seem a deprivation from which she would surely perish. The importance of drawing out a diffident male with carefully phrased questions, should the pantomime of active eyelashes and gently heaving bosom fail, had also been impressed upon me at that long-ago time (and promptly forgotten until this moment). I smiled at Bill across the table and studied the menu and could not bring myself to ask any of the questions that came rushing into my mind. Something about his reserve, the quality of it that was like the immurement of a troubled animal, the palpable interiority of it, told me not to require him to answer my questions—then and for all our years together and even in the time when we would be able to acknowledge our love.

"You've evidently been to Musso's before, you know the menu so well," I commented. "What do you recommend?"

"I set great store by their Cassoulet Toulousin." Bill smiled.

"Whatever it is, I'll have it."

Bill studied me wordlessly. Finally, "Tell me about yourself, Miss Meta."

"I wouldn't know where to start."

"How did anyone like you ever come to work in a Hollywood movie studio?"

Glad for his cue and relieved that the conversational vacuum would be filled, at least until the waiter brought our food, I talked about leaving the Platt Music Company for a job that had opened up in Columbia Studio's casting department when Mozelle Britton married Alan Dinehart, a stage and screen star. Mozelle and Katherine Strueby, both Studio Club girls, helped me convince Dan Kelly that I had the qualifications. A brief period followed at Universal Studios in the production office of Buck Jones, the cowboy star, and I was then hired by Howard Hawks to replace his pregnant secretary. When Hawks decided that he could not on the meager budget of $750,000 proposed by Universal executives produce and direct *Sutter's Gold,* a property he had been preparing with Gene Fowler as the screenplay writer, he moved on, I with him, to Samuel Goldwyn Studios to begin preproduction on *Barbary Coast.* Miriam Hopkins, the Southern-born actress who had starred as Temple Drake in the screen version of Faulkner's *Sanctuary,* and Edward G. Robinson were the stars. And Walter Brennan had his first screen role of any substance. Hawks valued me for my crisp efficiency and a willingness that compensated for my meager skills. My shorthand, a mix of incomplete night-school Gregg and arcane symbols, sufficed only because my employer dictated slowly, weighing each word to achieve the concision of thought on which he prided himself. I had only recently attained a degree of proficiency as a typist. When I wasn't being the magnolia-voiced, competent Miss Carpenter at my desk, I was major-domo to Hawks, superintending the moving of his office furniture and files (he was one of the first freelance directors) from studio to studio; seeing to it that his race horses were stabled, fed, and shipped to the proper tracks; helping Athol Hawks with sundry matters at their home; paying household and office and grocery bills (Hawks did not always remember the latter) ; uncomplainingly driving Hawks' two children on a Saturday morning, when I longed to sleep late or practice on the Studio Club piano, to Pasadena for a weekend with their grandparents; and generally relieving him of tiresome tasks that he delegated to me.

As I talked between bites of food, I realized that I was

being listened to with great absorption. It was one of Bill's graces that while he would wall himself off rudely from people he did not like, he gave himself as a listener, no matter who the speaker—savant or servant, the most ordinary of men along with the great thinkers of his time. Listening for him became a connection, a link, that bound him to the other.

"Is the cassoulet to your liking?" he finally asked.

"I'm enjoying it thoroughly," I admitted.

"That's good, hon'." It was the first time he had used that Southern endearment and he waited for my blush. Then, "Do you like seeing other people eat?"

"Why, yes, don't you?"

"Not 'specially."

"No?" I stopped chewing, afraid to swallow another bite and equally afraid of choking.

"People," said Bill, "should eat in the privacy of their rooms."

"But why?"

"There is something about human mastication that's downright unattractive."

"I take issue with you on that," I countered, breaking what I remembered to be a cardinal rule in my early education against the faintest disagreement with one's gentleman friend.

"Don't I repel you with my chewing?"

"No. Do I you?"

"Well, no, not a pretty thing like you."

"I find that most people are very attractive when they're eating," I said boldly. "When people eat, they're free and natural and happy."

"I've seen—and I expect you have too, ma'am—some mighty poor tables set down South for some folks." He cocked his head to the side and waited for my concurrence. "Hardly enough to keep the body stoked for the next day in the field."

"I still like watching people eat."

"The chawin', the greedy gobblin', the switchin' of tough

35

meat from one side of the face to the other, the swallowin', the boltin' down—all that?" He was being one of his own characters, born or unborn I knew not, and he acted it with leg-slapping humor, watching my face for its grin as he would watch the slack-jawed visages of a conclave of rednecks on the tin-roofed porch of a rural store, ready to guffaw with them and then to gather the spittle in his mouth for a mighty discharge of liquidy tobacco or snuff juice for emphasis. I laughed at the mimicry and he laughed with me.

He pushed aside his plate, a third of the food on it untouched, and wanted to know if I was happy.

"Happy?"

"With living out here, with your life, with your job."

"I'd rather be in the music world."

"Why aren't you?" Head cocked to one side. A father or older brother from back home come to reason with a rebellious city daughter or sister.

"I'm not good enough to be a concert pianist."

"Surely there are other ways to go in music."

"I played for a radio station in Memphis once," I mused. "In New Orleans, I was a pianist and accompanied singers on WCBE. And you know what? I was also one of the first women announcers on the station."

"You should be doing what you love, Meta."

"I guess I lost my way. I married and it wasn't what I expected of marriage and we came to California . . ."

Bill nodded his head understandingly. I busied myself with the white beans of the cassoulet and he did not ask me to go on.

"I'm reasonably happy working with Howard Hawks," I finally said. "He always treats me with respect. Besides, my job with him allows me to travel in style and with movie companies paying my expenses."

"That must be the best way, ma'am."

I told him of going to New York with Hawks to work with Ben Hecht and Charles MacArthur on the script of *Barbary Coast*. I had been ensconced in a suite, living room and bedroom, at the St. Moritz Hotel, where for five months I lived luxuriously. The living room became a workroom by day when Hawks, MacArthur, and Hecht would dictate to me. As I remembered that first trip to New York, I censored from my account a flirtation with Maurice Chevalier that had begun on *The Chief* when, sitting alone at a dining-car table—I did not want to take my meals with Hawks or Gene Fowler, who was writing another screenplay for him—I exchanged glances with the French star at a nearby table. The interest in his eyes was unmistakable and I looked away quickly. The next day, Chevalier prevailed upon Hawks to introduce us, and for the rest of the time on *The Chief* and on the *Twentieth-Century* out of Chicago, we had cocktails and dinner together, he amused at my Memphis finishing-school French, my naïveté, and, I feel certain, my fluster on the last night out when he suggested that I join him in his compartment and I pleaded *mal de tête* or some seizure equally unconducive to a night of love aboard a train. In New York, Chevalier found out where I was staying and invited me for cocktails at the Ritz. Dazzled all over again by his Gallic presence, the crooked smile, the jutting underlip, and the splendid celebrity that he was careful to wear casually but that I saw enameled over him like a glossy paint job, I debated with myself for a fast delaying minute, then sweetly declined dinner and its consequences. It was not that I would not have enjoyed whatever might have happened, but that I was overwhelmed and could find no coping grace within myself. The next day, Chevalier sent a dozen roses with a card inscribed *"Bonne chance,* Maurice." Edited out from the adventures of Meta Carpenter in the big city, too, was an incident with Gene Fowler, who, thinking it would be pleasant to have a little affair with Hawks' secretary, arrived at the St. Moritz suite to help me transcribe dictation I had taken from him on *The Chief.* He ordered a dozen martinis brought up, drank them all himself when I refused to join him, and at the end of the afternoon became abusive when I showed no interest in letting him lead me into the bedroom.

New York held a heady excitement for me. I went to see *Lohengrin* and *Carmen* at the Metropolitan Opera House, bought tickets to concerts and recitals at Town Hall and Carnegie Hall, and saw my first Broadway plays. I told Bill about weekends at Nyack, New York, taking dictation from Charles MacArthur, and being made comfortable by Helen Hayes in that quiet, unostentatious, beautiful house. (Years later, Helen and I became friendly when we worked together on *My Son John* at Paramount.)

For five months, I took down the dialogue and plot turns that Hecht and MacArthur dictated in rapid-fire fashion, MacArthur lying on the floor, feet on the couch, as he topped Hecht or was eclipsed by his collaborator with brilliant speeches, sight gags, and dramatic invention. In the last weeks, they took off the jester's bells and gave us a tight, well-constructed script, though I knew by then that Howard Hawks never filmed a screenplay as written.

"But you know that, don't you, Bill?" I asked. "And if you don't, you should."

"I don't look for anything I do in Hollywood to be used and I don't much care." He shrugged. "I'm a book-writin' man, not a scenarist."

"When I worked as script girl on *Barbary Coast*," I said, "I saw how Mr. Hawks took ideas from everyone on the set and changed almost every page."

"You were script girl on that?"

"Along with being a secretary," I said proudly. "Mr. Hawks asked if I could do both and I said yes. Besides, my salary jumped from thirty-five dollars a week to forty-two fifty and that made life considerably easier."

"Howard saved money on you doing double duty."

"Yes, but he made allowances for my mistakes and he had his own cutter, Eddie Curtis, work six weeks training me."

"Will you be on *The Road to Glory?*" Bill wanted to know.

"Yes. There was someone else on *Ceiling Zero* at Warners', but now I'll be back holding script on your picture."

"Howard's picture," Bill corrected me, "not mine."

"Perhaps we'll see each other on the set."

"Lord, no, hon', I'll be long gone from Hollywood by then. I'll be back in Oxford."

We walked along Hollywood Boulevard, peering into store windows, listening to newspaper hawkers in full cry on street corners. Grauman's Chinese and Egyptian theaters were disgorging patrons, and other moviegoers were queued up waiting to replace them. Everywhere people hurried or milled about. The Hollywood and Roosevelt hotels were great islands of light. Streetcars that would take passengers to downtown Los Angeles clanged by. In that day, when the boulevard was Main Street for members of the motion-picture and radio industries, one could occasionally glimpse a Barrymore, Joan Crawford, Constance Bennett, Carole Lombard, Ruth Chatterton, Robert Montgomery or almost any star out for an evening. While it would never be anything more than an overgrown small-town thoroughfare, tacky, dinky, funky, bland, it became on premiere nights a grandiose street of sweeping searchlights, chauffeured limousines, men in tuxedos and women in gowns by Adrian and Irene emerging from cars, and fans screaming hysterically in the bleachers as they recognized stars. The next morning, it would be its characterless, unprepossessing self, a commonplace broad slash through a commonplace area known as Hollywood.

Bill took my arm as we crossed the boulevard. Although I had worn my low heels out of consideration for the difference in height between us, I was still taller by almost an inch. We came to Larry Edmunds' bookshop, not wholly stocked then as it is today with movie memorabilia and books on film. Did I mind going in with him, Bill wanted to know, or was I one of those people who were not attracted to bright book covers, the smell of printer's ink, and the very heft of the volume itself. Inside, he asked the clerk if he had a copy of *A Green Bough,* a volume of poetry by Faulkner.

"Faulkner," the clerk repeated, squeezing his forehead into washboard lines puzzledly. "Faulkner?"

"William Faulkner," Bill added, clearing his throat. "You must have certainly stocked his novels—*The Sound and the Fury, Light in August, Sartoris* . . ."

"And *Sanctuary*," the clerk remembered. "I'll see if we have the book." He returned a moment later with a copy that delighted Bill with its pristine dust wrapper. After paying for it, he opened the book and wrote his name and the date on the flyleaf.

"I hear"—Bill grinned as he made his hieroglyphs—"that Mr. Faulkner doesn't pay any mind to the reviewers who don't think he's any great shakes as a poet. He just goes on versifying, poor fellow." He put the book in my hands. "For you, Miss Meta."

Turning back to the clerk, he asked if the store had any of Mr. Faulkner's novels or short-story collections on the shelves. The answer was a bored no. Faulkner did not sell well and there had been no reorders on his last book, *Pylon*, after the initial small order had been sold. There were occasional calls for some of the earlier books, but they were out of print, unavailable from the warehouse or the publishers.

"Mmmmmm." Bill sighed. "Mr. Faulkner must be doing poorly—all his books out of print."

In front of the Studio Club, he held my hand firmly and asked if he might have the pleasure of my company again.

"Of course, Bill."

"Tomorrow night?"

"All right."

"Same time?"

"Fine."

"I'll call for you at seven-thirty then."

Other girls were getting out of cars and hurrying into the building. I withdrew my hand from Bill's, suddenly aware of the electricity that surged from him and the heat of his skin. "Thanks for a lovely dinner and thanks especially for the book. Good night now."

"Good night, m' honey."

William Faulkner, of Oxford, Mississippi, creator of Yoknapatawpha County, author of a handful of books that would one day stand as beacon lights in Southern literature, walked out of the light thrown from the entryway and headed for his hotel, taking Lexington to Vine Street, then walking the two and a half miles north to Ivar Street to save taxicab fare.

In my room, fighting sleep and the numbing effect of unaccustomed wine, I finished *A Green Bough*, struggling page after page, where I would not have in music, to find precise or approximate meaning. Bill's imagery swept through me like great shocks of light . . . *"memories that swim between the walls"* . . . *"startled pigeons, like a wind beginning,/Fill the air with sucking silver sound."* . . . *"His brain floats like a moon behind his eyes . . ."* What did I really know of him? Which was the real Faulkner, the quiet, courteous Southerner with whom I had spent four hours or the wild, trumpeting poet of the book that I held in hands that were going boneless from need of sleep, his demons glowering behind him in the darkness? Suddenly I wanted him to be the only man who opened doors for me, pulled out chairs and paid me compliments. Sleep overtook me and I dreamed of William Faulkner in an airman's helmet flying low in a warplane over a foreign land, and of great caves open to the sea and the howling wind, and of my own hands—not those of the woman in Bill's poem—moving thunderously over a piano keyboard.

Chapter 4

Driving to work the next morning, I defended myself for having agreed to a second dinner date with Bill, and so close on the heels of the first. Why not? Even with his way of falling silent, he was, on balance, one of the most interesting men I had ever met and a relief after all the shallow Hollywood rakes I had come across. He was every inch my mother's definition of a true Southern gentleman, undeviatingly gallant where women were concerned. He had not suggested that I go to his hotel room, he had not put his hands on my body, he had not attempted to kiss me on saying good night but had thanked me for my company. Moreover, it was natural, I told myself, that I should go out with him. Weren't we both working for Howard Hawks on a movie and wouldn't we continue to be thrown together in the course of the screenplay development? Actually, we had talked briefly of *The Road to Glory* at dinner last night; tonight we might discuss it at greater length as a carry-over from the workday. It was all perfectly respectable, two co-workers, so to speak, having dinner after hours, being friendly and helpful. As for Bill being a married man, it no longer seemed terribly important to me since I was determined not to let anything happen between us. If he should forget himself, I was confident that with one word from me, one look of reproof, he would retreat at once, apologetic, covered with embarrassment. I knew my Southern gentlemen and the measure of their chivalry. He had asked me to dinner a second time and I had accepted. He was a man who did honor to my parents' state, the state in which I had spent a part of my youth. How could I have refused him? Here I was, a mere Hollywood secretary and slightly less-than-lowly script girl, valued by a writer whose books both pleased and enraged book reviewers—even if his books were out of print!

While I would cheerfully at the time have exchanged my job for one that allowed me to work with musicians or composers, I had to admit to myself that I was meeting people through the movie industry whom I would never have come to know otherwise. During the filming of *Ceiling Zero,* I had flown over Los Angeles in a Stimson with Amelia Earhart and Paul Mantz, the famous stunt flier who was to lose his life in a crash some thirty years later. Amelia, a pleasant woman, tweedy, baggy, given to a mannish stride in her wide-toed shoes, was a technical adviser on the aviation film, and Commander Frank Spigge Wead had helped the screenwriters with their script. While in New York, working with Howard Hawks in his Waldorf Towers suite, I had been introduced to Fannie Brice, Josh Logan, Nedda Harrigan, Tallulah Bankhead, she a whirlwind rushing in and out. And now I had been thrown in with William Faulkner!

That second night, as we were shown to our table at LaRue's on Sunset Strip, I was as close to being beautiful as I would ever be. Men—and women, too—turned to stare at me as I passed. Bill, alert to even the darting of an eye, proudly held out my chair for me. He examined the wine list with excitement. Bill had lived in Paris and New Orleans and New York, and he knew good wines. Now he bent forward, reading the wines as though they were the names of old friends whom he had all but forgotten. There was a gasp of surprise from him as he came to a particular vintage of Pontet-Canet, one of his favorite wines, the price a steep eight dollars for the bottle. Bill drew a deep breath and ordered it, then thumped an open palm twice on the table to express boyish pleasure. He would not have splurged on expensive wine dining alone. The desperate need for money to pay accumulated bills and put the farm on a paying basis drummed at his mind at that time like a disorder of the blood. Without me, he would have lived on soup and sandwiches in order to send home most of what he earned. Except for some drinking with writer friends and a dinner invitation or two that he could not avoid, he would have kept to his hotel room and worked on *Absalom, Absalom!* once he had finished his quota of screenplay pages for the day, using solitude and self-denial as fuel for the great furnace out of which his books came. Now, because I had come into his life, he kept back enough of his weekly check to cover the cost of our dinners together. He could not manage more than that because of bill collectors hounding him, notes to be met, many people to feed and clothe, a mother to support, and taxes to be paid, even though that weekly check was for approximately $750, a fortune in those days.

The Pontet-Canet was as Bill remembered it, the food superb. He was happy and expansive. Older and Wiser Man entertaining Unworldly Young Lady. Even if the ambience was for him pretentious, artificial, the stagecraft transparent, he endured oversolicitous waiters and self-conscious diners at other tables to give me a memorable evening. Over dinner, he told his favorite Mississippi stories, falling into dialect, rolling his eyes, making ladies' gestures with his masculine, vein-corded hands, becoming the personae of the anecdote, all not so much with the skill of an actor as with the recall of a born observer. My laughter encouraged him. He chuckled with me over the bullheadedness and the folly of Oxfordians and country folk and rural blacks. LaRue's made an unlikely setting—the shining silver, the china, the gleaming linen, the expensive clothes of its patrons—for tales about dirt farmers, Memphis whores, termagants, bootleggers and ruffians.

He had not yet spoken to me about his wife, Estelle, or his daughter, Jill, or his brothers or any other members of his family. But their names came up in his yarns. They had witnessed some priceless happening; they could substantiate the truth of this story or that story. There were references to Mammy, the black woman who had raised him and who now worked for him at Rowan Oak; to Phil Stone, who had first encouraged him to write and had paid for the publication of his first book of poems; to boyhood friends; to Oxfordians whose names I had never heard.

The check was staggering for a man who had to watch his money. I looked away as he paid it and the waiter brought change. On the Sunset Strip, we linked arms and agreed that a walk was in order after all the rich food. In that day, the Strip was the street of motion-picture agents and there were elegant shops and night clubs and small restaurants. A breathtaking view of Los Angeles, all glittering barnacles of light fastened to a black sky, was to be had at a point near the famous Trocadero, where the hill dropped sheerly to the street below. We watched a pinpoint of light move among the stars and metamorphose into a silver passenger plane.

"I wish," said Bill, following its course with a covetous eye, "that I could rent me a plane someday soon and take you for a ride up there."

"I'd like that."

"Not afraid of planes?"

"Not at all," I said. "In fact, I flew a World War I Jenny in Memphis."

"You fly, ma'am?" He looked at me incredulously.

"I did in Memphis. I gave it up when I left home though."

"I should have known that about you."

"That I fly?"

"That you fly, that you ride . . . You do, don't you?"

"Yes."

"And you hunt?"

"Except that I don't like killing living things."

"There. I should have known that day I first saw you sitting at your desk that you were not only beautiful and fine, but that we were alike. I should have known from the start."

I stared at him for an instant, observing the rueful set of

his earnest face, the look of a man who is seeing all that he might have had, then quickly drew him back to his love of flying. He talked easily about his own training as a flier with the Canadian Royal Air Force during World War I and of the combat missions he had flown overseas.

"When I crashed," he said, "I thought I'd never fly again."

"Oh, Bill." I broke stride and we stopped near the entrance to the Trocadero, whose dance music spilled into the street as doors opened to receive men and women dressed in the expensive fashions of the day. "You crashed?"

"Flying a mission in France."

I put my hand on his sleeve and we stood looking at each other as cars streaked by. "Were you badly injured?"

"There's a silver plate in my skull." He tapped his head over an ear and grinned. "The sterling in my head is worth more than I am down at the Oxford bank."

That night and for long years after, I believed that William Faulkner had been shot down out of the skies over the French countryside. I had no reason to doubt it until some time after his death when I learned that Bill had never been sent overseas from Canada and therefore could not have been shot down in a plane. Faulkner had told the "shot down" story to many people. It was not true, however, and he had refused to elaborate on it when newsmen who knew of the claim questioned him during interviews. It was an inconsistency in the life of a man otherwise given wholly to truth, the utterance of which sometimes hurt those around him.

Why had Bill told me, of all people, an untruth? More importantly, why in all our years together, when we were as close as a man and a woman could be, nothing concealed from each other, had he not let me know that it was a lie?

I believe now that Bill created his romantic fall to earth from the pleasant skies of France out of frustration at being deprived of active overseas duty by the sudden end of World War I. He had come to accept his fiction as real somewhere in the labyrinth of the mind where fantasy can survive. Everything else he invented went into his books, a whole county peopled with outsize characters, but this he would keep for himself. In time, it became truth to him, as I was to know soon enough. I still think of Bill spinning down out of the heavens in a World War I plane, flames shooting from the tail. The fiction persists for me as fact.

Before the second evening was over, Bill had not only claimed me for the next night, but for Saturday and Sunday as well. We were seeing each other two and three times a week when he told me that it was not enough; when I pleaded weariness or letters to be answered from my parents and my Aunt Ione, he complained that he was unable to concentrate on his novel or did not know what to do with himself in my absence.

"I have to see you every night," he insisted, his face pale and earnest. "It's everything to me that when I wake in the morning, I know you'll be there at the end of the day."

"Every night?" I was flattered, but his demand frightened me. What would I be getting into?

"You save my damned life out here, Meta. I swear you do. You keep me alive and sane."

"Oh, Bill, do I really?"

"I know that right now I'm a married man," Bill said. "I know I'm piss poor, pardon me for putting it that way, and that I can't give you anything. But if I'm not to see you every night, I may as well go home and let Howard get himself somebody else to work with Joel Sayre."

"No, you mustn't," I argued. "You need the money."

"I know that, I know that, damn it."

"And *The Road to Glory* will be a good screen credit. You'll get more scripts to do."

"If I never do another one until I'm old and bent and gray, it will be too soon." He held my hand in the vise of his own. "Meta, don't you feel just a little bit the way I do? When you're away from me, don't I cross your mind, don't you say you wish you were with ol' Bill tonight instead of doing laundry or talking to those Studio Club females or whatever?"

I laughed and he took it as assent, and it was.

After that he never had to ask if I would see him. It was a fact of our mutual existence that we would be together the next day or night. Parting in front of the Studio Club, we would fix a time at which he would call for me, walking to the club down Vine Street, past the radio stations and the Hollywood Ranch Market, or I would pick him up in front of his hotel—a neat, compact man in tweeds, jacket pocket bulging with pipe and tobacco pouch, straining his eyes anxiously toward Hollywood Boulevard for the sight of my small automobile. There were long drives to the beach on weekends. Bill would take the wheel when traffic thinned out and negotiate the long curves with steady hand and intent eye. Sometimes he sang the church songs of the South in a high, joyous voice; again, he would recite Swinburne and A. E. Housman to me, long, memorized stanzas, and when he was done, he would lean back against the car seat and comment, "That was some man."

Other times on our drives he spoke not a single word and there would be only the tinny grind of the motor and the singing of tires over pavements and the soft puff of his breath on his pipe. Gradually, I learned silence from him as I had earlier learned speech from my parents and music from my instructors. Silence was the surface of a country pond; broken momentarily by the dip of a dragonfly's wing or the plop of a stone tossed by a boy, it would recover from its agitation and settle back into stillness. Bill's silence and my own, as I mastered the nonverbal, became a ritual that bound us together. I had only to glance at him, bringing him back from his other worlds, to know whether he was thinking of Estelle and Jill back in Oxford or of a turn of a story or of a phrase that would bring a character into instant resolution. There were moments—looks, glances, smiles—that no spoken words could have given us. I would put my hand down on the car seat between us and he would cover it protectively with his own. I would incline toward him and be rewarded with a look of such contentment that my heart would rise in my breast.

I was falling in love with Bill. When I was not with him, he took full possession of my thoughts. I began to dream of him and toss restlessly, feeling the power of his eyes, heavy with melancholy, fixed upon me. Nothing in my limited experience had prepared me for an emotional involvement with William Faulkner, ten years older, my superior in intellect and reason, granite strong, but as unpredictable—to me—as a leaf in the wind.

But then, I asked myself, when had I been secure in a relationship with a man? My young husband had been a boyman and I had come to the marriage bed with the belief, passed on by older Southern women, that sex belonged to the dark side of life, not to be spoken of by a gentlewoman to her husband, but to be stoically endured for the issue of sons and daughters. I had come out of that brief and unreal union as though sewn into my bridal gown before the marriage ceremony. The men I had gone out with more than once in Hollywood had thought of me as nothing more than fair game for them, and had not thought of me again when it turned out I wasn't.

If Howard Hawks knew that William Faulkner and I were always together after office hours, he gave no indication of it. He genuinely liked Bill and the image that Bill presented, almost a reflection of himself. They were both more British than American in their reserve and in the careful distance they placed between themselves and everyone except the few people with whom they were intimately joined. One did not give Bill Faulkner or Howard Hawks a Rotarian slap on the back. Nobody told them ribald jokes. Each presented an almost interchangeable passive face, eyebrows slightly raised in warning, nostrils flaring, to vulgarians and loudmouths. They were moated men, closed off unto themselves.

One night, from holding the door bolted on his personal life, Bill finally began to talk of his daughter. Photographs were brought out. Jill with laughing eyes in a party dress. Jill in a bathing suit at the edge of a pond. Jill in Mammy's arms. Jill on horseback.

49

I was in uncharted territory, the piece of land in which his life apart from me had been contained, and I picked my way tremblingly through its spines and brambles before I spoke. With any other man, I would not have been afraid to ask questions, volleys of them, but not with Bill. From the beginning, I knew somehow that I had to be incurious. The insularity that he drew over himself like a second, tougher skin put him beyond common query. What enabled me to see the circles that this complex man drew around himself? I was able to sense recoil, the whole process that would be animated by the slightest assault upon his outer defenses, and yet I had not come into much wisdom about even the most transparent of people. Was it the love for him that grew within me, a whole vine of love, pushing its tendrils through my entire being? I know only that I would not let myself pry into his life or his work. Whatever small fragments of information he would tithe to me, that I would make do on.

Years later, thinking of Bill, needing his calming strength in a dark time of my life, I wondered what would have happened to us in those first weeks had I been unwilling to accept his terms of limitation, terms that he did not announce but that were there all the same. It was Bill who had come slamming into my life, not I into his. The advantage was mine. I could have demanded complete revelation between us from the first and damn his reluctance to talk about his wife, his daughter, his mother, his brothers, his friends, other women, if there were any. Had he known from the moment he saw me, by some intuition that matched my own about him, that I would never probe into the secret parts of his life? Did my voice, the set of my head, my back straight in the lady posture I had been taught, tell him that I would pose no danger to him, that he was safe with me, that I was incapable of guile?

I studied Jill's small face in the photographs, searching for a resemblance to Bill, looking to Bill and back again.

"She's a beautiful child," I finally said. And she was.

"Yes." The brown eyes glittered pride and love. "She is one very special little gal."

"I see you in her."

"Young'uns never favor you all that much." He put the photographs back into his wallet. "I wish you two could know each other."

"I wish it, too, Bill."

"She'd take to you, m'honey. She'd just naturally love you."

"And I know I'd love her, Bill." What was he trying to tell me? Jill was in Mississippi, with Estelle. Was he thinking of sending for the child?

He was thoughtful for a moment, perhaps putting the two of us together in fancy, sending us across a greensward hand in hand.

"Jill," he said solemnly, "is very precious to me. I think about her day and night. I worry about her."

"I'm sure she's—" I stopped myself, for Bill had not really addressed the confidence so much to me as to himself. His face, half averted, was strained and white. "I want, more than anything," he went on, "for Jill to be well and safe. I want her to grow up to be a fine young woman and a happy one."

"I'm sure she will. With you as her father, how can she help it?"

He groaned and worked his conjoined hands together as if he intended to break his ten fingers. "When I'm away, as I am now, I cannot protect Jill. I am powerless." He looked at me and saw only bafflement. "In my place there, where I should be, guarding her, there is nobody. Do you have any idea what I'm trying to tell you?"

"No." I glanced down at the wrestling hands and up again at his face, and, paradoxically, I wanted to shrink from whatever he was going to reveal, to make myself small and still and invisible.

"I worry, even with Mammy around, that something will happen to Jill when Estelle goes on one of her drinking binges. I worry that she will set the house on fire with her cigarettes and matches. I worry that she will do something terrible and catastrophic in her drunkenness."

I remained quiet, afraid to move, hearing my own breath

come and go under his own, harsh and rasping.

" 'Course I worry about Estelle's two children, too, since they are my responsibility now and not that of Cornell Franklin. They are nice children, good children, and I am very devoted to them."

"It wouldn't be like you not to be."

"What the hell am I doing, loading all this on you, m' honey?"

"Maybe because . . . because there has to be some openness between us." He shot me, almost as a reflex, a look of pure fury, but I would not be weakened. "I've never asked. I've left it to you."

He seemed to turn it over in his mind, examine it from all sides, then he called my name and pulled me around to him so that his eyes, abnormally bright, were level with mine. "Listen to me. You have to know this. When Jill was born, from that time on, Estelle and I have not had anything to do with each other as man and woman. Soon as she could, she moved upstairs at Rowan Oak to a room of her own. I swear to you, Meta, we have not had male-female sex since then. Estelle goes to her bed at night, I go to mine. You hear me, ma'am?"

The shock of what he was saying robbed me of speech.

"We are Mr. and Mrs. William Faulkner, and that is all, ma'am." He closed the glaring eyes for a moment. "It is hard on a man like me to be without a woman that way. A woman should be able to understand that as well as another man."

"Yes." It required a response beyond a nod.

"I know whores. I wrote *Sanctuary* out of what whores in Memphis told me. They were friends, but I don't bed down with whores. Not here, not in Oxford, not anywhere."

He had come swiftly to the end of it and he breathed heavily, like a man who had run one lap beyond his powers, and then he got out of the car and opened the door for me.

"Well, now you know."

I wanted to hold and comfort him, feel him slump in the harbor of my arms. "I'm sorry, Bill."

"It's God's truth I've told you."

"I'm sure of that."

He rubbed his forehead as if to press out of it a troubling image. "Pick me up tomorrow, same time?" The voice flat, almost inaudible.

"Seven. Yes."

What sleep came to me that night was shallow and fitful. A door had opened on the dark, airless, hidden part of William Faulkner's life, and while I had wanted it to be ajar, I was not prepared for the nature of his revelation or for the wrenching cost of it to him. Rage and self-pity and confession were alien to him. He was not a man to heap his troubles upon the backs of others; his family members, his friends, and sometimes strangers, drawn to him for his boulderlike strength, brought their woes and incapacities to him, and Bill bore them without complaint, never questioning the rights of others to hang new weights upon him. The people who depended upon his head-of-the-house solidity, adults and children alike, rode upon his sturdy small frame like wiry acrobats, legs encircled around the broad back of the strong man in a vaudeville turn. The men in Faulkner's novels were patient and stolid, as was Bill himself; they choked back the outcries that were born in their throats, kept their private agonies stoppered with self-containment.

I rolled from side to side in my bed, seeking deeper levels of sleep, like a mole digging fretfully in the earth. Was Bill sleeping in his lonely hotel room? I did not think so. The effort required to open himself up to another human being, especially to me, would have stunned him out of sleep. He would be lying awake in his narrow bed, the dark pressing down on his unclosed eyes.

It had been my expectation that if Bill would ever be able to bring himself to talk to me about his marriage, he would, characteristically, limit himself to the bald statement that he and Estelle were incompatible—no elaboration of it, no history, no postscript. Secretly, I hoped he would add that they had stopped loving each other; I wanted it to be a mutual ebbing away of feeling, absolving Bill of all guilt, preparing the way for us. But Estelle as an alcoholic, a danger to herself and their only child, was an aspect of his marriage that unsettled me profoundly. At the same time it put to rest a tiny misgiving curled up in the recesses of my mind: it was Estelle who was the drinker, not Bill, for an alcoholic would scarcely brand his own wife as a drunk; I would expunge from my memory the one time I had seen him unsteady on his feet, since it was clearly unimportant.

Well, I was no longer outside William Faulkner's life. He had drawn me into it, finally, and now I knew what only a few others in the world knew of his marriage.

Chapter 5

The week went by with Bill being only a shade graver than usual. He mentioned Jill's name more often than he had before, but of Estelle there was not a word. It was too much to expect that having admitted me into the area of his life that he kept closed and unlit, he would make more painful disclosures immediately. Letters from Mississippi often depressed him; I judged them to be from Estelle or from other family members. An unproductive workday could also slump the square shoulders.

"I hit a damned snag today," he would say, rolling his eyes upward to the muse that had not smiled down upon him. "You should see the balls of Fox Studios' paper crumpled up all over the room." He was actually on schedule with the screenplay and Hawks was pleased with the collaboration between Bill and Joel Sayre. "Will Howard have my hide, I wonder?" His concern was always for Hawks, who had given him the opportunity to earn money in Hollywood, not for the film project itself.

Another night he showed me a letter from Jill, with childish block letters spelling out "DEAR PAPPY."

The knowledge that Bill was without physical love, that he had been without normal sexual outlet for some time, pervaded my sensibilities. I found myself looking at him in a wholly new way, averting my gaze quickly when he became aware of it. I would see him walking rapidly toward my car as I pulled up to the curb and feel a consuming pity for this strong, brilliant, healthy man, not yet forty, still in the prime of his manhood. In one stroke, he had removed the wife as love rival, yet he did not press me for an intensification of our relationship; he did not ask me to grant him what he had denied himself in his estrangement from Estelle. Most men, I told myself, would have lost no time in arousing the woman's compassion. When we parted at night, it was still an enclasping of the hands; he made no attempt to kiss me. But womanwise, I sensed the tumult of his blood within him when we stood face to face, and the strain he felt at being close to a desirable young female.

There were other restaurants in the Hollywood Boulevard area—Lyman's, the Brown Derby, and Sardi's, which Charles Chaplin frequented—but Bill preferred Musso & Frank's for its comparatively reasonable prices, its honest ambience, and the friendly, unaffected waiters, most of them foreign-born. One night as we left the restaurant, we began walking toward Hollywood and Vine instead of taking the other direction toward the theaters and bookstores. As a rule, we touched hands lightly or interlaced fingers, but this night Bill held my hand tightly, kneading it in his own, and I found myself returning the pressure. At Ivar, he slowed his stride and looked at me intently. We walked toward his hotel, neither of us leading the other, as if propelled by some tidal force in the still air. My heart drummed wildly as I stepped into the brilliant light of the hotel lobby with him and I thought, I can still turn back, I can still say "No, Bill," but I was in love with him and I could not give voice to the pretexts running through my head. Bill led me to the elevator and to his room down a long hallway and locked the door behind us and took me into his arms.

He had not had a woman for a long, long time and the sudden reality of female flesh and form, not fantasied, made him tremble and fight for his breath. He muttered hoarsely, "Oh, my God," at the prospect that was now his—to behold, to explore with hands and mouth, to love without fear of rejection. Because I was young and not his equal in passion, he tried to control the male ardor that raged through his starved body and to be gentle and unhurting. Afterward, in an access of gratitude, he kissed my face, my eyelids, and my throat, and held me with all his strength, as if I might be torn from him. When sleep loosened his hold on me, I raised myself up on one elbow to look at him in his nakedness. His chest was massive for a small man, his arms and shoulders strong and muscled, his waist thick, not small and girlish, as one of his fellow townsmen with poor powers of observation has written. I began to dress in the half-dark. Hearing my rustling movements, Bill came awake.

"Don't get up," I said. "I'll drive home myself." All I could think was that I needed to be away from him, to be able to adjust to what had happened to me and to know whether, beyond the wild rapture I had experienced in giving myself to him, my body to him like bread, it was good and defensible and beautiful. The worm of guilt was already beginning to push its beetle head through flesh and tissue. I had slept with a married man, another woman's husband, and the precept I had broken was cutting deep into me. I wanted now to be in my own room at the Studio Club, door bolted, windows shut, arms flung across the bed, putting what had happened tonight against all that had gone before, and against tomorrow.

Bill brought me, half-dressed, to his naked body, begging for another hour, saying my name, speaking the poetry that came to his tongue.

"A half-hour then," he pleaded. "I can't let you leave me."

"It's after twelve," I protested, wanting him again, but wanting solitude more. "I can't get back to the Studio Club any later on a week night."

"Do you know what you've done for me?"

"Bill, I have to go."

"You've brought me out of a deep and bottomless pit, Meta. You and no one else. You!"

We clung together. Over his bare shoulder, I could see what I hadn't observed before—the table where he worked, papers neatly arranged. There were books on end tables and books piled on the floor.

He walked me through the lobby, ghostly empty, past the glazed eye of a room clerk, holding my arm, being my lover and protector for then and for all the stolen time we would ever have together. At the parking lot, I insisted that he go back to his hotel. I was a big girl and I could drive the short distance to the Studio Club blindfolded, no need of him riding shotgun.

"I'll pick you up tomorrow, same time," I promised, turning to start my car with a frantic push-pull manipulation of the choke. As the motor rasped and caught, Bill withdrew his hand from mine on the steering wheel and stepped back. At the corner, I turned in my seat to wave to him. He was still standing where I had left him, face obscured at the edge of the pool of soiled amber cast by the streetlamp.

It was after one in the morning when the night watchman opened the door for me at the Studio Club, squinting to make certain it was I, who had never before been late. I showered and slipped into bed to think, grave and solemn as a child who has committed a terrible wrong. The self-accusations would not parade across my mind. The questions I had planned to ask myself sank like suns below the horizon. The columns would not add up. A languor I had never before known warmed my body. William Faulkner was my lover. My eyelids became weighted down and I slept.

Chapter 6

"Why, dear one, exactly why?"

Having listened to my suggestion that we drive to the beach and lunch at the Miramar with Sally Richards and John Crown, my close friends, Bill asked the question in a voice that was stiff with unconcealed irritation.

"Because," I sighed, shaking my head hopelessly at his insularity, "if you had your way, we would never see anyone. You'd let nothing intrude on us. We would live suspended in the world."

"I don't need anyone but you, Carpenter."

"Yes, but I'm not like you."

"For that biological difference, I am most beholden." The grin that followed instantly melted me; the eyes, dark and alive with mischief, were fixed on me. "Praise the Lord."

"You can sit for hours like some Indian swami, not saying a blessed word," I protested. "I can't, Bill. I need people."

"You just think you do."

"Not a lot of them. A few. A handful. Sally and John."

"What if I don't like Sally and John?"

"You will."

"And what if I'm short with them? What if I can't help myself?"

"It won't be like that."

"That would break your precious heart."

"Bill"—I put my hands to his cheeks, feeling the hollows under the prominent bones—"do it for me."

"I'll be poor company."

But I sensed his sudden acquiescence as he said it, heard the rumbled snort of resignation, and kissed him gratefully. It was my first victory with him. We met, we had dinner together, we made love. Because he was deeply in debt, he would not, dared not, take from his earnings more than a modest weekly allotment, enough to cover food and drink. Concerts, recitals, and plays were expensive, and dancing was completely out of the question. An evening at the Cocoanut Grove or any night club was for richer men than he, and besides, he didn't dance. Movies were a luxury, and why did I want to see them when I was in the business of helping make them? Despite his eagerness to please me, I found myself restive, boxed-in, longing for something outside ourselves that we could share.

We broke our pattern of isolation and frugality only on Saturday afternoons when, at Bill's wish, we would stop by at the back bar at Musso & Frank's. The small room, now boarded up, was always filled with writers then, some just in from New York to begin screenplay assignments, some taking time off from books in progress, some only minutes before released from the cubicles they occupied at major studios. At times, so many writers were crowded into the small space that it was impossible to pass between the crowded bar and the tables. It was, nevertheless, the one place where he could meet writers he liked or, if he chose, turn a chilly back on others. The bar was always strident with the nervous conversations of men and women freed for a few hours from the drudgery and loneliness of their craft, and there was hearty laughter and difference of opinion, strongly expressed, sometimes with table pounding and invective. Bill sat drinking with me, smoking his pipe, laughing freely. He did not mingle much with his colleagues, yet he was happy to be among writing men. While he talked more at Musso & Frank's bar than at any other time, he was by all odds the least communicative person in the room. When we sat longer than was our wont, usually because of a colloquy that Bill found himself listening to or the late arrival of a writer he had not seen in years, we ordered dinner at our table. Over the years, Bill was one of the habitués along with Nathanael West, F. Scott Fitzgerald, Budd Schulberg, S. N. Behrman, Dashiell Hammett, Max Brand, Jo Pagano, Joel Sayre, A. I. Bezzerides, Lillian Hellman, Horace McCoy, John Fante, and other writers, many of whose books were popular in their time but whose names, unlike Bill's, are all but forgotten.

He was polite to waiters (never complaining of poor service, loath always to send back food that was inedible), bartenders, and clerks. Inevitably, we ran into people I knew, but never his own acquaintances except at Musso & Frank's. If I were not quick enough to steer him out of my friends' immediate trajectory, there would be introductions to make. Bill steeled himself for their "Oh, you're from the South, too, just like Meta" or "Name some of the books you've written, Mr. Faulkner." Once when Bill let me coax him into an art gallery, effusive friends materialized from behind a sculpture; Bill, curbing an instinct for sudden, bird-like flight, a fast swoop into the air and away, pointedly moved to the other side of the gallery and kept himself equidistant from them until they left. There were other collisions with people I knew, for Hollywood will always be a small town in its high incidence of chance meetings. Bill was never troubled by what others took to be arrant rudeness, blinking innocently when I would reprimand him for the back he had turned on another person or the vanishing act that took him into the street, there to wait, puffing unconcernedly at his pipe, until I joined him.

Had Bill then or later refused to open up our lives to Sally and John, I would have accepted the decision calmly. I had grown equanimity like an extra limb in my adjustment to this volatile and sometimes arrogant man; my docility, far from lessening me, gave me an inner feeling of new resilience. We were as close now as groom and bride, discovering new wonders in each other, hating the hands on the clock beside Bill's hotel bed as they moved punishingly toward the moment when I must struggle out of his locked arms. In the act of love, Bill, the restrained, remote man by day, was seized with a consuming sexual urgency. Desire and sensation shook him as a storm wind buffets a stout tree.

"I've always been afraid of going out of control, I get so carried away," Bill said. "I'm not myself anymore; I'm somebody else. There was a time I worried about myself with women a whole lot. I still do, in fact."

My own response to him was womanly enough, but I did not need him in the wild, insatiable way he needed me. Mine was the surrender of the female to the aggressive, overpowering male, the sweet bliss of being rapturously loved and gratefully cherished afterward. He wanted me whenever I was willing to go with him to his hotel room, but he did not press me to turn from Hollywood Boulevard to the Knickerbocker. The dark eyes flashed their entreaty into mine and if I said I was tired or sleepy or under the weather, he would nod in acknowledgment of my right as a woman not to sleep with him that night, and he would accompany me to my car, hiding his disappointment with a story or a little song that he forgot as quickly as he made it up. He was happiest when he could lie with me in his arms for as many hours as we could have together. Sexual gratification made him voluble and outgoing. He told bawdy stories and kissed the blushes that inflamed my skin. One day when I had finished his unexpurgated copy of D. H. Lawrence's *Lady Chatterley's Lover,* a paperback edition smuggled in from Paris, he touched himself and with a sly smile announced: "Mr. Bowen."

I put my hand to my mouth to suppress a giggle.

"Not John Thomas but Mr. Bowen." He snuggled closer and his hand found my inner thighs. "And not Lady Jane but Mrs. Bowen."

The first of a number of poems from Mr. Bowen to Mrs. Bowen was written by Faulkner a few weeks later:

To Mrs. Bowen. Sweet, the maiden's mouth is (not) cold, (by a damn sight)

Her breast blossoms are simply red; (I know why they're red)
Her hair, mere brown or gold (one where, even less brown than gold
Since no sun kisses there, but only one of earth's sons seeks delight
When lover's dark limbs cover the beloved's white)
Fold on simple fold (she holds and he is holed)
Binding (let it be 'heads' then, if the censors require it) her head.
    (Yes, 'heads' then, if necessary for the censors)
    (When we're in bed)
        (The same bed, that is)
          Respectfully,
            Mr. Bowen

The hotel room was a poor place for the love with which we filled it, but it was all Bill could offer. I tried not to let him see how difficult it was for me to pass with him through the hotel lobby, looking straight ahead, stiffly avoiding accusatory eyes that might tell me too piercingly what they knew of us. If only I had a place of my own, where Bill could come to me! The apartment would be filled with vases of fresh flowers and curtains would billow at the windows. I would awaken Bill—how did he look in the mornings?—to a breakfast of eggs, country ham, and grits with yellow butter melting like lava in a volcano cone. I would draw his bath for him unless he preferred a shower. I would sew on new buttons to replace lost ones, brush off his jackets, restore with a hot iron the creases that had vanished from his trousers. It would all be straight out of the hit-tune repertoire of salesgirls in the sheet-music departments at Woolworth's. Moon, June, spoon, blue heaven, a cottage small by a waterfall, just a love nest. The scenario of the other fantasy that I allowed myself was amorphous, incomplete; in it, I stepped off trains with Bill as vast throngs cheered and people extended books to him for his signature. Could it have been the dream landscapes of France and Germany, where his novels and short-story collections had never gone out of print and where he was recognized even then as one of the great writers of the day? We always seemed to be traveling in my random visions, moving through other hotel lobbies, other hotel corridors. In that period, I sometimes consciously gave serious thought to the possibility that I would one day be Mrs. William Faulkner, and that we would live in Oxford. But realistically, I saw the South as a threat to us. Those great plowed, curving acres and courthouse squares and forlorn depots would wrest him from me. Better keep him away from the South in my reveries. Safer territory.

With no money for entertainment, we spent hours at the Studio Club on Saturday and Sunday afternoons. Bill complained that the air was charged with female energy, but he was comfortable enough after the first few times. In the game room, we played vicious rounds of Ping-Pong, slashing the ball back and forth. When I won, he was delighted.

"Good girl," he complimented me, meaning it, taking pride in my agility. "Let's see you do it again." And I did— often and invariably to his gleeful surprise.

One Sunday, I brought my camera, a cheap box model, to the Knickerbocker.

"What's that for?" he asked, eyebrows descending suspiciously.

"I want a picture of you."

"Of me?"

"You've never given me one, you know."

"I don't have pictures taken of myself."

"By the window, please, Bill," I begged. "More to the left, so you're in the light."

I teased a half smile from him and pushed the lever down. That he would tolerate being photographed at all by me was astonishing; I had fully expected him to roar out his objection, to regard me sternly and say, with finality, "No, ma'am." Encouraged, I pleaded for another shot. He nodded patiently and I took a series of pictures, even persuading him to stand still for a difficult mirror shot. Nothing would do after that but that I pose for him.

On another Sunday, with the Studio Club parlor deserted, I went to the Steinway grand piano and played for him.

Glancing his way, I was startled to see that he was squirming in his chair. He had written in *A Green Bough* of *"music of lustrous silent gold."* Why was he restless? Later, "You didn't like my playing"—the accusation offhand, lightly admonitory.

"You play very well, m' honey."

"But it didn't do anything for you."

"I don't appreciate music as much as I ought to," Bill apologized. "It's one of my flaws, I reckon." He shook his head in self-deprecation.

"Why, Bill, I would have thought . . ." I was baffled at a side of him that could not respond to music.

"Language is my music," he said. "All I'll ever need."

"I'm surprised."

"A man has to have his failings."

Lunching in the studio commissary with another secretary, I overheard the end of a conversation at the next table. The speaker was talking about William Faulkner.

"The man's an alcoholic," he said with the authority of someone who knew his subject personally. "He can't stay away from the booze."

It was as though I had been lashed. My skin burned and stung. The food in my mouth turned to rocks.

"What's the matter?" my lunch partner asked.

"Nothing, nothing." I forced a weak smile and wondered whether I had misunderstood what was said.

"Hawks will have trouble with Faulkner, mark my words," the voice suddenly boomed. "He'll go on a drinking jag—he's done it before—and he won't be any damned good on the script after that."

It was a despicable lie, I told myself, a slander on a man who rarely ordered more than two drinks at dinner and was not affected by them. He kept no bottles in his hotel room that I had been able to see. Perhaps Bill had imbibed when he was in Hollywood before—that was a possibility—but if true, what right did anyone have to hold past excesses against him now? Leaving my table, I shot a look of concentrated fury at the libeler, whose mouth fell open in surprise.

Just as I had excised the canard from my mind, ascribing it

to pure hearsay or, at the most, exaggeration, an actress at the Studio Club asked if she might speak to me on a personal matter.

"It's about someone you're seeing a lot of," she began. "William Faulkner."

We sat down in chairs a distance from the area where girls were clustered around a radio console and she inclined toward me in an attitude of dramatic confidentiality.

"I have been told by someone who should know that he is a very heavy drinker."

"I doubt that," I said firmly, amazed at my unhesitancy and anger. "I doubt that very much."

"But this friend," she went on, "knows what he's talking about, Meta. When I told him that I had seen Mr. Faulkner here with you, he said I would be doing you a kindness if I told you that the man has a terrible weakness for liquor."

I thanked her coldly and made a mental note to cut her dead in the future. The next time Bill came into the Studio Club with me, I deliberately paraded him past her. She looked up sharply, then went back to the script she was studying.

There were Saturdays when I was commandeered for afternoon driving duty by Howard Hawks; because Bill would be at loose ends, I suggested that he find someone, a writer friend perhaps, with whom he could play golf.

"No'm, I don't think so," Bill objected.

"But you're a physical man," I said. "Back in Oxford, you play golf, you ride, you swim. You'll feel better."

"No'm." He was adamant. "I'll just wait here at the hotel until you've done your chore for Howard. That way there won't be any overlapping of time."

One weekend, I persuaded Bill to try miniature golf at an outdoor amusement area where there were also Ping-Pong tables. He guffawed contemptuously at the course, with its miniature palaces, millponds, and waterfalls, but played the game with complete enjoyment. My own score was miserable. To escape the crowds of children and doting parents, we would meet at six in the morning on weekdays, have breakfast, then drive to the putt-putt, as Bill called it, for an hour of diversion before I had to report to work.

At best, miniature golf was a token sport, not the same for Bill as bending his body and driving a ball down the fairway in a coordinated action of eye, arm, and hands.

I had not anticipated further resistance when I arranged for him to meet John and Sally.

"But I'm not a good mixer," Bill protested. "I'll pull my head in like an old mud turtle."

I would not let him retreat. "Not with them, Bill."

"You're tired of me, I'm thinking." He put on a mournful face for me. "Old Bill just ain't compelling enough for you."

"You know better than that."

He flung out his hands in bewilderment. "Then why do we have to accommodate to others? Why can't we go on just as we have been?"

I was on the point of giving in. Then and later, whether through a lack of self-love, an inability to evaluate my own worth, I tended to acquiesce to the love interest in my life. To what extent it was a part of my Southern conditioning where men were concerned, I'm uncertain, but I always ended up deferring to the man, sacrificing my own pleasure.

This time, activated by the fear of what we were coming to, I stood my crumbling ground. I had to. We were consuming each other in our self-isolation. It wasn't natural. Bill had placed us in a bubble and we were using up the air in it; one day we would not be able to breathe. I could not believe that I would always be endlessly fascinating to him, that he would never tire of my company. I was a woman, not a series of Chinese boxes within boxes. We needed others to impinge on us, others to relate to.

"Bill, I can't do without friends anymore," I said resolutely. "Please let me have some balance in my life. It may be right for you, but it's wrong for me this way."

"All right, Meta," he agreed almost instantly. "I'll do anything you want me to, meet anybody you want me to. What will happen is another matter, but I'll go through the motions and I'll try damned hard."

We drove to the Miramar Hotel in Santa Monica on a dazzling Sunday morning; the ocean, viewed from the last high turns on Sunset Boulevard, hurled light back to the blue dome of sky and carried toylike fishing boats on its agitated skin. I spotted my two good friends on the beach and drew Bill along with me over the crunching sand.

Squinting good-naturedly against the strong sunlight, Bill had his first look at Sally, with her heart-shaped, dimpled face, soft brown hair drawn back in a bun, and laughing brown eyes, and at John, a humorous, lovable young bear of a man with reddish-blond hair, handsome, far taller than Bill, expansive and outgoing. Both were in bathing suits, their tanned bodies flecked with white sand. Sally made her conquest of Bill with no effort at all, for he was susceptible to demure Southern women. After the first half-hour, he began to laugh at John's hearty banter and to let himself be gathered into the net of absolute warmth and charm that John cast over people. If Bill, for all his resolve to make me happy, lapsed occasionally into stony silence, John jolted him out of it with his wit and his great appetite for life. By the time we were at lunch in the Miramar dining room, Bill was completely at ease with Sally and John. He had been accepted as Meta's friend, not as William Faulkner the writer, and now he was their friend, part of them, as I was. No questions were asked about his books or his personal life. The subject of music, into which I would normally fall after the first few minutes with them, was studiously avoided. Bill looked out at the heaving sea and the bathers, then turned his full attention to me and his new friends. He was as happy as I had ever seen him.

Sally Richards and I became friends when we were brought together in Memphis by Betty Walter, the other member of the triumvirate until I left for California. Pianists all three, we competed with each other, principally for the honor of playing solos on the local radio station. (As guest artist the first time, I proudly rendered Grieg's "March of the Dwarfs" and "La Guirlandes" by Arabella Goddard; the critical consensus among friends and family was that I was on my way to greatness and I believed it until I realized that both Sally and Betty had the edge on me.) Sally arrived in Hollywood a few years after I put uncertain roots down in its arid soil. My recently widowed Aunt Ione and I cheerfully shared our small apartment with Sally and her baby grand piano. Aunt Ione, a small, fragile woman with a translucent skin and big, warm brown eyes, mothered her until she had recovered from an unhappy emotional experience.

Sally played in bars, restaurants, rehearsal halls, and at private parties to earn a living, and finally was able to afford a modest apartment of her own. I remember the elation my Aunt Ione and I felt when she brought John Crown to meet us for the first time. They had been drawn to each other when Sally joined a chamber music group of which John was a member. Lucky Sally, she had been wise to come to Hollywood. John, an extraordinary young pianist, was beyond anyone she had ever dreamed of attracting.

Now she was self-effacing about her virtuosity as a pianist and was content to stand in the brilliant light of John's greater talent. The idea of a life devoted wholly to music no longer appealed to her. At John's prodding, she would spend an hour or so at the keyboard each day playing classical music, but at night she performed as a jazz musician.

John, on the other hand, lived for his music, as Faulkner lived for his writing, pouring the very substance of himself into his playing. Although he was the most highly disciplined of musicians, technically correct, he infused his music with a fire and strength that made the listener feel he was hearing the work played for the first time.

The four of us struck it off unbelievably well. An exciting equation of personalities, each interacting with the others, was formulated: the three musicians and the writer tone-deaf to the thunderous miracle of music. Learning that Bill had been on a walking tour of Europe, John brought it all back to him by describing cities and towns, the different looks of the countryside, the tourist traps best avoided, and the wonders he hoped Bill had experienced. Marvelously funny travel stories came to his mind and Bill threw back his head and laughed at a storyteller as gifted in the manipulation of humor as himself. When we said goodbye to our hosts in midafternoon, John shook Bill's hand in genuine regard, not for Faulkner the novelist, although he knew his work, but for a pleasant, warm, interesting man whom I had brought around for him to meet. As for Bill, he had forgotten after the first few minutes that John was younger than he by many years, hardly out of the stripling stage, to hear Bill grumblingly tell it later. Sally had completely ingratiated herself with him; she was "home folks" to him, a counterpart of any one of a score of girls whom he knew in Oxford.

"Excuse me." Bill drew me off to the side and spoke in a whisper. "Dear one, would you like for us to spend the next weekend here at this place?"

"You mean overnight?" I reddened and he saw it. "Saturday and Sunday?"

"If you're free. If Howard doesn't work you."

"Well . . ." I saw Sally and John watching us a few yards away.

"We'd have to check in as husband and wife, ma'am."

"I've never done anything like that."

"It's up to you."

For another moment, the last of my parents' stern injunctions about men buzzed in my head like bees aroused from dormancy, and then I thought, Dear God, I'm a grown woman, I've been married, I sleep with Bill Faulkner in his hotel room.

"All right," I managed to say, vexed with myself, resentful of parental admonitions and prohibitions that could fuse into nasty tumors of guilt. This was Bill, my lover, my friend. "It's fine. A good idea."

"You be sure now."

"Oh, Bill, I am. It's just that sometimes, as you perfectly

well know, I have to be helped over fixed notions of what's proper and what isn't."

"Do I debauch you, ma'am?" His eyes danced with delight.

"Yes, you do."

We made our decision known to John and Sally. Would we be trespassing on their Eden if we joined them at the Miramar next weekend? Would they be uncomfortable with us around?

"Hell, no." John grinned. "It will make it all the better."

"I'd love it," Sally agreed. "At least I'll get to see Meta."

"Well, then it's settled," Bill announced. "How expensive would a bungalow be, John?" Beyond his head I could see Sally smiling impishly. Later tonight, I knew, we would be on the telephone to each other and she would tell me candidly what she thought of Bill and what John thought and what they had said when we left them.

Bill drove back to Hollywood along the treacherous winding turns of Sunset, singing church hymns, Confederate camp songs, and Negro spirituals in a high-pitched, exuberant voice when there were no cars near. I leaned my head against his hard shoulder and felt my love for him surge through me like a strengthening current. I had not given more than a perfunctory thought to Estelle in the last few weeks. I had kept her in the dark of the wings, powerless, immobilized, while I occupied the stage with Bill. Now I allowed myself to think of Bill writing to her for a divorce. Perhaps she would fight him at first, but in time she would agree to it. Where we would live, I didn't know. Hollywood? He wouldn't be happy here. Northern California? No matter, it would all work itself out. Jill would spend months on end with us and I would be an adoring stepmother. I would have Bill's other children.

"Happy?" Bill gripped my hand.

"Look at me."

"I like them—Sally and John."

"They like you."

"How do you know?"

"I just know."

"How old is he?"

"Twenty-two, I think."

"Twenty-two? Good God, ma'am." Bill turned toward me, incredulous, and the little car swerved into the next lane before he could right it.

"He's brilliant, admit it."

"He is that, yes, ma'am." Bill shook his head in disbelief. "He also has the doggonest laugh of any man I ever met. I never before in all my born days heard such a laugh."

Bill started to ask a question, then thought better of it. I knew what it would be and why he was hesitant when it finally came.

"Why aren't they married?"

I told him of how John's father had lost his money and how that had necessitated the postponement of the well-financed, stage-managed concert career that John had been promised. "Sally," I added, "contributes in her small way, though John's parents have no idea she does."

"That a fact?"

"She earns about five dollars a night playing jazz in night clubs around town. What she doesn't need to keep herself going, she adds to what John makes so that the family can eat and pay the rent."

"And they don't know it?"

"Even if they did, they wouldn't approve of her as a wife for John."

"Why not? She's a pretty little thing."

"They think she's dowdy, no style, no taste in clothes."

"Nothing wrong with her in a bathing suit."

"Families like the Crowns," I explained, "families in music, Europeans, expect their gifted sons to make advantageous marriages. They've brought him up to be a great concertizing artist on the world stage. They expect him to marry a wealthy woman or at least a woman from a great musical family."

"Hmmmm . . ." Bill pondered it. He knew all about

Southern aristocrats who arranged brilliant marriages for their sons and daughters.

"Poor Sally thinks the Crowns already have a girl picked out for John."

"I'll tell you something."

"What?"

"I've just met him this once, but I don't think he'll be pushed into anything like that."

Suddenly we were bumper to bumper with other cars and Bill, unnerved by heavy traffic and impatient drivers, flashed me a look of distress. We exchanged seats and I drove us back to Hollywood.

Over Christmas, I reluctantly left Faulkner to spend the holidays with my parents. I was not to stay an hour more than necessary, he complained, else how was he to survive without me in this terrible place? The brief separation was as much of a torment to me as to him, and I returned to Hollywood a day earlier than I had planned.

Chapter 7

The love poems, thrust into my hands, left upon pillows, slipped slyly into my purse and pockets, moved me as only music had before. Years later, reading the yellowed sheets and scraps of paper I did not destroy when I was attempting to make a new life for myself, it occurred to me that while Bill may have guarded that part of himself that had to do with Estelle, nothing of his interior life with me was shuttered. Far from the verses being mere paeans to the loved one, they sang rapturously of his own uplifted spirit and the new tide of his passion. It was as if he were saying to me: This is what I feel, this is how I am with you.

One of the first love lines he wrote to me was in French: *"La bouche de ma fille n'e pas froid."*

When I repeated it to him at night in his arms, he wrote another declaration of his love in his imperfect French:

> *Se tiarait coup de fusee aimez vous la Française,*
> *Parce-qu'elle*
> *Bien dige d'etre aimee.*
> *Je t'adore, ma douce cygne*
> *Blanche, ma coucheuse, ma*
> *Bien aimee.*

Books were stacked in an uneven skyline on the floor of his hotel room (chambermaids simply walked around them). He was pleased when I asked him to read from my copy of *A Green Bough*. I remember every word of the last eight-line poem:

> If there be grief, then let it be but rain,
> And this but silver grief for grieving's sake,
> If these green woods be dreaming here to wake
> Within my heart, if I should rouse again.
> But I shall sleep, for where is any death
> While in these blue hills slumbrous overhead
> I'm rooted like a tree? Though I be dead,
> This earth that holds me fast will find me breath.

When he had finished reading it the first time in that flat, soft Southern voice, he caught his breath and looked away.

"That last line is my epitaph," he said. " 'Though I be dead/This earth that holds me fast will find me breath.' "

Another time, after he had explained allusions and hidden meanings to me, he opened my *A Green Bough* to the blank afterpages and wrote:

Meta
Bill
Meta
who soft keeps for him his love's long girl's body sweet to fuck.
Bill.

The inscribed volume of verse is now in the Berg Collection at the New York Public Library, not to be made available to anyone in this century, along with erotic drawings that Faulkner gave me. One series shows us, recognizable, in the act of lovemaking, with a final sketch of Bill stretched out beside me, visibly exhausted, penis shrunken. Among other Faulkner items in the collection that are to be kept under lock and key until the year 2039 is an erotic letter in which Bill drew a stop sign to convey to me the buildup of his passion when he recalled our nights together in Hollywood and a paragraph that reads, "For Meta, my heart, my jasmine garden, my April and May cunt; my white one, my blonde morning, winged, my sweetly dividing, my honey-cloyed, my sweet-assed gal. Bill."

He loved reciting for me poems of others that he had committed to memory, and he would seize with trembling excitement upon a new volume he had acquired, to share with me an old favorite or a new discovery. I was introduced to James Joyce's "Watching the Needleboats at San Sabba," from a paperback copy of *Pomes Penyeach*, on one of our drives to Santa Barbara:

> *I heard their young hearts crying*
> *Loveward above the glancing oar*
> *And heard the prairie grasses sighing:*
> No more, return no more!
> *O hearts, O sighing grasses,*
> *Vainly your loveblown bannerets mourn!*
> *No more will the wild wind that passes*
> *Return, no more return.*

Breakfasting one Sunday morning on the veranda of the Knickerbocker Hotel, he decided to write a variation of part of Keats' "Ode on a Grecian Urn" for me.

"What sounds best to you?" he asked. "Should I say I have seen music or I have heard music?"

I spooned into a golden papaya half, doused with lime juice, and refused to render an opinion.

"Being a musician, you'd naturally prefer 'heard,'" Bill accused.

"You're the poet, dear one," I reminded him.

Within a few minutes, he had reworked the lines and I had my Keats/Faulkner poem:

> *I have seen music, heard*
> *Grave and windless bells; mine air*
> *Hath verities of vernal leaf and bird—*
> *Ah, let this fade: it doth and must.*

> *Nor grieve.*
> *Forever shall I dream*
> *And she be fair.*
> *Meta, my darling, my love.*
> *My dear love.*
> *My dear, dear love.*

Some of his erotic poetry frankly puzzled me. If I asked its meaning, I don't recall that he offered any clarification that, at the time, I could understand. I was on firmer ground with his French love poems to me than with:

> *Red thy famble,*
> *White thy gan,*
> *And thy quaranon.*
> *Dainty is couth*
> *Couch thy moons.*
> *Mid with me then*
> *In the darkness*
> *Clip and kiss.*

The age difference between us no longer existed for me, who had restored his youth and his sense of fun, but for Bill it had strangely widened. Although he made love to me as a man to a woman, there were times when he saw me as being far younger than I was. A girl-child. With one flourish of his mental blue pencil, he would edit out all the facts of my life since Memphis—my birthdays, my marriage, my work—and behave toward me as if I were just out of high school. I don't remember making an effort to play my assigned part at these times, for, if anything, I was confounded by his need to turn me into a sweet, tremulous girl.

One day he presented me with a box in which there was a ribbon for my hair.

"I can't afford presents for you," he apologized, "but I couldn't resist this."

Although I thanked him and wore it, I was troubled by his

choice of gift. The idealization of me as a girl far too young for him was to last for a number of years and to appear in some of his letters to me. I never protested, and my acceptance of his vision of me as a maiden nourished his fantasy.

Our first weekend at the Miramar and those that came after intensified my own feeling that I was actually married to Bill. Mr. and Mrs. Bowen, shown to their bungalow by a polite bellboy, chattered away in husband-and-wife fashion about the car and the milkman and the dog—would she howl? would she refuse all food?—that they had left at the kennel. Bill's hotel room was dreary, but this spacious cabana bungalow was golden yellow with sunlight and smelled of ocean brine. Alone, bellboy properly tipped, we broke into laughter over our inept performances as the Bowens and kissed joyously to be in such a cheery place on a Saturday afternoon, with a whole night and the best part of a Sunday ahead of us, and the company of John and Sally, whose room in the main hotel was cheaper. We unpacked the respectable suitcase (Bill's) in which our clothes were mingled for the first time. A curious solemnity came over us with the unaccustomed intimacy of hanging them up and putting them away. Bill watched as I shook out my Sunday dress, placed toiletries on the bathroom shelf, arranged inexpensive jewelry on the dresser, and laid out my bathing suit. He was clearly fascinated, as men often are, by the small rituals of feminine women. Then we were undressing and slipping into our bathing suits in bold daylight sight of each other and rushing to meet our friends, though Bill would have had us stay inside for the rest of the afternoon.

At one with the strong light pouring down and the crashing waves and the cat sounds of sea gulls, my lover that Saturday did not once, I swear, think of Oxford, or the wife who drank herself into a helpless wreck, or the debts still unpaid, or whatever else would darken his beleaguered mind when the other existence intruded. He splashed into the water, a lake swimmer in the treacherous Pacific undertows, and with sure, strong strokes took the rising waves. On the beach with

John and Sally, we turned our faces to the sun and accepted its lovely fire. Bill and John parodied the muscle men we had seen by posing together in stylized tandem, heels digging into the sand, chests pushed out, muscles flexed—my serious, grave Bill, antic and uninhibited.

That night when I came to Bill in my new nightgown, he had covered the bed with gardenia and jasmine petals. Where he had found the flowers, where he had concealed them until the moment of surprise, I was too stunned to ask. He stood, shyly waiting for my approval, like a set decorator for a movie director's nod. I could only look from the blossom-strewn bed to the unabashed romantic who had emerged from the many selves of William Faulkner. Lover at the forefront, all other aspects of himself banished for the night—the dour, the silent, the desperate—he beseeched me with his eyes to find pleasure in what he had done. If Script Girl found it extravagant, straight out of the Swinburnes and Lord Byrons to whom he had introduced her, an excess of sentiment that would have made Howard Hawks groan, Finishing-School Graduate, who had not yet relinquished her hold on me, saw it as a declaration of elegiac love. Eyes misting, I moved into Bill's arms and wept on his chest out of the joy of being loved as I had always dreamed, of being treasured and pedestaled.

We made love with the windows open to the sea, curtains aflutter, and moonlight so brilliantly white that I could see my lover's face afterward, peaceful and eased. It was the first time we had been together for a full night, no clock hands to send me hurrying back to the Studio Club. I could doze in his arms without alarm bells going off prematurely in my head, jerking me like an electric prod, so that Bill would draw me to himself protectively, calmly, and murmur, "Not yet, m' honey, not yet," and I would ask in panic, "What time is it?" and he would say, "Never mind. There's almost an hour yet." In the morning, with the young light feeling its way into the bedroom, searching the corners, I saw for the first time how sleep transformed his face and how handsome he was with the creases ironed smooth in his forehead and the strong mouth slightly parted. The four of us had a bountiful breakfast—"A Paul Bunyan breakfast," Bill pronounced it— in the glassed-in sunroom of the hotel. Later that day and through subsequent weekends, he drew a series of sketches for me. The first panel was of the two of us at the breakfast table, a tower of pancakes before us; the next was of himself knocking at the door and the next of his Meta in bed, and written under the drawing, "Since you have just waked up, this won't be a good night but good morning. And here's the morning paper all ready for you." He captured us playing Ping-Pong, then added a panel in which he sagged with defeat as I stood victorious over him. In a drawing of us in my little car, he put himself at the wheel, placing me so close to him as to almost be in his lap. There was a sketch of us running along the beach, Bill a head taller than I. In two companion panels, we are on the beach and I am powdering my nose as the sun rises; again we are stretched out face to face on the sand as the sun falls below the horizon. There were sketches of Sally and John, he with a folio under his arm lettered "Something Bach." And the crowning effort: our bungalow room seemingly empty of its occupants, our clothes neatly hung, a "Do Not Disturb" sign on the door.

Sally called attention to Bill's feet as we sunned ourselves on the beach.

"I've never seen such pretty feet on a man," she said in the tone of one who has made a remarkable discovery.

Bill grinned and wiggled his pedal extremities for us.

"Downright pretty," Sally continued, pressing the point. "Haven't you noticed, Meta?"

"Yes, and I've complimented him on them."

"Bill, are you the least bit aware that you have pretty feet for a man?" Sally asked.

"So my mama told me." He arched his feet and squinted at them.

"He's vain about them," I commented.

Bill half sat up. "I'm short and not much to look at. Now don't you think I'm entitled to have at least drawn pretty feet in the lottery of good looks?"

"His feet look," I said, "as if he'd never worn shoes."

John, feigning jealousy, demanded to know what was wrong with his feet. He held them up for our inspection.

"Not in Bill's class," Sally said, tossing sand at the man she loved. "Yours are just ordinary and Bill's are a Greek god's."

"Bill's," announced Bill, "are a Mississippi dirt farmer's." Then he narrowed his eyes against the sun and turned over on his stomach.

In the late afternoon, with the sun withdrawing its warmth, a cold wind blowing in, we checked out of the Miramar and headed for the Hofbrau on Sunset Boulevard. I had gone often to this Hollywood restaurant with Sally and John, but this was Bill's first visit. He could not bring himself that time to join us in singing German songs or in swaying to the oompah, oompah-pah of the musicians, but he clinked his stein to ours, drank his beer with gusto, and laughed at John's rollicking humor. We had given Bill back his youth and the years fell from him. The heavy German food did not appeal to him, but he said "Fine, just fine" when I asked how he liked it. As we dined, I looked up from my plate at him and thought him particularly handsome with the healthy glaze of sunburn on his face.

It angered Bill that he was too poor to make a ritual of Miramar weekends. From time to time, however, he found the money for it and we would drive to the hotel, Mr. and Mrs. Bowen living it up with the rich, their own cabana, mind you.

"Why don't we take a room next to John and Sally in the hotel itself?" I once suggested. "It's far cheaper and I'd be just as comfortable."

"Meta, my honey"—he put a flaring kitchen match to his pipe and worked his cheeks to ignite the tobacco—"I've never been as happy in my life as with you right here. In the name of love, let me be impractical."

Some weekends were shared with John and Sally, who could no more afford even the Miramar Hotel on a regular basis than could Bill. When we were all broke, we would drive out to the hotel, have breakfast as drop-in customers, then spend the day on the beach. For lunch, we would consume ten-cent hot dogs and drink soda pop so that we could still afford dinner and beer at the Hofbrau. The weekend foursome broke up when John, unable to find concert bookings, opened the Crown house on Bronson Canyon for Sunday-afternoon musicales; the dollar admission entitled music lovers to hear him or his musician friends-in-need concertize. Since Bill would not sit through an afternoon of music, I missed those concerts that became part of Los Angeles' music history.

Bill's affection for John and Sally, genuine and wholly independent of his feeling for me, grew each time we were with them. At least one night a week was shared with them when we were deprived of their company on weekends. They were to become Bill's good friends, this man who did not easily give of himself and who could not accept with grace the friendship proffered by others. He was to visit them unfailingly in the years ahead when he returned to Hollywood to earn the money that his books failed over and over to yield him in royalties.

Their marriage, when it came, delighted him as a clear victory of wonderfully stubborn lovers, nose-thumbers at convention and opposition. He marked the growth of the two daughters born to them with avuncular pride. The Crowns were his closest link to me and the years in which he had been exuberantly happy in Hollywood, and he would sit quietly in their presence, as if to draw something of me from them, asking nothing but to be caught up in their lives for an hour or so. Had they heard from me, he would finally inquire. Was I well? Was I happy? Waiting for the question, Sally would tell him where I was and then read the latest of my letters.

The occasional Miramar weekends gave Bill therapeutic release from his hotel room and studio office, and from the strain of working on *Absalom, Absalom!* after a full day with Joel Sayre on the script of *The Road to Glory*. At the time, I had no inkling as to what the escapes to the beach helped overcome and sublimate in his nature. He became darkly sunburned. The whites of his eyes flashed imperiously against his bronzed skin.

"You look," I told him, "like an Armenian or a Sicilian."

"Good!"

"A desert chieftain."

"Oh, Lord." He surveyed himself in the mirror after lunch. "I'm pretty dark at that. They just might ride me out of Oxford."

Bill wouldn't let me take the full sun for more than a few minutes at a time, motioning me back to the shade of a beach umbrella or the shelter of our cabana when I overstayed my limit.

"No, ma'am," he said firmly. "I won't have that rare white skin marred by ugly red and blistering. No more than I'd stand for a great painting to be left out in the rain."

He would let his eyes, sprays of deeply intaglioed lines radiating from the corners, scan my face and body.

"I have to find a way to describe that white skin," he said. "It's not blanched-out white but a white with a suffusion of ivory and alabaster. I've never before seen any woman with such a skin."

There was no repeat of the love bed of flower petals, that Busby Berkeley-*Arabian Nights* Faulkner whim, but only because I made it clear to Bill that he had been grossly extravagant. He settled on pinning a fresh gardenia to my pillow. It was his secret how he brought it to the Miramar, concealed from me, and found the opportunity to put it in its place under the coverlet.

"You're sweet," I said, fitting myself into his arms the moment he slipped into bed. "But it's not really necessary."

"It's most necessary, ma'am. I want you to breathe the fragrance all through the night."

He had almost finished his final screenplay draft of *The Road to Glory*. Howard Hawks, greatly concerned about melding the new scenes with the extraordinary footage from the original French movie, asked Bill to work full days for

83

the time left in the office assigned him in the writers' building at Fox; Hawks could then discuss with him and Sayre each morning the pages he had read at home the night before, and at lunch they could confer on new dialogue. Predictably, the return to his writer's cubicle depressed Bill and he was unable to overcome the feeling that the move demeaned him. The dreary building added to his misery and he complained of not being able to work as efficiently as he had at the hotel.

"It's like a hospital prison corridor," he railed. "Those damned gray walls, those damned wide corridors, all those closed doors. And everything so damned hushed and still. I hate it."

Sometimes, following their luncheon meetings, Hawks would send me to Bill's office to take his dictation. If nobody was about, we would kiss, then reluctantly get to work. I had found with Ben Hecht and Charles MacArthur during the writing of *Barbary Coast* that I was far more effective recording their bursts of invention on the typewriter than in shorthand. The pages would be there for them to go over as soon as they had finished their work. Bill, unused to dictation, more comfortable writing out his dialogue in longhand, paced as he spoke the lines to be said by his characters, described their actions and emotions, indicated camera angles. At times, particularly when his back was turned, his soft voice became so indistinct that I would have to say, "I beg your pardon," and he would with the utmost patience repeat himself. When, momentarily, he ran out of ideas, he would lean over my shoulder to peer at what I had written, brushing my hair with his lips.

Since, as script girl, I would have to deal with screenplay inconsistencies, I questioned him about a line of dialogue.

"Now, Bill, in this scene you say—" I began.

"I didn't say it," he corrected me. "The character said it."

"The character?"

"Yes."

Although I nodded as if I understood, I did not really

comprehend that Bill was telling me that his characters had a life-force of their own. What they did, what they said, came from them. Once he had created them, given them shape and color, they were then the authors of their own speeches and triumphs and follies. Throughout our years together, he would say, "A character of mine once said . . ."

The final section of the screenplay went rapidly, but Bill made no reference to it when we were together. He was working harder in these last weeks than at any time before, and it became increasingly clear to me that it was for more than the reason that Howard Hawks needed the final screenplay draft for distribution to Darryl F. Zanuck and the casting and legal departments. When Bill talked about Jill, a new excitement crept into his voice. There were unexpected allusions now to Mammy and to Phil Stone and to Oxfordians who were his friends. More and more, he spoke of Rowan Oak and projects still uncompleted, plans to be put into operation. Of Estelle, he said nothing.

I had nurtured a wild hope that Bill would remain in Hollywood once the screenplay was completed. Now I knew that he wanted to go back to Rowan Oak and to Jill. A thousand things of which I knew nothing were exerting an intense pull on him.

I came back to the bed where he lay with his arm over his eyes. "When are you leaving?"

"Maybe next week." He cleared his throat nervously.

"You can't help yourself?"

"No, ma'am."

"A week." I wouldn't let myself cry. "That's all the time we have then."

"Give or take a day or two."

"I'll make your train reservations with the travel office at the studio. You tell me what day you're leaving."

"Soon as I know for sure, ma'am."

I had gone beyond the bounds I had rigidly set for myself in bringing his departure into the open, but it had not angered him. Now he would not have to hide it carefully from me day after day. When I left the hotel room, I knew that he was wrestling with his decision, but I would not turn back to force him to change it.

I waited for him to talk about us. Was this the end of it or would he come back to me? Did he have a plan to divorce Estelle and marry me? Would he boldly tell his alcoholic wife that he loved me and could no longer live with her? Would he retain a lawyer? Searching his locked face, I realized that short of my demanding candor of him, he would not say a word to me. If that was Bill's way, I told myself, then so be it. I would not maneuver him into a confrontation.

On his last Sunday in Hollywood, Bill was asked by Howard Hawks to meet him on a troublesome story point. For the first time since we began seeing each other, I had to face a whole afternoon without him. The prospect of even brief separation with time running out upset me, but I busied myself writing letters, then rushed down to the music room of the Studio Club for the Sunday-afternoon radio symphony from New York. There were a number of other girls present, all of them trying for careers as actresses, singers, musicians, and dancers (Tamara Geva was one of the young ballet aspirants). I was greeted as a long-absent member of the group and for the next hour was lost in a great, vaulting symphony.

That Monday, I began to type the last pages of the screenplay. Unreasonably, I kept believing there would be a last-minute reprieve. Howard Hawks would ask Bill to stay on to rewrite. There would be another screenwriting offer, one that he could not refuse for the money and the extra margin of time it would give him to complete *Absalom, Absalom!* The miracles failed like ill-calculated special effects. Suddenly the work was done, the finished script was sent to the secretarial pool to be retyped and mimeographed, and Bill's weekly salary was terminated.

With John and Sally, Bill paid a last visit to the Studio Club, and I photographed them with my box camera in the courtyard. There was a farewell supper at the Hofbrau. John, as I knew he would, kept the conversation light and insubstantial, moving in quickly with a pun or a witticism whenever Bill and I, remembering how little time was left, looked at each other in stricken silence.

The following night, I brought Bill my poor presents: a matte photograph of me that I had asked a studio still man to make (feminine to the end, I did not give Bill a choice of the proofs but picked the picture I wanted him to have) and a sunbonnet for Jill.

"Beautiful," he said. "Exactly like you."

"Will you be able to keep it—hide it somewhere?"

"Yes, ma'am. I'll look at it every morning and that will get me through the day."

"I know you don't like being photographed, but have a portrait made for me, please."

"I promise." He examined the sunbonnet. "She'll love it. Jill loves presents."

"I couldn't think of anything else."

"It's just right, dear heart. I'll send you a snapshot of her wearing it." He had not forgotten me. From the hotel-room closet came a huge box with the Bullock's-Wilshire logo. Inside, there was a double-breasted full-length brocade evening coat. "For you."

"Bill, you're out of your mind," I cried. "You can't afford this."

"I know I can't."

"Did Howard Hawks give you a bonus?"

"No, ma'am."

"Bill, I can't let you spend all your money on me."

"I'm a hardheaded man. Nothing you say will send me back to the department store yelling 'Refund, refund.'"

I slipped into the beautiful coat and pivoted for him, arms extended to the side, head flung back. He caught me in a pirouette and we moved together, body to body, in a slow dance.

"My beautiful Meta," he said joyously. "My lovely long-legged, big-mouf, white-skinned gal."

A few months later, I saw a Bullock's-Wilshire ad. The coat had cost Bill a sacrificial seventy-five dollars. What uncanny divination of the future had prompted him to buy it? Not many years after, in Frankfurt and in New York, the coat served to cover my threadbare dresses and to conceal my abject poverty.

It was the last night we would be together. His love-making was furious, as if he had to put his physical stamp upon me forever, and afterward we rested exhaustedly in each other's arms.

"I don't want you to be alone," he said after a while.

"I'm used to it."

"No, I want you to have a dog. You've wanted one." He explained that he had made arrangements with the Knebworth Kennel. "You're to go there and pick out any puppy you want."

"Faulkner, I can't let you spend another dime on me when you need money so desperately."

"I want to. Besides, you'll think of me when you look at the puppy and that will give you pleasure."

"Bill . . ." I kissed his forehead and his eyelids, my hair cascading over his face.

"Ma'am?"

"What about us?" I could no longer keep it tamped down.

He turned his head and there was no answer from him. I felt the hurt spread in my throat and chest. When he faced me again, he put one finger to my lips, entreating me to ask no more. Over my protests, he rode back to the Studio Club with me. I cried as we parted, something I had never done before, and he regarded me with startled face before he abruptly wheeled around and started back to his hotel, head bent slightly as if braced against a whipping cold wind.

The next evening I drove him to Central Station at Fifth and Central in downtown Los Angeles and we had dinner at the station restaurant, white-tiled and bleak. Neither of us ate more than a few bites of the heavily gravied beef or the sodden vegetables. I blotted my fresh lipstick with a paper napkin and was taken aback when Bill reached for it and placed it in his jacket pocket. I looked at him questioningly, but he had retreated into massive silence, as remote as a holy man on a mountaintop in India, even more distant than he had been on our first night together. I gave up my feeble attempts to re-establish verbal contact with him. Arms linked, we walked under the vaulted ceiling, past benches on which people sat in attitudes of resignation, redcaps pushing baggage carts, pigeons foraging for food morsels. Other passengers rushed down the stairway, but we walked slowly, delaying the moment when he would have to board his Pullman car.

The train groaned, wheezed, and blew plumes of white, scalding steam from its underside.

"You write to me now," Bill commanded.

"How can I?" I was already weeping inside and there was a great something stuck in my throat. "Do I write on the envelope 'Mr. William Faulkner, Rowan Oak, Oxford, Mississippi, return in five days to Miss Meta Carpenter, Hollywood, California'?"

"No. Write me care of Phil Stone." He scribbled an address on a scrap of paper that he found in his pocket. "Phil's my closest friend. He will see to it that I get every letter."

"You're sure?"

"Don't put a return address on the envelope."

"Will you write to me?"

"Every chance I get, ma'am."

For the rest of the time, we stood silently at the Pullman car steps. We had said nothing to each other of our inner anguish and now there was less than nothing left to say. People were boarding the train, a porter was calling "All aboard," and Bill said, "Go on back to the Studio Club, m'honey, and don't wait, for God's sake, for this train to pull out. Don't make me have to see you standing on this platform. Damn it, Meta, please go, or I'll not get on this damned train."

I did as he bade me before he could see the brimming tears—climbed the metal stairs to the upper level and walked back toward the great shell of the station. At the telegraph office, I wrote out a wire to be delivered to Bill at some stop along the train's route: "I will wait for you forever. Love, Meta."

Driving back to Hollywood, I tried to envision Bill on his seat in the Pullman car. He would be looking out at the lights of Pasadena by now or reading one of the volumes of poetry he had packed in his shaving kit. I hoped that he had not drawn a garrulous seat partner, else he would edge away fastidiously, inch by inch, until he could put no more space between himself and the talkative one, then escape to the smoking car.

He would smile to himself as he puffed on his pipe, oblivious of his fellow smokers. Was he thinking of me? Or was it of the beloved child, the tiny daughter whom he would soon swoop up in his arms? Or Estelle? Dark misgivings scudded into my mind like clouds and massed there. It had all come to nothing with Bill Faulkner. Of the men I had known, he was the one who was most nearly right for me, the only one who could keep me living in a fever pitch of pure exhilaration, yet the bright, flaring circle that enclosed us had broken and I was alone once more.

Approaching Western Avenue, I hit the brakes hard when a car in the next lane swerved into my path, then shot through the red light. Waiting with fast-beating heart for the signal to change, I let the image of a train wreck, cars twisted grotesquely, flash across my mind. Dear God, let Bill be safe, I petitioned; bless the engineer's hands at the throttle, if they still use throttles, and bless the tracks and the signals and oncoming trains. Was he praying for me at this moment as I was praying for him? Were my questions his questions? Why, since he loved me, had he not broken decisively with Estelle weeks ago? What kind of life was it for him in Oxford—damn its sacred soil—with a wife who drank herself into insensibility and could not be trusted with their only child? Was he bound to Estelle by pity, by obligations beyond the marriage vows? I punished myself sadistically by saying aloud to the dashboard, the bug-splattered windshield, the worn upholstery, the rear-view mirror, that Bill Faulkner did not want a divorce; he had no desire to exchange Estelle for me. Suddenly there were stinging tears and I quickly pulled the car over to the curb until I could clear my blurred vision. If there were passers-by staring at me, I didn't care. I sang song after song, anything that came to mind—songs from movies, songs I remembered from childhood—until I was dry-eyed once more. Where, when, had I first started singing aloud as an antidote to pain?

By the time my head touched the pillow, I had purged myself of suspicion. I was certain that William Faulkner loved me. A few months ago, I had not been mature enough to take the real measure of a man's love. So there was growth of a kind. What was needed now was an inventory of possibilities.

I must first face the fact that Bill Faulkner had made no promise to me to come back. He had kissed me and boarded the train, leaving unsaid all that I thought would be made clear in our last few moments together. The chances of any director other than Howard Hawks signing him for a screenplay were remote. He had no Hollywood agent that I knew of. And I could not say that Bill would take another Hollywood assignment if it were offered; the money would be no goad if his new book sold well.

What was going to happen to me? Twenty-nine, though I looked nineteen, I had almost run out of margin for blunders with men. I could not—I must not—let myself count on Bill. Marriage? I worked in a vast dream factory. Robert Taylor as prince/playboy/doctor gave up his throne/inheritance/practice for Joan Crawford as shopgirl/streetwalker/ruined woman. There were fantasies enough without my spinning another. Parting from Bill had been like the tearing of live flesh. But there was an Estelle. There was a Jill. There was a Rowan Oak. And there were Estelle's two children, Bill's mother, all the people, black and white, dependent on him.

"Why does all the responsibility have to fall on you?" I once asked Bill.

"It just does."

"But why do you have to accept it?"

"I guess I was built for it."

I beat into my mind the certitude of his life apart from me, willing it to remain there like a bruise. Yes, yes, he belonged to Estelle and Jill and those others—not to me. Tomorrow morning when I opened my eyes he would be that much closer to the train connection that would return him to Oxford. The reality of the Mississippi town in which he had spent most of his life, the locus that was his Jefferson, the whole countryside that was his Yoknapatawpha, would dim out his time with me.

Bill would have his writing and the maintenance of Rowan Oak to poultice the raw pain of separation, but what salving balm could I find? I would have to quickly fill up my life with things that would lessen the anguish, diminish the cold sense of loss. There was music, yes, but at best there were only a few concerts a week in Los Angeles. It had been years since I had studied piano. Could I go back to it now, regain the excellence I had reached in Memphis, then go on from there? An old daydream in which I sat at a grand piano in a vast auditorium, tremblingly aware of the thousands of people in the darkness, pushed itself up from nowhere. No! Cut! It was too late. I would never reach that pinnacle. I couldn't be Howard Hawks' secretary/script girl and still have the time, the boundless energy, the discipline, the purity of spirit—that last above all, my girl—to devote myself to the piano again. Even if I had these qualities, where would I find the money to pay a top teacher? I thought of my purse on the last day of the week, with never more than a crumpled dollar bill or two, smelling of face powder, and a few coins. Something—anything—to take my mind away from Bill, blindfold the eyes so that I would not be reminded of him. What if I enrolled for night classes or extension courses at UCLA, rushing to the campus after work and coming home too exhausted to think or feel? Suppose I again applied myself to the task of understanding art? Before Bill came charging into my life, Richard Day, an art director at Samuel Goldwyn Studios, had given me access to his office library of art books. Each great artist, he explained, had a unique angle of vision; nobody before him had painted this way, had seen the world beyond the mass of himself in quite the same perspective. Here was an El Greco. Could I, without looking at the text, pick out another reproduction of this artist's work after studying his identifying style? A Turner? A Klee? A Modigliani? Not enough, my forays into art. I needed to be wholly possessed by something. But what? The fortune cooky was without a message from the Hong Kong Noodle Company, the card that issued from the weighing machine was blank, Dorothy Dix would have no panacea. The antidote I needed to William Faulkner was William Faulkner himself. I could, of course, leave Hollywood altogether. My parents in their letters continued to remind me that Hollywood was little more than a sinkhole, unsuitable for a young woman descended from Usserys and Dohertys, and that my place was with them in Arizona. They would provide for me. I could live with my Aunt Ione, but could I ever again live with my mother and father? The no's became multiple images, flashing lights in a pinball machine.

Chapter 8

Howard Hawks gave me a penetrating look when he arrived for work the next morning. I presented an unclouded face. I would not be, because he expected it, Lillian Gish betrayed, Helen Hayes suffering quietly, Janet Gaynor wringing expressive hands. My typewriter clicked away. I took the morning's dictation and had my employer's letters ready for his signature before lunch. Braving the crowded Café de Paris for lunch—Was anyone staring at me?—Those two writers with their heads together there, did they recognize me as the blonde who was always with William Faulkner at Musso & Frank's?—I found a seat at a table with three character actresses dressed in Western frontier garb. Good! I was saved from joining all-knowing studio secretaries at a nearby table. With my elderly ladies in their costume-department bonnets, I could stop smiling for the next half-hour, allow my vulnerability to hang out, grind my teeth if I wished. The drone of voices and the clanking of silver seemed oddly remote, faraway sounds heard through a window when one is ill abed. I darted my eyes right and left, and saw—or imagined it—a number of heads turned my way. Studios in the golden era of Hollywood, when the contract system flourished, were hotbeds of gossip. There was an incredible network of rumor and exaggeration from which professional radio gossipmongers mined most of the inside news that entranced the public; today, the interest, as witness the number of newspapers without Hollywood gossip columns and television stations with no movietown scoops, is almost nonexistent. Secretaries assigned to producers, directors, and writers not yet in preproduction stages had little to do other than read the morning trade papers, take messages, and write an occasional letter. To alleviate numbing boredom, they telephoned each other from office to office to pass on fact, half-truth, and falsehood. At least twenty secretaries now in the commissary would know that William Faulkner had left for Mississippi the day before, ending his affair with the Southern girl who worked for Howard Hawks; by clock-out time, half a hundred would have heard it.

Hawks left for the races, not to return until the next day. I finished my work like a run-down, secondhand automaton and later, at the Studio Club, shuffling the letters in my box, hoping to find a telegram, I heard my name called out.

"Meta." It was a girl who worked at MGM. "You haven't come dancing with us for months."

"I know."

"You remember that CPA, the one you thought was such a good dancer? He's asked about you a dozen times."

I had no idea whom she was talking about.

"How about next week at the Grove? We're all going. I could tell him you're available."

"Thanks. I'll let you know."

Even as I promised, I knew that it would be a long time, if ever, before I could bring myself to go back to the mindless good times. It was a way out—better than anything I had thought of—but I simply wasn't going to take it.

The next day's performance was wretchedly B picture, poverty row. My smile was anemic, my jauntiness palpably contrived, and my eyes red-rimmed from weeping. Hawks noticed it at once but made no comment. I managed a record number of typing mistakes and blundered outrageously in spelling names. Lunch—I could not face the Greek chorus of secretaries—was half a sandwich and a cup of coffee in the office. By the day's end, I knew that I was near emotional collapse and that it was doubtful whether I could make it to work the next morning.

There were letters in my box, but no telegram. Dazedly, I glanced at the return addresses on the envelopes. The last letter was from Bill, my name and address written in his distinct and arcane hand. In my room, I read it in one hasty scanning, like a thirsty man gulping down water.

"9 P.M. on the Golden State Limited. Darling, love, dear love, dear, dear love—I had to be cold and still when we said goodbye; if I had let myself go and hold you, I would not have let you go and boarded the train."

An hour before, I had wondered whom at the studio I could ask for a sleeping pill. Anything to bring me oblivion through the night in my tiny cloistered room. Now I was almost making tatters of Bill's letter, reading it, folding it, putting it away, opening it again. I was Bill's love, his dear, dear love. Nothing had ended. We had only begun. Great walls had moved and there were open spaces never there before and a fresh wind was blowing through. I rushed down to the dining room before it was too late to eat the evening meal to which, along with breakfast, my weekly payment entitled me. Saved from being Ophelia, I ate ravenously to be strong and vital and beautiful for my lover.

Later, the letter placed reverently on tables, dresser, bedspread; regarded, smoothed over, hidden, retrieved, I committed every word of it to memory. Bill had credited me with an intuition I did not have. How could I have guessed that he had cut himself off from me at the station in order to leave me? Now I was seeing it all as it might have been; Bill weakening at the last minute, holding me, the porter shouting and beckoning, the train moving out of Central Station with his bags and books and manuscripts placed in the rack over his seat. No. I let the scenario fall to the floor for the cleaning crew of reality. I was glad he had been able to board the damned snorting, puffing train that had carried him away from me. He was a strong man who needed to believe in his

Nine years old, back from a summer spent on the plantation at Tunica, I posed for a Memphis photographer, with my mother approving the stained-glass window background and the assorted props.

I was thirteen and had given my first important piano recital after passing the Mississippi-Arkansas-Tennessee Tri-State musical examining board. Dreams of concert fame spun in my head.

Demure, soft-spoken, given to romantic dreams, I approached my six-teenth birthday in Memphis with the determination to dedicate myself to music and become a renowned concert pianist. My talent was not that extraordinary.

Henriette Martin was my closest friend—a handsome, magnanimous, gifted woman whom Faulkner found entertaining. Her career as a screenwriter suffered when she was blacklisted by Hollywood studios during the terrible years of the witch hunt and the House Un-American Activities Committee. Unable to find work as a writer, she pounded the pavements as a census taker to keep body and soul together.

At the Studio Club. That's me in the last row on the left. Marjorie Williams, the beloved director of the club, is third from the left, last row.

With Faulkner in the courtyard of the Studio Club, whose alumnae included Gale Storm, Janet Blair, Norma Jean Baker (later to be known as Marilyn Monroe), Kim Novak, designer Georgia Bullock and author Ayn Rand.

John Crown and Sally Richards in the days before their marriage, when there was opposition from the Crown family to Sally as a suitable wife for the brilliant pianist.

Chloe, our puppy, was a year old when my beloved Aunt Ione came to visit me in Hollywood.

There was still film left in my cheap box camera on a warm Sunday afternoon in the Studio Club's courtyard, so Sally Richards took her turn as photographer to snap a picture of Bill Faulkner, hands in pockets, John Crown and me. The dress was one of the few in my scant wardrobe, and Bill's Harris tweed jacket was the same one he had worn at our first meeting.

A bare-chested William Faulkner taking the sun on the beach at the Miramar Hotel, where we would spend our weekends when he had the money for a cottage, which wasn't often.

The sweetest picture (in my opinion) ever made of William Faulkner, the gentleness and loving kindness of him radiating from his face as he sat on the edge of the fountain in the courtyard of the Hollywood Studio Club, where I lived.

When Faulkner beseeched me for a portrait of myself that he could keep in his hotel room, I prevailed upon Milton Gold, an outstanding photographer at the Samuel Goldwyn Studios, to photograph me alone and with Chloe. I did not give Bill his choice but, like any young woman in love, picked out the pose I wanted him to have—a profile shot, idealized and romantic.

The camera was on Tamara Toumanova and Leonide Massine in the Warner Brothers film version of the Ballet Russe de Monte Carlo's Capriccio Espagnole, *with Jean Negulesco, kneeling, as director. Note my early pants suit.*

A very young John
Huston (I am in the
background) leans
over Humphrey
Bogart and Walter
Huston, who dropped
in to observe filming,
on the set of The
Maltese Falcon.

Helping Bette
Davis with her
lines on Now
Voyager.

Director Raoul Walsh would
turn his back when a scene was
being played, roll a cigarette,
then ask me, "Met, how was it,
were all the words there?"

The Road to Glory—*hanging on every word from director Howard Hawks with two of the stars, Warner Baxter and June Lang.*

Warner Baxter prepared a chili luncheon for the cast and crew of The Road to Glory, *and it was served on a sound stage. I am sitting between Fredric March and June Lang on the left; on the right is Howard Hawks, flanked by Warner Baxter and director of photography Greg Toland.*

*Although at first I was reluctant, Bill persuaded
me to go along with him to Marc Connelly's house
in Hollywood, and there we found Dorothy Parker
and Ben Wasson, Bill's agent. In a 1975 biography
of Faulkner, I am identified in the same picture
as—was it one of Estelle's little jokes?—someone
named Mrs. Ernest Pascal.*

*Walking along Hollywood Boulevard, Faulkner
spotted one of those automatic quarter-operated
photography booths and nothing would do but
that I have my picture taken—so that he could
have my likeness in his wallet. He snipped off his
favorite and I kept the rest.*

Bill had no photograph of himself to give me, so I brought my box camera to his room at the Knickerbocker Hotel and snapped this picture of him.

Bill took pride in this picture he made of me in his hotel room. He can be seen looking through the box camera in the mirror on the wall.

I wore my mother's bridal gown when I married Wolfgang Rebner in 1937.

Wolfgang Rebner as he looked when we were married and dreamed of a good life in the world of music.

Hollywood, 1937. Wolfgang and I were about to be married and I had closed Faulkner out of my life (I thought).

The first years back in Hollywood as Wolfgang Rebner's wife, with Perky, right, and Chloe at my feet.

While I was on my honeymoon in Frankfurt, a leading woman photographer was attracted by my American look and asked if I would pose for a series of portraits. The photograph she chose to give me out of the many she took showed me looking far more German than American.

A photograph taken of Jill at the beach by her doting father and proudly given to me.

Helping Richard Burton and Elizabeth Taylor in a highly dramatic confrontation in Who's Afraid of Virginia Woolf?

A reunion with Fredric March in Hombre *on location in Tucson.*

I took this snapshot as we entered Oxford and approached Rowan Oaks, years after Faulkner's death, when I found myself in Mississippi as script supervisor on The Rievers.

Standing at William Faulkner's grave, at the time of that visit, I was only dimly aware that my friend Mel Traxel was photographing the scene. MEL TRAXEL

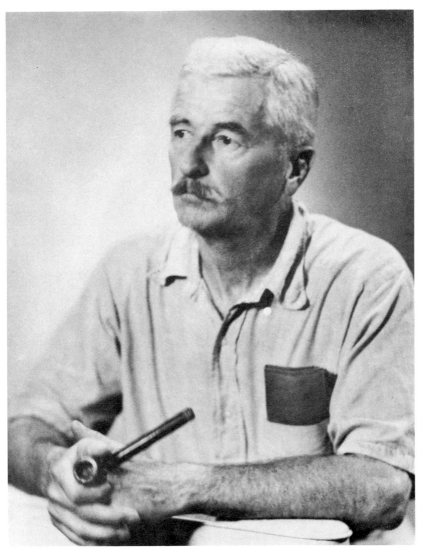

In one of my letters to Faulkner in the last years of his life, I asked if he had a recent photograph that he could send to me. He replied that he had no pictures of himself but would have one made. A month or so later, this white-haired, dark-browed likeness arrived.

I held script on so many routine films, giving all of them my best efforts, that now they have all become a cinematic scramble in my mind and I am unable to remember the titles. BOB WILLOUGHBY

strength as he believed in his genius, and I had helped him unknowingly with my loving acceptance of his behavior.

I wrote to Bill that night, declaring my love for him over and over, feeling gloriously reprieved. It was the first of many letters that were sent to him in Oxford, all delivered in accordance with arrangement to Phil Stone. What happened to them, I never found out. I think Bill would have destroyed them only if their discovery threatened him—or me—in some way. *Did you bury them, Bill? Are they in some secret cupboard somewhere, bound with decaying string, each letter in its proper envelope?*

In his second letter, he referred to the paper napkin with the "maiden's autograph."

". . . it is in my left hand as I write this. And when I put this period down, it is going back into my left breast pocket where it lives."

With Bill's first letters, I began to feel that an alteration of some kind was required in my life. It was akin to the menopausal compulsion that some women I have known experienced, without knowing the why of it, to change the placement of furniture in a room; they try to ignore it at first, then the insistent force within them will not be denied and they find themselves pushing heavy furniture over rumpled rugs until, at the point of collapse, gasping for breath, they survey a made-over room. What I was to overturn, move, transform, I did not know until Bill's reminder that I had not yet written him about the puppy.

My reason for not immediately going to the kennel was the Studio Club's ban against pets. Marjorie Williams was flexible about minor rules, but the one taboo she would not modify in any way had to do with animals. Relax the prohibition for one girl and the building would swarm with tail-waggers—yelping, mewing, spitting, growling, pulling at leashes, lifting hind legs. Now, wondering how to explain to Bill that I was not allowed to have a dog, it suddenly occurred to me that he had known it all along. There had never been a four-legged creature within the walls of the club when he visited me. The gift of the puppy was his way of telling me—of course!—that it was time for me to move away from the Studio Club. He would not, sparing, unhurting lover that he was, rudely take me by the shoulders and point out that to continue living among seventy-five women in a structured mini-society was to remain childlike and ingenuous. The club was an extension of my Memphis finishing school, a kind of amber in which I could be preserved as I was. Here I would not grow, toughen up, learn to parry the aggressions of other people. To accept Bill's gift, I would have to resign as club president, move to a place where pets were permitted, and live as a woman independent of a group.

Very well. So be it. Since Bill wanted me to leave and had taken an indirect way of telling me, I would look for a small, cheap apartment. Bill had become in his absence not only the lover who had cruelly withdrawn his warm, ardent body from mine, widowing me in effect, but a strong male figure in my life, not father so much as older mate. I had never regarded my own father and mother as dominant figures; because of their own emotional conflicts, I thought of them as my children. Now in Bill I had the stable force that had been missing from my life. It was not only that he propped me up but that he knocked childish notions out of my head, patiently taught me about human relationships, forced me to look at the spherical whole to find my own truth. When I was less than an apt pupil, he put off further instruction until tomorrow.

Unlike other men who had hurt me out of their own emotional insecurities or had lashed out at me when the pressures of life became too grinding, Bill had no need to injure or cripple. He was a punching bag, a tackling dummy, designed to take endless hurts and shocks from others. He raised up, restored, and healed those he loved.

The problem of how to afford even a room with a private bath was unexpectedly solved by the reappearance in my life of Betty Walter. Unusually tall for a woman at that time, painfully thin, with a ravaged look, she was, nevertheless, arresting and vivid. In Memphis, when Betty, Sally, and I walked along Union Avenue past the Peabody Hotel, it was Betty who attracted attention. We found a corner away from everyone at the Studio Club and Betty catalogued her private woes. She had not recovered from her divorce in Memphis. Although she was regularly seeing Victor Kilian, a fine and reasonably successful actor, she could not ward off abject depression.

"I could live with Victor, he has a house in the hills, but I can't bring myself to do that," Betty said. "Oh, Meta, why did I ever leave the South? I feel so cut off from everything."

"Have you thought about going back home?" I asked sympathetically.

"Yes, but I don't want to. There's no place for me there."

I thought quickly. By sharing an apartment with another woman, the rent and utilities would be half. Besides, I had real ties to Betty. Her mother and mine had attended Belmont Private School together in Nashville, and Betty and I had been friends since girlhood. As a woman who had been married herself, she would understand my involvement with William Faulkner—if he ever returned to Hollywood. I had only to suggest the idea of an apartment together to bring the light back to Betty's eyes. We would begin at once to look for a furnished place within our combined means. Large living rooms with space for grand pianos were out. We would avoid the high-rent districts. I wrote Bill that I would be telling Marjorie Williams in the morning that I would leave as soon as we had found a place. Once Betty and I were settled, I would go to the kennel for "our puppy."

It was Betty, with more time for combing Hollywood, who discovered the bungalow court on Crescent Heights Boulevard, almost directly behind the Garden of Allah, where many actors and writers from New York and London stopped when they were in Hollywood. Bill had stoutly resisted the temptation to live there. The Garden of Allah and the nearby Château Marmont, another favorite with writers, were steeply expensive; the former was a particularly hazardous place to work because of the endless drinking parties, and Bill had learned firsthand while living at the Algonquin in

New York how literary camaraderie could impede his work. I hastened to inspect Betty's find. There was a small living room, furnished with a sagging couch, that had the look of the Hollywood of poor actors reduced to hopelessness, one bedroom with two beds, a bathroom with ancient plumbing, and a dark kitchen built for only one person at a time. I thought of the capacious drawing rooms and library at the Studio Club, then said yes, it was fine, and since it was all right with Betty, why couldn't we move in the next weekend? I informed Bill of the new address and received an answer from him within the week.

It was hot in Oxford, but there were wonderful hours with his Jill. They would lie on his bed and watch the horses from his window and once they had gone swimming in the spring branch creek. He was not drinking, he wanted me to know, and his flask had not been touched. No credit to him, it was just too damned hot.

"Also—most of the usual uproar has blown over. It didn't worry me anyhow. All the while I was not listening much. I was thinking about the maiden's mouth. My white, my beautiful, my swan. Don't I know? Don't I?"

That Sunday, I drove to the Knebworth Kennels and found among the small, awkward furry creatures a big-eyed, plump female cocker spaniel, newly weaned, that licked my face in instant love and trust, and would not be diverted from me by a biting brother. I said I would return for her when she was paid for, but the kennel people would not hear of it. The arrangement with Mr. Faulkner was that I was to have the dog of my choice immediately. I drove home with the bundle of fur on the seat beside me and in my purse her pedigree with blue-ribbon-winning sires and dams going back for yelping generations.

Bill was notified by a letter posted the same day. The puppy—our puppy—was adorable. Now I awaited the name Bill had promised to give her. By return mail came his check for the kennel and a name for the small creature sleeping at my feet: Chloe.

"I can see you going out to see her, entering and seeing her, and I imagine you say, like I said one day when I came in a door, 'There she is.' "

When he was in Hollywood, the tug of Oxford kept Bill in a restive state. Now that he had let it draw him back, there was a counterpull to me in Hollywood, a retortion, and again peace of place was denied him.

He was not happy, he wrote, but he had not thought to be and had also accepted that. Although he knew that he should not admit it to me, he had hope. He longed by day and dreamed a little by night. It had been his intention to leave me free to do with my life whatever I wished before he would see me again, but he hoped, and it was as well that I knew it. Did I know? Could it be that I knew and that he had guessed it? Perhaps that was why he had put the hope into words, breaking his vow to himself.

The clear admissions that came from Faulkner after the months of silence and obliquity dumfounded me. Now I must connect the warm, outgoing man of the letters with the man who was largely a cipher to me. For the first time I began to understand actions that had cut me to the quick, responses that I had misinterpreted. His hope? I had not known that he had hope for us. Through no flaw or fissure in that terrible armor had I been able to perceive signs of dream, expectation, intent—only his own darkness. But holding me fast or lying alone with me in the night, he had actually seen us as man and wife, yoked us together, moved us through the years —Bill and Meta, Meta and Bill—and I had not guessed it. How many times, thoughts straying from his work on *Absalom, Absalom!,* had he faced the wife in his imagination and patiently explained that their life together was untenable, that nearing forty he had a clear right to what happiness he could find, that she would somehow be provided for, and that Jill would be better off with him and his Meta; remonstrating, pleading, offering her everything he possessed, then, finally, shouting, accusing, putting his life on the table as the poisons of anger darkened his face, and sweeping that life away in exploding fury. Bill had hoped as I had hoped; in his own kind of dramaturgy of the mind, he had dreamed too. Now I knew there was a chance for us and the conviction of it shot through me like a tremolo.

The letters I wrote were affirmations of my love for him, accounts of Chloe's progress at canine training school—she would soon be home with me, housebroken, tractable, non-chewing—communiqués on the casting for *The Road to Glory,* and the conveyance of warm affection from John and Sally, who took me with them to concerts, plays, and movies. I chronicled the most minute evidence of my personal growth, knowing it would lift the corners of his mouth into a proud smile. In reply to a letter from my parents calculated to fill me with guilt for a purposeless way of life (they still did not know that Mr. Faulkner, of Oxford, was my lover), I pointed out that I was a grown woman with my own life to live; I would not be manipulated. Bill had said, "You must assert yourself with them. You are a person separate from your parents," and I had finally found the strength to define myself without alienating them. As I made judgments about others, I learned to weigh them and to subtract biases as I would small sums from greater sums.

Bill sent copies of his books, each inscribed to me; those that he couldn't supply, I found at the library, though often it meant waiting until the Hollywood branch had requested a scarce, one-copy-only Faulkner title from other branches. I felt my skin grow clammy when Joe Christmas murdered Joanna Burden, mourned for Quentin Compson when he drowned himself in the Charles River, felt my scalp tighten when Temple Drake hid in the corncrib. I also tried to read writers of whom Bill spoke most often—Thomas Wolfe, Willa Cather, Erskine Caldwell (Bill was not sure he would fulfill his early promise), Ernest Hemingway, and F. Scott Fitzgerald—though not in depth, for I was a late starter.

Wearing sensible low heels, I stood in front of Renoirs, Van Goghs, Manets, Turners, and Rembrandts at the Los Angeles County Museum; Gainsboroughs and Reynoldses and Whistlers at the Huntington Library; Groszes and Klees and Kandinskys at the few art galleries that existed in Los Angeles in the mid-1930's. Occasionally, I would go back to the Studio Club on Sundays to have dinner with Miss Williams or a few of the girls I particularly missed. One Saturday afternoon, I drove to Musso & Frank's, thinking it would assuage my loneliness to have a drink in the back room, but I no sooner entered the restaurant than I turned about and left; seeing all those familiar faces but not Bill's, grave and reflective, would have only saddened me.

I dreamed once that Bill's face had been erased from my memory. To the great, elongated shadow figures moving in the background of the nightmare, I protested that I did, indeed, remember my lover's face, needed only time to bring it back from the shafts of memory, but I could not force Bill's image to materialize. I came awake, instantly remembering every aspect of my beloved's countenance—the thick hair, the brown eyes alive with intelligence, the moustache with its jutting hairs, the quality of his skin, the good, strong jaw. Taking care not to waken Betty, I dressed and gave Chloe a walk. For a moment, I thought I saw Bill sitting on the curb in the early morning light, as he had many times on Lodi Place.

An earlier letter had hinted of "uproar" at home. Now he began to confide more about his difficulties with Estelle. He had discovered that in spite of his warnings to local merchants, she had managed to charge up to about a thousand dollars during his absence. Among the items were some overstuffed pieces of furniture and a radio.

"So I have given myself (I have a small soul after all) a certain amount of sadistic pleasure in ejecting from the house pneumatic divans and Cab Calloways and so forth. Also I have . . . No I won't tell you about it."

The image of Bill Faulkner, angered beyond the limits of endurance, as he threw Estelle's purchases out of Rowan Oak stunned me. My good and gentle Bill? But then I did not fully know, I told myself, what had gone on between husband

and wife before I came into his life. My gaze went back to the three words, "Also I have . . ." Why hadn't he finished it? What was it that he couldn't bring himself to put into a letter? Had Bill finally asked Estelle for a divorce? It was a dangerous speculation for me, too much daydream in it for a woman with a weakness for the illusional, but it insinuated itself in my mind and would not be torn out. I went back to an earlier letter in which he had written, "I should not say this. I have nothing to base it on, nothing particularly new, that is, but I have a feeling that I'm going to be free soon. I don't know why I feel it." Steady, girl. Put it away in its box. If I had learned anything at all from Hollywood, it was that nothing was to be counted on until it happened. I had seen too many actors replaced at the last moment, too many writers with empty hands on the day that contracts were to be signed for movie rights to their books.

One evening, arriving at the bungalow from work and opening Bill's letter with packages still tucked under my arms, I began to screech with joy.

"Meta, what in the world?" Betty appeared from the kitchen, alarmed.

"Bill's coming back." I danced around the drab living room holding the letter aloft. "He has a new screenwriting job. He'll be here"—I had to consult the letter—"soon. He doesn't say when. Just soon."

Knees threatening to buckle, I sat down and stared straight ahead for a moment like a cataleptic, then hastily scanned the letter again. I hadn't misread it. There had been an offer— from whom he failed to say—and he had accepted. How could he announce it to me so calmly? I grabbed Chloe and informed her that Bill was returning to me.

"He gave you to me." I laughed. "You're not just mine— you're ours."

Betty, happy for me, mixed us a highball, then another— she always seemed to have a bottle of whiskey about—and we celebrated until the room whirled about and I crawled into bed, happy and exhausted.

Chapter 9

There was no money for new clothes, but I splurged for three dresses, anyhow. I attempted to brighten up the bungalow with bright pillows and ashtrays. Whatever was washable was washed, scrubbable scrubbed. I wrote Bill that I was in the grip of the strongest emotion I had ever known and that I lived for the day when I would see him again and wherever my love for him led me, there I would happily go. Our private history until Bill's departure had been played out for the most part in a pantomime of glance, sign, gesture, and touch, few declarations of love from him except in moments of passion and in his poems to me, and little enough on my side because of his own constraint. Now I put my feelings into my letters to him and it was a release that lightened my heart and clarified my very blood.

Production started on *The Road to Glory*. I moved through each day self-confident and composed. The letters from Bill and the certainty that he was coming back to me were my amulets against the crassness, the small cruelties, and the rampant egomania that rise to the surface on a Hollywood set when millions of dollars, combustible personalities, and madmen are involved. I used the textual memory of them as a black woman in Mississippi wore her conjure bag against evil spirits. Nothing could ever again harm me. *The Road to Glory*, filmed on Twentieth Century-Fox sound stages and on the vast studio backlot, was a far more difficult assignment for me than *Barbary Coast* in my dual capacity as script girl and secretary. Late at night, having finished the last of my liner notes to the film editor, Betty sound asleep in the next bed, I would write Bill about the film. Although he was not a movie fan, he knew stars by name and had seemed secretly pleased when I pointed out celebrities to him. Fredric March, I wrote, was playing the young Lieutenant Michel Denet, Warner Baxter the aspirin-gulping Captain Paul La Roche, Lionel Barrymore the crusty Papa La Roche, June Lang, in company far too fast for her, was Monique, and in featured roles there were Gregory Ratoff, Victor Kilian (I had mentioned him to Bill before as Betty's friend), John Qualen, Theodore Von Eltz, Paul Fix, and Leonid Kinskey. I did not tell him that precious little beyond structure was left of his and Joel Sayre's screenplay. Howard Hawks knew how to use actors for more than their talent and physical presence. His was not so much direction of his players as it was an adroit channeling of their personalities into the roles they portrayed, so that the actor without fully knowing it infused his whole idiosyncratic self into his character. To remove that last barrier between the actor's naked libido and the part itself, Hawks would ask his cast members to paraphrase their dialogue.

"Say the line as you would say it yourself in this particular situation," Hawks would suggest, and I would be there to record the improvisation in shorthand. Rarely were actors, who often find it difficult not to tamper with the writer's words, at a loss for replacement speeches. If the words had the ring of truth, Hawks would go with them, convinced that since they were being uttered by a player caught up in the emotional flux of the scene, they were therefore far more valid than the words of professional writers who might have worked for weeks on the jettisoned dialogue. He was a man who had the most inordinate respect for novelists and play-wrights, quicker than most of his peers to recognize the new giants on America's literary horizon, yet he had little regard for their art in the long run. The critics of the day accepted the dialogue in Hawks' canon as the authentic work of the screenwriters. Unfortunately, the critical fraternity is no more clairvoyant today in fixing credit or blame; many a screenwriter is blasted for lines written by the director in the new omniscience conferred upon him by reviewers and noisy film buffs.

In all fairness to Hawks, the improvisational approach was risky and he knew it. Far safer to shoot line for line from a screenplay that has been rewritten many times for concision, impact, and visuality, and, most important, the transitions and connections in story line.

The deification of Howard Hawks by movie cultists decades later caught me by surprise. I had regarded him as a knowledgeable, gifted director, but not a film maker to stand with William Wyler, George Stevens, Ingmar Bergman, Federico Fellini, and Bernardo Bertolucci in the pantheon of great masters of the film form. While he tended to improve on the screenwriter's contribution minutes before the camera turned, he was guarded and conservative in all other aspects of the director's hegemony, mindful of budgetary restrictions, rarely self-indulgent, and even more rarely seized by inspiration. For the most part, he took no chances with writers and actors, backing himself with the best of their guilds, and further protecting himself with top cameramen, film editors, art directors, set decorators, sound mixers, unit production managers, and assistant directors. Rehearsals were extended; some mornings, Hawks would ask his actors to work on a scene until noon without going for a take, then break for lunch, or he would instead ask, "Does anybody feel like trying it for the camera now?" The care he lavished on nuances and details held him to two setups a day at this point in his career, but there never was a time when he did not prefer to shoot slowly and with the greatest deliberation. Interpretations were left largely to the actors themselves. There were no quiet sideline conferences between director and actor such as I witnessed working with other film makers who had the ability to liberate the actor, drawing from a pedestrian player a performance of rare power and magic. Hawks was not an actor's director, but then neither are most of the venerated members of the craft today. The D. W. Griffiths are gone, the von Sternbergs are nowhere to be found, the alchemists have all but vanished. As we shot *The Road to Glory,* it was obvious that Hawks did not have it in him to be Svengali to June Lang's Trilby, and her performance, as a result, was uninspired. On a Hawks film, his actors would be positioned where he wanted them, and their movements would be carefully blocked out for them, but the rest was a matter of the actor's own skill and the director's choice of takes.

An unnatural quiet fell over the company when Hawks, after a seventh or eighth take, turned to Victor Kilian and asked irritably, "Would you just mind doing it my way?"

Victor, who had received no direction whatever, cast a mild look at Hawks and said, "Why, sure, only I didn't know you had a way." Nor did any of the other actors.

My latter-day wonder at the honors paid to Hawks was as nothing compared to my shock on reading not too long ago that his films not only celebrated the friendship of strong, physical men, but that in most of his work there was the archetypal Hawks heroine—Jean Arthur in all her variations, incapable of guile or artifice where her man was concerned, straight-shooting, accommodating, undemanding, sweetheart and pal all in one. Clearly, Howard Hawks knew far more about his blonde secretary and her relationship with William Faulkner than I had deduced from his uninquisitive manner and masklike face. I make no pretense to having served as the model for the classic Hawks heroine, comfort and joy of the noble, stalwart Hawks hero. The coincidence of timing and likeness, however, cannot be entirely ignored. If any part of me as I was then went into her creation, Hawks and the directors who borrowed from him are welcome to the bits and pieces.

The war scenes for *The Road to Glory* were shot on the studio backlot, now Century City with its thrusts of stainless steel and black glass. Night filming in particular was an exhausting, bone-chilling business. As we sat huddled in the camera perimeter, warming ourselves in the heat thrown by powerful arc lights, the actors and extras shivered in trenches and dugouts. Shells burst over us in gaudy special effects and rigged explosions ripped up the earth within camera range. When battle scenes were at their bloodiest, rain pouring down on soldiers as they fell or moved ahead into enemy fire, according to the assistant director's instructions, I had to look away, so real were the sequences. The sight of Lionel Barrymore lying on his stomach in a water-filled shell hole and Leonid Kinskey, caught on barbed wire between opposing forces, unable to free himself from the hundred spikes, screaming for his comrades to help him, affected me in spite of the moviemaking equipment visible only a few feet away. Like others of my generation, I lived in constant fear of a repetition of World War I and believed that munitions makers might lead us once more into global suicide.

Matching Hollywood photography to the graphic footage from *Wooden Crosses,* each frame like a dark mezzotint, made filming doubly complicated. Unsatisfied with dailies, Hawks would reshoot endlessly to achieve the photographic quality of the French movie. Despite the arduous schedule, the company remained friendly. I recall Warner Baxter cooking gallons of chili in his dressing room to serve at lunch next day to the cast, staff, and crew; Fredric March's unfailing geniality and youthful good looks; and Gregory Ratoff's rich, rolling Russian accent.

John Crown telephoned one night to announce with barely restrained excitement that his good friend and quondam fellow *Wunderkind* Wolfgang Rebner was in Hollywood for a brief stopover before embarking on the next leg of a world tour as accompanist for Emanuel Feuermann, the renowned cellist. They had known each other, John and Wolfgang, since they had been prodigies in Frankfurt, Germany, where Wolfgang's family lived, and had both studied there under Edward Jung. Virtuosi at age ten, they both appeared as guest artists with symphony orchestras through-out Germany and Austria.

"Wolfgang loves movies, can you imagine?" John said. "If he could see one being made or just even visit a film studio, it would be a great thrill for the foolish boy. I don't want to impose on you, Meta, but can you pull a wire or two?"

John and Sally came along the day I arranged a pass for the visiting German musician. On the sound stage where inte-riors for *The Road to Glory* were being filmed, the three stood at a remove from the camera area, my friends, who had visited studios before, only mildly interested, Wolfgang Reb-ner awed by everything, even the clapper. When the camera was being reloaded, I left my chair to talk to the visitors. Wolfgang hardly looked at me, so fascinated was he by the magic circle of light that defined the area of photography, the walls of other sets visible in the semidarkness, men overhead in the flies adjusting arc lights, carpenters hammering away. I thought him a handsome man, tall, dark, lean, with an aris-tocratic European face; thick-lensed glasses rode the bridge of his curved nose. His English, refined by residence in London, was faultless, marred by only the slightest of accents.

"I hope I will have the privilege of hearing you play," I said, meaning it, visualizing him at the piano in a swallowtail coat.

"It would be my greatest pleasure, Miss Carpenter." He bowed, almost from the waist, with a quick, easy grace, then turned a hypnotized gaze on Warner Baxter, Fredric March, and Lionel Barrymore as they took their places in front of the camera. As filming continued, I would glance back and marvel at his rigid attention. An hour of observation was enough for John and Sally, exasperated by the repetition, the time consumed in relighting, the flubs of actors, and the thick-ening tensions. Wolfgang, however, was rooted to the spot and reluctant to leave. During a move to another part of the sound stage, I drove my guests to the backlot, at that time as extensive as any in Hollywood. Wolfgang gasped with wonder as we passed standing outdoor sets: Western streets, a small town square, a Chinese temple, a European street, a lake with a steamboat afloat in the middle, whole blocks of brownstone fronts, a vintage train at a depot stop.

"It's incredible," Wolfgang marveled. "They all look so real—more than just false fronts with nothing behind them."

"Like some people," John commented.

"The most admirable workmanship goes into all of this," the German pianist went on. "The people who create these sets are near-geniuses. The fine detail is astonishing."

We passed an ante-bellum Southern mansion and Sally tapped Wolfgang on the shoulder. "Meta once lived in a house like that."

"Oh, yes, the South." Suddenly he caught sight of a waterfront set and clapped his hands delightedly. "I recognize backgrounds I have seen in many movies," he said. "I am sure I have seen many of them before."

"Yes, and you'll be seeing them again, old boy." John laughed. "Over and over and over again."

Driving back to John's parked car, I tried to answer Wolfgang's barrage of questions. Of an investigative mind, he wanted to know about process shots, glass shots and the construction of miniatures. Could we drive past the crafts building, where sets were built? Did composers who wrote music scores visit the set when the picture was in production? He liked the films of George Cukor, Clarence Brown, W. S. Van Dyke, Mervyn LeRoy, William Wellman, and Frank Capra—"Mr. Hawks, too, of course; I remember seeing *The Dawn Patrol* when it showed in London"—and he vastly preferred American films to the European variety. Who were the other directors with whom I had worked? How many thousands of people were employed by the studio?

"Forgive me for asking so many questions," Wolfgang apologized as we parted, "but this has been very stimulating for me."

"I'm surprised," I said, "that you know so much about the American film industry."

"Oh, I read everything I can get my hands on about the making of movies. Also, wherever I am in the world, I find time to go to them. In Tokyo, I plan to see the Japanese cinema. As you can see, I am hopelessly addicted to movies—any kind."

Saying goodbye, Wolfgang kissed my hand with a flourish and thanked me for a rare experience. Would I, John asked, join the three of them for dinner that night? Ever since Bill had written that he was coming back, I had shunned the company of others after work hours, content to talk to Betty when she wasn't rushing out to meet Victor Kilian, walking Chloe around the block, and rereading the letters from Oxford. But how could I refuse an invitation from John, who, with Sally, had filled in the emptiness of my life when Bill left? And how could I disappoint the German visitor, his face alight with hope? I would be happy to meet them at the Hofbrau, I agreed, but I couldn't promise to arrive on time; Howard Hawks generally wrapped up early, but there were times when he wanted to dictate after we had finished shooting for the day.

Wolfgang Rebner, who had hardly looked at me that afternoon, made up for his inattention that evening. He held my chair for me, jumped to his feet when I stood, fussed over my comfort. A superb raconteur, he moved his witty stories forward with the assurance of one who knows how to build tension so that the tag line excites pure mirth and relief. He clowned, punned outrageously, and delivered himself of epigrams that could only have come to him at the moment. At one point, having suggested to the waiter a German dish that was not on the menu, he invaded the kitchen to satisfy himself that the dish was being prepared to his specifications. Even thinking in an access of guilt that it was not Bill but a stranger sitting across from me at our favorite Hofbrau table, I was not immune to his charm.

Whether I wanted to or not, I was having a good time. I was familiar with the music over which they argued and I had at least heard of the glamorous personages whose eccentricities sent the friends into paroxysms of laughter. How different from my evenings with Bill when he would talk to me about writers whose names were wholly new to me and quote from books I would never read. Later in the evening,

Wolfgang talked about his tour with Feuermann and I listened fascinatedly. Out of the wing of my eye, I noticed that Sally sometimes turned her head away, unable to conceal a certain coolness, almost a hostility. Was she resentful of this man who had known John far longer than she and who now commanded his undivided interest? I watched Wolfgang for an indication of his response to Sally. It came soon enough with the arching of an eyebrow at an ingenuous comment or a suffering look when his European humor completely escaped her.

At midnight, I announced that a half-comatose script girl next day would cost Twentieth Century-Fox several thousands of dollars and contribute little to the good dispositions of Howard Hawks and Darryl F. Zanuck. It had been a marvelous evening and I had completely forgotten how exhausted I was at the beginning of it. I put out my hand to wish Wolfgang bon voyage and a successful tour of Japan.

"Surely you'll be with us tomorrow night," he said.

I explained that I had a great many things to attend to in the next two weeks, that I was worried about leaving Chloe alone, and that a close friend, as Sally and John knew, was coming back.

"Not all that soon," Sally reminded me. "Oh, come on, Meta."

Behind his glasses, Wolfgang blinked bemusedly.

"It won't be the same without you," John argued. "I thought it was understood that we would all be together."

"I'm sorry."

John overrode my every excuse. "We'll show Wolfgang the town together. We'll even get him to play for us." He raised his hands in a grandiose sweep. "You have never heard piano until you hear our Wolfgang play."

"All right, John, all right." I signaled my surrender. Who could contend against this tall, assertive young man who gathered everyone, Bill Faulkner along with the rest of us, into the magnetic field of his personality as if we were so many iron filings.

Although I told myself that I was breaking my rule against

seeing any man other than Bill only because of my friendship with John and Sally, I enjoyed the evenings that followed. There was something almost schoolboyish about the exuberance of the two men when they were together. More anecdotes were recalled, all of which they told with unflagging zest and *brio,* but always with that little-boy edge of mischief, as if, having been deprived of normal childhoods, sitting hour upon hour at a piano while other children played and teased and fought, they were now, grown men, compensating for the release they had been denied. Again, they would enter into long and serious philosophical discussions that made me realize how far their minds ranged beyond music. Sometimes I would turn back to listen after Sally had diverted my attention and hear them speaking of National Socialism and of Adolf Hitler. A number of times I heard, without attaching any significance to it, the words "Aryan" and "non-Aryan." They pitched their voices low and would leave off abruptly when Sally or I came within hearing distance. Sally, liberal and informed about the world in which she lived, a liberated Southerner before she left the South, would have understood the concern that made them grave and guarded, but to me Hitler was a ridiculous buffoon with a postage-stamp moustache who gestured and fulminated in the newsreels.

On Sunday, at the Crowns' house, Wolfgang did not choose to perform, as I had hoped he would. Instead, the two musicians, each drawing the other out, engaged in disquisition, with great brandishing of arms, on compositions that interested them above all others. What had been the composer's intention? What was he really saying? How would Wolfgang interpret this curious Chopin passage; John this rich, powerful phrase of Bach's? Each would expound his beliefs, his theorems, then rush to the piano to demonstrate. Never having been privileged before to be in the presence of artists probing for meanings and nuances, I sat spellbound. Once John sought to enlist Sally in an argument over a Schubert sonata, urging her to come to the piano and play a middle passage, but she would not move from her chair. She had given stage center to John at the very beginning of their relationship and every day she retreated farther into the wings—a pretty young woman with shining hair and full cheeks and a radiant smile that redeemed the drabness of the unbecoming clothes she chose to wear. Occasionally, John's father would drift in, listen, nod his head, then depart, to be replaced by Mrs. Crown, still handsome, still the elegant diva in the proud tilt of her head and her erect carriage.

That Wolfgang Rebner was all John had represented him to be—and more—was evident in the fragments of music he played to illustrate a point. It might be only two or three minutes in duration—for he could not wait to spring up from the piano bench shouting "See what I mean?"—but his music struck at the heart with its purity and power. At the piano, in the act of merely bending over the keyboard, he was instantly transformed; his sharp-featured face became almost beatific, his body an angular extension of his instrument. In his assured command of the piano, the technical and intellectual grasp of the work he was concerned with came through clearly. There was a range of tonal variety. The phrasing was spirited, scarcely mannered. He could by merely rippling his fingers over the keyboard evoke in me feelings of exaltation and nobility.

"What shall we do tomorrow night?" Wolfgang asked. "Meta? Sally? John?"

"Dancing," Sally said. "Let's go dancing."

"Would that please you, Meta?"

"I'd love it."

"Then dancing it will be." Unlike the rest of us, he had money to spend and would not hear of our passing up the more expensive attractions of Los Angeles.

We went to the Biltmore Bowl. That whole day I had smiled to myself at the prospect of an entire evening with a man who was surely a superb dancer. Tall, slim, with an elegant stride, shoulders thrown back, he would be European in his dance style, but he would lead authoritatively and I would follow with no difficulty. I could hardly wait to take to the floor with him. When the anticipated moment came, I realized that I was in the arms of the world's worst dancer. This man with the exquisite sense of timing at the piano pushed me about the dance floor with all the grace of a kangaroo. We collided with other dancers. My sandaled feet were trod and retrod upon.

"I'm very sorry," Wolfgang apologized.

"It's nothing."

"Have I hurt you?"

"No, not at all." Spoken as my mutilated feet throbbed with pain and as visions of toes mangled and bleeding flashed through my mind.

There were flowers the next day. A few hours later, he managed to get through to me on the sound stage for a brief "I know you're busy, but I suddenly needed to hear your voice. Will you please say 'Good afternoon, dear Wolfgang' and then I will let you go back to your actors and your director." Each day thereafter until his departure, fresh flowers were delivered to the office for me and a telephone call would reach me just as I returned to the sound stage from lunch. Two nights before he was to leave, we had dinner together, an arrangement I had agreed to with some hesitancy, even after being assured by John and Sally that I had no reason for misgivings.

"Bill would see nothing wrong in it," John insisted. "You are not interested in Wolfgang Rebner romantically. You will be going out with him only because he is my good friend. You are doing us a favor."

"What do you think, Sally?"

"John is absolutely right. You know how fond we are of Bill Faulkner. We wouldn't for anything in the world tell you to do something that would make Bill unhappy."

"Of course," John added, "he's fallen in love with you."

"Wolfgang?" I colored, feeling the sting of blood in my cheeks. "Oh, no."

"It's true, Meta," Sally said. "He may not show the signs and symptoms, but he's in love with you, all right."

"He's enchanted," John broke in. "Straight out of Max Reinhardt's *A Midsummer Night's Dream*, wandering love-struck through the forests of Hollywood."

"He's too much a man of the world," I insisted.

"Wolfgang?" John laughed quietly.

"I'm sure he finds women wherever he goes."

"My dear Meta," John corrected me, "all of Wolfgang Rebner's life, most of it anyhow, has been spent at the piano —practicing, rehearsing, playing, composing. Dalliance requires time. And time away from the piano is a commodity that he has never had."

I was suddenly uncomfortable, caught in a complication I didn't want.

Betty Walter telephoned to say that a letter from Bill had arrived and for the rest of the day at the studio I was on edge. Dear God, let Bill not write that he had put off his trip. I rushed home to read the handwriting, no longer odd to me, all thoughts of Wolfgang and my evening alone with him swept from memory's cells. My relief was enormous. Nothing had changed. I could expect him on the twenty-second. Bill's communications during this first period and for all our future separations affected me almost physically. The envelope that contained the letter, the minute strokes of his pen, the plain paper on which he wrote—all arranged themselves into a kind of conduit through which was transmitted to me, or so it seemed, the very force of his being. A Faulkner letter made me shut myself off from everyone and allow images of our days together to cut like flung golden disks across my mind. With Chloe snuggled at my feet, I would go to bed early, sometimes without food, and think on Bill happily, as a novitiate on her lord. I snapped on Chloe's leash, thinking of the warm bath in which I would luxuriate after our walk and the poems in *A Green Bough* that I would reread before I fell asleep, then with a jackhammer jolt I remembered my date with Wolfgang. It was out of the question. I had demonstrated my friendship for John and Sally by being their visitor's partner for the past evenings and on Sunday afternoon, but how could I be alone with any man tonight? I went to the telephone a half-dozen times with prepared excuses, only to hang up before the connection was made. Finally, there was nothing to do but walk Chloe, dress hastily, answer the doorbell at the exact minute we had agreed I was to be called for, and go to dinner with my German escort.

By the time we each had a drink, he had dispelled my reserve and I was laughing at his banter.

"Will you please read the menu to me?" He smiled. "Top to bottom, please."

"It is too dark for you?" It was one of those restaurants of studied gloom, unfair to the myopic and the astigmatic.

"Oh, no. It's simply that if I read it, I will be required to take my eyes from you longer than I care to."

I asked question after question of him, thinking how a fraction of the fusillade would have snapped Bill Faulkner's equanimity, and listened pleasurably to the clipped foreign voice, so different from Bill's soft, blunted Mississippi tones. He was the son of Austrian violinist Adolf Rebner, the former leader of the Frankfurt Museum Orchestra and the well-known Rebner Quartet. His first teacher had been Edward Jung and later he had been a pupil of Artur Schnabel's at the Berlin Hochschule. Paul Hindemith had lived in the Rebner house and taught Wolfgang composition. Where had he concertized? There had been recitals in Frankfurt, Bremen, and Berlin, then he had appeared in Copenhagen and London. After coaching orchestras and serving as musical conductor in Bremen, Dresden, and Prague, he had returned to London, where he was assistant conductor to Sir Thomas Beecham at the Covent Garden Opera House.

In Japan, he would conduct the Tokyo Symphony Orchestra, with Feuermann as soloist of the evening. A tour of the United States would follow—Los Angeles, lamentably, was not one of the cities on the itinerary—and then he would return to Europe.

"Frankfurt," he said without joy. "Home for me."

"What's home like?"

A hesitation, a sudden tightening of the mouth, then, "A very large house. Many servants. Formal gardens. A concert grand piano. Paintings, many old paintings. A magnificent Goethe library that is now mine; my grandfather left it to me in his will. Another life from this entirely."

"It sounds . . . storybook."

"No." His exhalation of breath was like a groan. "Not anymore."

"What happened?"

"Don't you know, Meta?"

"Should I?"

"I'm Jewish. Didn't John tell you?"

"No."

"Well, I am. It is very difficult today in Germany for Jews —even those who, like my family, have given so much to the country." He looked inquiringly at me. "Does it make any difference to you that I am Jewish?"

"Not at all." He needed reassurance. "Not in the least." I put my hand over his, feeling with my palm the ridged, long, pliant bones.

"That's good. That's very good."

"Did you think it would matter to me?"

"I didn't know."

"Now you do." I withdrew my hand as he began to caress it. "I've never seemed to have the capacity for prejudice. Even as a child, I never quite believed that I was the superior of my black playmates or their parents."

"You were taught that?"

"It was poured into my head like thick molasses," I said. "I remember feeling so sorry for my mammy and the other Negroes who worked in the plantation house because they couldn't sit at the table with us at meals. They had to have separate dishes and glasses."

"Have you known Jews before?"

"Not in the South, no. But my work brings me into contact with Jewish directors, producers, and writers. It's never occurred to me to look upon them as different."

"You have Jewish friends?"

"Henriette Lichtenstein is as dear to me as Sally or Betty. And John's half Jewish, though I never think of him as being anything but John."

"You're a remarkable lady."

His volubility and charm were stimulating. He was as sure of his talent as Faulkner was of his. When his tour with Feuermann was over, he told me, he would never again accompany another musician. But for the political climate of Germany, he would not have accepted the offer to tour with Feuermann at all, though his admiration for the cellist was unbounded.

"On my next visit to your country," he promised, "it will be Rebner in recital."

"Will you recognize me if I come backstage?"

"In an instant."

"Pushing my way through all the adoring women and the baskets of flowers?"

"I will permit no one but you to enter my dressing room."

The next night, his last in Los Angeles, Wolfgang was not his ebullient self, less than an inventive match for John's rollicking gambits. More than once, I thought I saw uneasiness and worry in the lean, sensitive face. He was leaving a boyhood friend and the wrench of it would be painful for him. Ahead of him were thousands of miles and weeks on end without a familiar face. John would be appropriately waggish when they parted tomorrow, hiding his own feelings, but then John had Sally as his love and refuge and ballast. Wolfgang had no one.

I said goodbye to him a second time. He kissed me on the lips and asked if he might write from Japan.

"I hope you will," I said brightly.

"And may I see you when I return to Los Angeles?"

"We'll have a reunion." I had to keep it on the level of friendship. "The four of us."

Chapter 10

The evenings that had made me forget the tensions on the set and my own fatigue had come to an end. At night, after the long hours, the grinding monotony, the inescapable crises, I worked on my cutting notes and turned in by ten o'clock. My spirits were buoyant. Bill was coming back and that was all that mattered. Exigencies found me calm and resourceful. Raw displays of vulgarity by crew members, often calculated to shock me as the only female on the set most of the time, failed to touch me. I watched exercises in monumental temperament with pity for the fire-breathers and wondered what it was about success that caused grown men and women to grow dragon scales. Even the narrowness and bigotry of the typical Hollywood union crew—Jew-haters, Roosevelt-cursers, Communist-fearers, denigrators of Catholics and blacks and Mexicans, espousers of the Silver Shirts, opponents of liberal legislation—would not bring down the sky kite that was my heart.

Toward the end of June, Bill wrote that he was counting the days, as he had as a child before Christmas, and that it would not be much longer.

"I think myself to sleep every night with you, only one night I thought too well: it was too much for Bowen and he waked me later in the throes of a natural phenomenon, so I know I've been away long and long enough."

On July 15, the day of Bill's departure from Oxford in his rattletrap automobile, his black employee Jack driving, I moved onto a plane of high anticipation. Bill was on his way! Money had brought him from Oxford other times because of grocery bills that had to be met, mortgages held by the bank on his 1840 house, taxes, stacks of invoices for services rendered and materials supplied. He had gone through periods when fifty dollars would have been as manna from heaven. Now it was different. He had chosen to come back to the Hollywood of power-drunk movie executives and swaggering stars, crimp-haired old ladies, hollow-cheeked, shuffling old men watering dry lawns, and tourists lining up for radio game shows at NBC and CBS for only one reason: to be with me. While he would for years to come need money desperately, there was enough saved from his earnings on *The Road to Glory* to keep his creditors from plaguing him for some months at least. I needed no other proof of his love for me than his decision to work once more in the Hollywood for which he had such contempt.

Daily, I studied a section of map concealed beneath my marked screenplay of *The Road to Glory* to guess where Bill might have spent the last night, where he might stop for lunch, where he would be by dusk were the weather clement and the roads passable. I could see his car passing along main streets with tin awnings extending from squat buildings on either side, moving through sun-stricken Southern towns with their endlessly repeated courthouse squares and ugly signs advertising snuff and chicken feed and patent medicines; a freight train would outdistance the slow, clanking vehicle in which he was a passenger, children would wave from the porches and galleries of mean houses along the roadside, whole black families would peer out from mule-drawn wagons. By the third day, pulse racing, I begged Henriette to let me take a rain check on dinner with her and Fletcher Martin, and asked John and Sally to give my ticket for a violin recital to someone else.

"Meta," Betty scolded, "it's a long drive and he can't possibly make it to Los Angeles in less than a week."

"I know, I know." Fussing with drab furniture. Wiping tabletops. Gathering up magazines in a neat pile. Brushing Chloe until her coat was silky.

"Then stop acting as if William Faulkner can make it from Oxford in four days."

I was worried about Betty, but I gave her no direct indication of my concern. Betty, gentle, soft-spoken, talented Betty, was drinking far beyond her meager tolerance for alcohol. Victor Kilian adored her, but his love was not enough. Something—was it the career she might have had or the wounds inflicted in Memphis?—guided her to the bottle with increasing frequency. By nightfall, whiskey made her critical and argumentative. For the past weeks, she had been unable to keep up her end of the rent and the full burden fell upon me.

I was glad for the nights when Victor, still wearing studio make-up, sounded his horn outside and she would hurry out to his car, drink in hand, for the rest of the evening. It had been a mistake to try to live with another woman, but I was not ready to admit it. Somehow, things would work out for us. I would have to take courage in hand and shock her back into some kind of self-discipline. In no event would I desert her or let her down. Along with Sally, she was bound to me, as Wolfgang was to John, by filaments of the powerful past; we trailed them after us wherever we went like the drooping fins of exotic goldfish. We were also three disoriented women trying to wrest some lasting happiness for ourselves in Hollywood. Why had we thought we could make new lives for ourselves here in this town of so many defeated, stunted, and maimed creatures? What had led us to think that we had a chance as musicians in a marketplace glutted with remarkable talent from all over the world? I would wait until Bill arrived, when some normalcy was established in my life, and then I would try to help Betty over her need to drink away her phantoms, whatever they were.

On the fifth night of Bill's departure from Oxford, I rushed home from the studio, bathed, put on a blue-and-white dotted-swiss dress with puffed sleeves, and stood at the screen door waiting for a sign of Bill. Chloe, sensing my nervous expectancy, whined as she watched my movements. By midnight, I gave up on Bill and fell into a troubled, twisting sleep. The waiting ritual was repeated the next night, but still no Bill. On the seventh night, I was wild-eyed with apprehension. There had been an accident on the road, I was sure. How would I know it if Bill were unconscious in some hospital or had been taken back to Oxford? I jumped out of my chair and raced to the door whenever brakes screeched outside or the headlights of a car swept across our walkway. A few minutes after nine, I heard footsteps and suddenly there was Bill in the doorway before I could stumble to unlatch the screen. We clung together, afraid it would all dissolve into dream if we let go.

"Bill."

"Meta."

"Bill."

"Meta."

Haggard and almost at the point of exhaustion, he had driven nonstop with Jack the night before; they had spelled each other at the wheel and slept by rounds in the back seat; except for food and steaming cups of coffee, they had pushed themselves since morning.

"I had to get here before you went to bed," Bill said, "otherwise there'd be another darned day before I could see you again."

Chloe, circling nervously, wanting to join in but wary of the stranger, finally made herself heard. Bill hunkered down to meet the furry animal he had bought for me, letting her know the smell of his hands, then stroking her; she turned over on her back, ecstatic, hypnotized.

"She's just the kind of puppy I figured you'd pick," he said. "No big, ol', flop-eared country bird dog but a sassy, fat, li'l, spoiled, no-count plaything bitch dog." He looked up, forehead furrowed. "Has it helped you to have her, dear heart? Has it been less lonesome for you?"

I nodded and knelt to join him on the worn carpet, taking life from his ardent mouth, feeling his strong body under his jacket, inhaling his sweat through his shirt.

"Bill," I murmured, "stay this time, please."

"I hope," he said, "that it will be for a right good spell. I'll know more in a few days."

"When you're away, I can't think of anything but when you'll come back. And now that you are here, I'm feeling this dread that you'll pick up and go away."

"You don't think I ever want to leave you again?" He pulled away suddenly. "Oh, Jesus, I've plumb forgot about Jack."

He found Jack Oliver waiting unobtrusively on the walkway where he had left him and brought him inside. I held out my hand, and when he didn't take it, I grasped his large, coarse hand.

"Thank you," I said, "for getting Mr. Faulkner here safely. I'll fix you something to eat, Jack."

"Oh, no, ma'am, thank you, much obliged. I ain't hongry."

"Bill, tell him he's welcome."

"It's his first time out of Miss'ippi, ma'am," Bill said. "Don't overwhelm him."

He would find a place for Jack to live—he had been told just where to go—and then he would return to me. An hour and a half later, having rented a room for his faithful black man, he was back, fatigue miraculously gone. We embraced, rocking, laughing.

"My sweet Lord, you're so lovely, ma'am, so white-skinned, so soft," Bill whispered hoarsely, his face sheened with perspiration and the grime of the road. "I didn't invent you. You're just like you've always been. The way I've remembered you—every day, every hour, every minute."

He found fresh linen in his battered suitcase and I brought him a clean towel so that he could wash up in the cramped bathroom with its jars and bottles of female unguents. Skin luminous with health, thick hair restored to order, a clean white handkerchief tucked into his jacket sleeve, he presented an appearance largely unchanged except for the coppery burn of the Mississippi sun and the first signs I had ever noticed of great, crushing strain around his eyes. It had come from more, I guessed, than the long hours of driving.

The restaurants in the vicinity of Schwab's drugstore were closed. We finally found a small Italian restaurant, only a few other couples dining. Bill had a whiskey neat, then another. The food was hot and spicy, and we washed it down with common red wine.

"Guess what?" Bill grinned as I began to apply my lipstick. "I still have this." He reached into his breast pocket for the Central Station napkin, now rumpled and torn. "Well, I won't need it now. I've got the real thing." He shredded the souvenir into an ashtray, set fire to it, found my hands across the tablecloth.

Betty would not be home for hours yet, but I would not let Bill make love to me in the bungalow. I drove him to the Beverly Hills Hotel, where he had a reservation for several nights, and boldly accompanied him to his room after he registered, chattering away to give the impression that I was a close friend who had met him at the railroad station. The hotel was even then, with its rise over Sunset Boulevard and its apartness from it, a hostelry that gave immediate peace to the heart of the traveler. Bill's love-making was fervent and afterward he lay breathing hard from the visceral depths of himself. I held him fast, this composed, plated man who suppressed a raging sexuality, wrestling with it constantly, man against savage angel, moaning in his sleep for remission, glancing up suddenly from his writing to see the fearful intruder advancing across the room to take him from his holy work, flying planes and riding fiercely to hounds to overcome the blood's involuntary rush and thickening. He was not, as he has been termed by a *New York Times Book Review* critic, "a womanizer," but a man whose carnality would have destroyed him as a writer had he permitted it, had he not for long periods by sheer exercise of will purged himself of the tickle of physical passion and consciously used the accruing power to feed his genius. In any case, he was not, as I knew him, a man who could easily spend his seed in any available woman. His sexual key was the image of a young woman, fresh and fragrant of skin beneath her summer cotton dress, tremblingly responsive to his desire. He could not complete the act of love after the first years of marriage with his drunken, quarrelsome wife or at the nearby bawdyhouses of the local Reba Riverses. When his fame and his mystery made him a magnet to women everywhere—in New York, Hollywood, Charlottesville, the cities of the world, even Oxford—he remained, except for one brief, twilight love affair, more self-denying than voracious. Sensualist, yes, as some of the drawings he made for me and his letters confirm. Womanizer not at all.

Released, drowsing, Bill stretched out and I pillowed my head on his chest, hearing the timpani of the great, vigorous heart.

"I have so much to tell you, m' honey," he said, winding fingers into my hair. "I went back to pure hell."

"That's over for now," I whispered. "You're with me."

"It was bad."

"I can imagine."

"But not as bad as it might have been. I could shut her out just thinking of you. She'd holler and scream and carry on, and I'd just see your sweet face—yours and Jill's—and not hear any of it."

"Really and truly, Bill?"

"Yes, ma'am, that's so." I thought for a moment that he had drifted into sleep, but he was wide-awake under his tired, closed eyelids. "She is drinking worse than ever, getting blind, staggering drunk, and that is a worrisome matter to me." A sigh of despair shuddered from his constricted throat. "I set things up this time so no harm can come to the children, but I will not be able to leave her many times more, the way things are getting to be."

He felt me tense and gathered me in his arms so that we were face to face. "The trouble is that in Miss'ippi—and I've sounded out more'n one lawbook lawyer on this, letting 'em think I needed the information for my book—the trouble is that the Miss'ippi courts always award the child to the mother."

"Always?"

"Every time. Estelle is not a woman who can be proved bad or unfit on moral grounds. There's just her drinking and that ain't enough for a Miss'ippi judge to take Jill away from her and give her to me to raise."

"But if she's a danger to Jill—"

"That won't make any difference. Estelle would get Jill sure as Sunday follows Saturday. Jill could see her ol' pappy once a week, but it would be Estelle raisin' her, not me."

"It's not right, Bill."

"You're not that long from the South, Carpenter, that you don't know how the mother is held to be the fit parent." Bill's "Oh, Lordy" was sonorous, weighted with pain. "In court, Estelle's recital of my drinking would more'n match mine about hers, and she'd find witnesses to back her up."

"But you haven't been drinking . . . that way."

"No, ma'am. As I wrote you, I've abstained. And I hope to continue not letting it get to me. But that's now—not last year." He was thoughtful, lower lip trapped between his teeth. "Now in my drinking, I can rouse myself from the effects. Of the two of us, I am the more responsible. Do I make a grain of common sense to you?"

"Bill, I've never seen you inebriated—"

"Inebriated?" He began to laugh, pulling me closer to him.

"—but that once . . . in Mr. Hawks' office."

"Inebriated! Oh, ma'am, I was drunk as a lord. I woke up that morning and thought, Here I am in Hollywood again, how am I going to stand it? I couldn't think of a way so I got drunk." Suddenly he was serious. "I wrote you that I had hope."

"I know you did."

"I still have it, ma'am."

128

"Then so do I."

"There's a possibility that Estelle and I will be able to reach some accommodation."

I had waited to hear it and now my eyes burned with salt tears that he could not see, that could be wiped dry if I moved my head quickly against the pillow.

"Where Jill and, of a certainty, Estelle's two young ones, Cho-Cho and Malcolm, won't in any way, shape, or form be damaged by divorce. Where there won't be recriminations and backbiting and downright misery." He shook his head convulsively, as if to ward off dread images of sorrow and ruin and death. "I cannot promise you anything, ma'am. You must keep it in mind that while I love you as I have never loved a woman before, I cannot—" The soft voice became clogged and gritty. "Let me say it this way: I want you for my own always, but I don't know—I do not know—whether it can ever be."

I left him sinking into the deepest abysses of sleep, too subterranean to be startled from by the sounds of my dressing and the closing of the hotel room door. Chloe whined as I turned the key in the bungalow lock. Betty, stirring, mumbled "Meta?" as I slipped into bed, Chloe at my feet, and I smiled myself into sleep. Bill was no longer thousands of miles from me but in a hotel bed five minutes away, his body and spirit quiescent for the first time since he had left me. For now, my emotional poverty was over.

Within a few days, Bill was back on salary at Twentieth Century-Fox, his salary charged to a small-town comedy for which he could draw on his fund of country humor. Denied his request to work away from the studio, he reported to the bleak office assigned him without complaint. The claustrophobia he experienced was a small price, he confided, to pay for the delight of being with me once again, and for another thing, he was away from the quarrels with Estelle—quarrels that "skinned me alive," he would say. There were other saving graces, too: he was again making a four-figure weekly salary and letters from Oxford assured him that watchful eyes were being kept on Estelle during her drinking bouts. From New York came word of the impending publication of *Absalom, Absalom!*

We resumed our pattern of life together as if there had been no separation. John and Sally, whom he telephoned almost immediately, met us for a reunion at the Hofbrau, where Bill's earthy Mississippi stories, some on the gamy side, came as fast as John's shafts of wit. No mention was made of Wolfgang Rebner or our evenings with him. On Saturday afternoon of Bill's first work week, we appeared at Musso & Frank's back room—Bill had missed it—and found ourselves surrounded within minutes by writers, some from our earlier visits, others newly arrived in Hollywood from the East. The conversations in the bar were rarely weighty in content and never, as I recall, concerned with the state of the nation or the world beyond, where Hitler was beginning to throw an outsize shadow. Saturday afternoons were primarily for laughs, for exchanges of the latest Hollywood anecdotes. Had we heard the one about the movie executive's relative who was kept on salary because he owed thousands of dollars in poker losses to studio moguls? Pressed for an explanation of his brother-in-law's duties, the movie satrap answered: "He is paid to keep a steady lookout from his office windows and notify us if he sees a glacier coming." Had Bill heard what Dorothy Parker or Robert Benchley had retorted to their respective producers? What Carole Lombard told her director he could do? Occasionally, there would be references to movies or new books written by back-room habitués. That summer, *Gone With the Wind* was the subject of endless discussion. No, Bill said, he had not read it and therefore could not comment on the picture it presented of the South during the Civil War. More than one scribe referred to me as "Miss Scarlett" to Bill's mild amusement. Hollywood writers were savagely critical of colleagues' books, plays, and screenplays. Bill had his own opinions of the literary worth of other American writers whose works were being published, but he was careful not to express them in the context of table gossip and exercises in literary denigration. In fact, he listened more than he spoke, and I, painfully aware of my intellectual limitations, held myself to dazzling smiles when they were appropriate.

Bill found a room in a small hotel near the studio; there Jack would pick him up every morning for the drive to the studio and call for him on the evenings when I wasn't able to join him for an early dinner. Our return to the Miramar was delayed for weeks until John and Sally could afford to join us. We left them to walk to our cabana from the dining room under a sky ribbed with gray washboard clouds. In the doorway, we watched winking lights far out at sea and held our faces to a late wind from the north.

Throughout the darkened morning hours, the wind lifted white sand from the beach and sent it lashing against the cabana, peppering the windows, stinging the walls. It was a manifestation of nature unknown to me, threatening and punishing, and I huddled in Bill's arms as in childhood I had clung to my mammy's protection when the thunder rolled over the Delta and the sky opened up to release its furies on the planted earth.

The morning was bright and still. I stretched out under a beach umbrella while Bill, John, and Sally swam and sunned themselves. Half asleep, I listened to the drone of the three voices—Bill's pure Mississippi, John's with a slight British overlay, and Sally's, girlishly pitched—and awarded myself a gold star for giving Bill Faulkner two good new friends with whom he was completely at ease and for whom he bore demonstrable affection. I had never seen him more relaxed and forbearing. The frustration he had suffered on not being able to complete *Absalom, Absalom!* was gone and he was not yet sufficiently under the thrall of *The Wild Palms* to be discomfited by the rush of time, lost or stolen. A letter from Oxford or a bad day in his studio cell would throw him headlong into gloom, but he would pull out of it almost immediately when he was with me. I sometimes caught him off guard, the inverted V between his eyebrows signaling worry, and I let myself think that he was preoccupied with the legalities of divorce.

"Tell me about Phil Stone," I asked one night in Bill's apartment.

"Phil?" He blinked puzzledly, as though I had no right to be curious about his close friend.

"Our go-between," I said.

Bill shrugged, then proceeded to talk freely about his friendship with the attorney who early on had encouraged him to write, who had literally stood over his shoulder in the beginning, and who had borne the cost of printing Bill's first volume of poetry, *The Marble Faun,* a mint copy of which today brings $3,000 on the first-edition market.

"Phil," he said reflectively, "thinks I ought to stay married to Estelle."

"But he knows about her!" I was dismayed to learn that the man whom I had trusted with my letters was aligned against me.

Bill scratched the side of his nose, almost as if this was his first chance to consider Stone's opposition. "What I think it is, on Phil's part, is a kind of feeling for the place he thinks I will have in American letters and for the kind of exemplary life that should go with it."

"Good husband, good father."

"Something like that."

"I don't know about writers," I said, "but nobody thinks any the less of great composers for having led morally ragged lives."

"Well, Phil didn't put his reasons into so many words." Bill stretched out beside me and let his hands glide over my body. "Phil's a country lawyer and something of a churchgoer and it may not have a lick more to it than that."

He allowed the circle of people around us to increase in number. Henriette he admired inordinately for her quicksilver mind, but while he responded to Fletcher Martin's highly masculine art—boxers, wrestlers, stevedores with great hulking bodies and massive biceps—he was never wholly comfortable in his presence. Since just being Southern gave most women extra points with him, he liked Betty Walter at once and there were some fine, easy evenings with Betty and Victor Kilian at Victor's home off Laurel Canyon; once Bill demonstrated his skill at parlor games by excelling at something called Red Cap; other times, he would sit cross-legged on the floor with me, back propped against a wall, listening intently to Pete Seeger and other folk-singer friends of Betty's play their banjos and sing lustily of American mountains and plains and rivers, of unrequited love among mountain folk, of freedom and justice, of rascals and rogues. To please me, he agreed to an evening with Sally and John at the Cocoanut Grove, a sheer extravagance for all of us, but only on the condition that he would not be expected to dance, having "two left feet and the grace of a lumberin' bear after bee tree honey." He dressed for the occasion in a dark wool jacket, snowy white shirt with a narrow tie, and white duck trousers. I told him, whispering so that John and Sally would not hear, that he looked like Ronald Colman.

"I sure as hell don't talk like him."

"No, Bill, you don't."

He was actually, at that time of his life, young, a mere thirty-nine, a handsome man in his own strong, authoritative way, with penetrating brown eyes, a strong curved nose, and a clean jawline. When he was not troubled, he would walk into a room glancing neither right nor left, letting his assurance carry him forward like a strong, sweeping wave. Stoniness and severity were not to come into his countenance until his fifties, draining away the bright dyes of youth, impounding the warmth of his younger years when, defenses unmarshaled, he laughed and sang and gave of himself without stint.

Bill's misery in crowds was very real, but this night he concealed his unwillingness like a competent actor working from a script. His face asked of me, "Have I made you happy?" and I let him know by my pleasure in the dance music and soft lights and elegantly dressed ringsiders that he had, indeed. I wore a strapless gown and he kissed my bare shoulders as he surrendered me to John for a dance, then, with Sally, watched us swirl and dip together to a mélange of Broadway musical-comedy tunes by Cole Porter, George Gershwin, Harold Arlen, Richard Rodgers, and Arthur Schwartz.

I longed to get him on the dance floor, if only to do no more than move from side to side in his arms, but I had given my word. We sat holding hands as John and Sally spun by us, John warning the DeMarcos and Veloz and Yolanda that a new hotshot dance team was on the way up.

"You're sweet to stand still for all this," I told Bill. "I know you don't care for it."

"I want you to be happy."

"I am."

"Sometimes I think to myself how much I'm depriving you of and I feel downright guilty about it."

"You've no reason to."

"I impose my unsociability and my reclusiveness on you."

"Have you heard me complain?"

With the completion of *The Road to Glory* I moved with Howard Hawks to the Samuel Goldwyn Studios to prepare *Come and Get It* from Edna Ferber's best-selling novel. Bill finished his assignments at Twentieth Century-Fox and shifted to the RKO Studios on Gower Street to help shape a screenplay from Rudyard Kipling's "Gunga Din." One day at Goldwyn's, I introduced him to Jo Pagano, who had been signed by Hawks as one of the writers on *Come and Get It*. Bill, familiar with Pagano's stories about Italian-Americans in *Scribner's Magazine* and *The American Mercury*, liked the handsome writer at once for his gusto and honesty. Even Jo's admission at Musso & Frank's bar that he preferred F. Scott Fitzgerald's work to Bill's—though he conceded the grandeur of Bill's body of work to date—failed to abort the friendship. Jo, in turn, admired Bill for his genuine simplicity and his own considerable skill at throwing the lance into the sacred, decorated bulls of American literature in the 1930's. Years later, when I was out of the country, Bill and Jo were downing drinks at the Melrose Grotto near Paramount Studios. The bartender fairly groveled when he discovered that one of his customers was the famous William Faulkner and announced to Bill that his wife considered him the greatest of all living writers. "She's read everything you've written, Mr. Faulkner," he boasted. "Just wait till I tell her I served William Faulkner today." A short time later, he asked whether Bill would accompany him to meet his wife, who lived only a few miles away. Bill readily agreed, as if visiting a bartender's wife were a normal event in the course of a day.

"He was the kind of man who would accept a bartender's invitation," Jo tells it even today, "but wild horses couldn't drag him to Louis B. Mayer's house."

Bill did accept, though he hated dinner parties and all formal social gatherings, an invitation from Samuel and Frances Goldwyn. Whether it was at the urging of the Hollywood agent who now represented him or whether it was his esteem for the distinguished films that Goldwyn made, I cannot say, but one day he told me that for this one time he was constrained to break his rule about Hollywood parties.

"I haven't asked you to go with me," Bill said quietly, "and I hope you are not hurt by it."

"I wouldn't go in any case," I assured him.

"Then you agree with me that it would be imprudent for us to be seen together at a private dinner party and that it would only cause a lot of unpleasant gossip."

"I do agree." There was no injury to my feelings. The thought of a roomful of people whispering about us chilled me. And what if our names were linked in a gossip column?

Mustering his last ounce of civility, Bill appeared at the Goldwyn mansion on time, suffered himself to be introduced to stars, movie executives and their spouses, stoically and monosyllabically answered questions about his opinions and work; dinner over, he fled, having observed most of the amenities like a true Southern gentleman and endured shallow conversational gambits for longer than at any period in his life.

I picked him up in my car at the RKO Studios' gate at the end of a workday and asked how he was coming along with the screenplay. Curiosity about his movie assignments was permitted, but even the suggestion of inquisitiveness about his novels would send him scurrying back into the shell of himself like some addled sea creature.

"The trouble with the script," Bill said, scowling, "is that these damned fool people"—he gestured toward the administrative building—"don't begin to realize that Gunga Din was a colored man."

Betty Walter's drinking had now become a serious problem to herself and her friends. Bill, ever sympathetic to heavy drinkers, assured me that he was in no way upset, but I could no longer bear to see him flinch at her rude parries. I had always wanted to live in one of the small cottages in Normandie Village, a complex of apartments that fronted on the Sunset Strip and descended the hillside to a narrow, short street below. Hearing of a vacancy, I rushed over to look at it without telling Bill. Although the quoted monthly rental stupefied me, I signed the lease. I would somehow manage the rent, even if I had to demand another raise from Howard Hawks or subsist on crackers and cheese. Now Bill could come to me and stay the night; I would no longer have to dress in the early-morning hours and, over his grumbling protests, slip into the dark, lonely night for the drive home. I would cook breakfast for him on Sunday mornings. He would be more completely mine and I unreservedly his.

Friends contributed oddments from their homes and apartments—chairs, tables, lamps, kitchen paraphernalia, rugs —and with money borrowed from my parents, still unaware of my involvement with the literary man from Oxford, I purchased the rest. Bill, lifting and carrying, pipe clamped between his teeth, helped me make the move to the first real place of my own. He proved to be astonishingly skilled at carpentry, connecting appliances, painting, and repairing. Betty and I parted on cordial terms, no breach in our long friendship. Somewhere in the recesses of her mind was the raw knowledge that she had almost caused a rupture between us, but she would never admit it to herself, then or in time to come; and when she no longer found it necessary to drown her woes in whiskey, the memory of her brief addiction was like a stab of black guilt. My new home made it possible for Bill and me to experience the closer relationship that men and women know only when they are thrust for most of their time together within the circumscribed space defined by walls and ceilings, though Bill returned on weekday nights to his hotel room to work on his new novel. The imperfections of the beloved, the human peccadilloes, are unseen when lovers meet in secret, their hours together measured out, M. d'Albert transformed in his ardor to godlike grace, Mlle. de Maupin leaving the love bed before the harsh light of morning, each partner moving in an amber glow of ideality. As we discovered our common frailties, they became the staves that held our love together. Bill's lapses from the sublime endeared him to me all the more and he, in turn, came to love me equally for my shortcomings. I could live with this man for the rest of my life, I told myself; the dark moods, his lack of attention to me when his characters possessed his mind, his aversion to self-revelation that would be with him all his life, his coldness to others when they pressed in upon him—none of it would be more than I could rationalize.

One Saturday afternoon, listening to a Metropolitan Opera radio broadcast of *Tristan and Isolde,* I waved Bill away as he approached calling my name. For a moment he gazed at me in absolute disbelief, the impact of my impatient gesture drawing the blood to his face, then slammed out of the room. When the love duet that held me mesmerized was over, I found Bill sitting on the outside steps, angry and remote, Chloe at his feet.

"Bill, I'm sorry. I just wanted to hear the love duet through to the end."

"Yes, ma'am." His mouth was still compressed, his strong shoulders rigid and held high.

"When I hear great music like that, I get lost in it, that's all."

Another "Yes, ma'am."

"Nothing else seems to exist for me." I reached for his unyielding hand and kneaded the resistance away. "Can't you see that music is to me what books are to you?"

"I just don't know, ma'am."

"There are things that are yours that I can't share. Not just your writing. You hunt. You ride. You go to air shows. You fly planes, which I don't do anymore. Everybody has something that is his own."

A nod. The language of a man's hand enclasping a woman's. The gentle pressures, the exploration of fingers, and finally the peace of two hands fitted together, a sculpted diptych.

"I know sometimes when I'm listening to music that you think I'm half out of my mind."

He laughed heartily. "You are a sight to behold, my beauty. Those hands flailing the air, that maniacal look on your face."

The day came when I could no longer put off telling Bill about Wolfgang Rebner, whose letters arrived daily, a whole white avalanche of them from Japan. My Southern voice, he wrote, had stayed with him and he could recall, when the strident Japanese street noises assailed his ears, the lilt and musicality of it as he could a Schubert *lied*. My face swam before him at the most unexpected moments. What a stroke of luck to have met me and how odd that it had come through his good friend John Crown, with whom so much of his earlier life was intertwined! Wolfgang wrote of the gratifying response of Japanese audiences to the concerts, of his meetings with brilliant Tokyo musicians, of his excursions from hotels and inns into streets where few, if any, foreigners had walked before, and of Japanese women, whom he found superior to Japanese men. From letter to letter, he became more self-revelatory. His whole life had been changed in Los Angeles; everything he had previously planned for himself was abandoned, since it would not include me. He had wondered why he had not, before we met, become seriously involved with a woman. Now he knew that life, by some powerful predeterminative force, had directed him to me.

"Bill," I apologized, never taking my gaze from his un-readable face, "I never believed Wolfgang would fall in love with me. Even when John and Sally told me, I discounted it. I thought there would be a few postcards from Japan and that I wouldn't hear from him again."

Bill dug strong fingers into Chloe's fur and she lifted her head in rapturous gratitude. "I'm not surprised that this mu-sician fellow is taken with you. What concerns me, ma'am, is how you feel about him."

"You don't have to worry on that score."

"You write to him?"

"How could I not answer? He writes every day."

"And what do you tell him?"

"That I wish him well. That I hope the tour continues to be successful for him and Mr. Feuermann."

"Is that all?" Gently asked, nothing of the inquisitor about him.

"I also write him about Hollywood. He's interested in what goes on."

"Have you told him about me?"

"No. There was no reason to."

He tapped the stem of his pipe against his teeth, thought-ful, puzzled. "This fellow—"

"Wolfgang," I prompted.

"Wolfgang. He writes of his feelings for you?"

"Yes, Bill."

"And you haven't returned his affection?"

"No, Bill."

"No?"

"His letters to me and mine to him—they don't touch what I have with you."

I could see the beginnings of a smug, swaggering male smile start to form, then he pushed it back and the mouth became a straight, noncommittal line once more.

"Honest?"

"You're the man I love."

"Well, now." He drew me down to his lap and kissed me gratefully. "I feel a heap better."

Bill thrust Wolfgang from his mind. He could not harbor jealousy for long without its blunting his powers as a writer and he knew me to be incapable of guile. But the realization that music possessed me, that I was bonded to it as I could never be to a lover, troubled him at times. Estelle, who "played piano right well," according to Bill, had never been passionate about music; hers was an accomplishment to be shown off in the front parlor rather than any special brilliance as a pianist. Remarkably prescient, able to receive startling auguries about total strangers who broke the seals of his privacy, Bill began to think of music as a rival and more than once asked how I could be under vassalage to something that he considered "white and opaque and distant." He could no more follow me into my world of symphony, chamber music, recital, and opera than I could enter his innermost domain, where he sat hunched over paper making tiny bird's-feet tracks with his pen.

His own work was my rival. As the pages of *The Wild Palms* increased, he became obsessed with the novel. Although we continued to see each other daily and on weekends, Bill began to leave me earlier at night. Sometimes he would go straight to the table that served him as a desk in his hotel room and sometimes he would catch a few hours' sleep before he would begin writing. All too soon came Jack's knock on his door and the moment when he must leave for the studio.

"You're so drawn in the face," I complained.

"I feel fine."

"You're not getting enough sleep."

"I never required much."

"You worry me."

He reproved me with a vigorous shake of his head. "It's nothing to cause you concern. I'm excited about *The Wild Palms*. I think I have something fine going."

We could hardly wait for the weekend during an oppressive heat wave to drive northward like refugees from sweltering, airless Los Angeles.

Temperate weather returned and there were pleasant evenings with Ben Wasson, Bill's agent for some of his literary efforts. A Mississippian by birth, witty and cultivated, he was, I am certain, hopeful that Bill would gain his freedom and marry me. His tacit approval, if only because I made his good friend and client happier than he had seen him in years, salved the hurt of Phil Stone's opposition. One afternoon, over my "Please, I don't think it's wise," Bill took me with him to spend an afternoon with Dorothy Parker and Marc Connelly at the latter's rented Hollywood house. Their immediate acceptance melted the ramrod in my back and I began to enjoy myself. Connelly took a photograph of Dorothy, Ben, Bill and me and later gave Bill prints for himself and me. I was taken aback to see the same photograph reproduced in the two-volume biography of William Faulkner by Joseph Blotner published in early 1974. I was identified as Mrs. Ernest Pascal, a woman I never met and of whom Bill had never spoken to me. As a rule, where writers he had known in New York were concerned, Bill was as wary as I of provoking gossip that might reach Estelle's ears, but with Dorothy Parker and Marc Connelly, with my own circle of acquaintances, few of whom had an idea of his stature as an American novelist, and with the scribes at Musso & Frank's, he had no qualms.

Bill, to my real surprise, next agreed to escort me to a cocktail party given by one of John's friends and important to me for some obscure reason. We drove with Sally Richards and John Crown, John negotiating the incline up to the high, twisting spine between Los Angeles and the San Fernando Valley that is Mulholland Drive with complete aplomb. We made a happy, jocular foursome, and at John's prodding, Bill softly sang "Steal Away to Jesus," a hymn that conjured up visions for me of black prayer meetings on the plantation. When we reached the proper address, Bill declined to come in with us.

"No'm," he said sweetly. "I'll just sit here in the car or take a stroll while you enjoy yourself."

I motioned to John and Sally to walk ahead. "You're sure?"

"Yes, ma'am. I'll wait out here till you're done."

I was sufficiently hung up on convention to want to die at the thought of walking through that doorway as an appendage to John and Sally, but I was incapable of pressing or reproaching Bill. My love for him overrode all disappointment. He watched my back as I walked bravely to the house; at the door, I looked back and saw that he was leaning against the car and filling his pipe bowl with tobacco. Never again did I suggest that he go with me to parties. I could not fully understand his aversion to people en masse, but I did not want to cause him even the small pain of boredom.

The intelligence from Oxford, from whomever it came, grew more ominous and Bill began to move inward into himself once more. Estelle was drinking heavily, and Jill, frightened at seeing her mother lying unrousable on the floor in an alcoholic heap, had cried out for her pappy. On weekends, unable in his anxiety to devote the morning to *The Wild Palms,* Bill would have Jack drive him to my hillside cottage at six o'clock and there he would sit on my "stoop," as he called it, and drink from a full bottle of wine until he heard me bestirring myself inside; by the time he knocked on the door, the bottle would be almost empty.

His consumption of whiskey increased, too. Where before he was content with one or two straight shots of bourbon at dinner, he now had as many as four or five before the food was brought to the table. Since the whiskey barely affected him, I made no comment. Secretly, I was worried that the control he had achieved since I entered his life was slipping precipitously. His drinking was no longer casual and free. I saw futility in his eyes as he gulped down bourbons neat.

A Sunday work call from Howard Hawks took me to the studio for the morning. When I returned to the Normandie Village cottage, where I had left Bill, Chloe met me at the front door in abject canine distress, all whimpers and squeaks as she led me to the bedroom. The bag of groceries I had bought on the way dropped out of my hands as I saw Bill huddled on one corner of the bed, hands stretched out, palms foremost, as if to ward off something menacing. His head was bent, eyes mercifully turned away from whatever it was that threatened him, and he moved as I observed him into a crouched position—knees up, shoulders sagging. The bottle of whiskey he had brought with him the night before was only a quarter empty. It was my first indication that the quantity of whiskey he poured into himself had no relation to his lapses into drunkenness; he could at times drain a fifth without losing control of himself; again, two drinks would be sufficient to hurl him into total inebriation.

"Bill," I called out, my stomach knotting in alarm and shock.

He looked up, no recognition whatever in his face, and screamed, "They're going to get me! Oh, Lordy, oh, Jesus!" He covered his head with hands that alternately flailed and supplicated, shouting over and over in a litany of dread, "They're coming down at me! Help me! Don't let them! They're coming at me! No! No!"

He was a man I no longer knew, and when I tried to touch him, he recoiled from me convulsively.

"Who?" I asked him. "Who's trying to hurt you?"

"They're diving down at me. Swooping. Oh, Lordy!"

"Faulkner, what are you talking about? Who's after you?"

He turned a face as white as library paste toward me. "The Jerries! Can't you see them?" Suddenly he was doubled over, trying to crawl into himself. "Here they come again! They're after me! They're trying to shoot me out of the sky. The goddamn Jerries, they're out to kill me. Oh, merciful Jesus!"

I held my own hands to my stomach, corseting myself against nausea, and groped for the telephone. Calmly— where did the presence of mind come from?—I asked Information for the home telephone number of a young violinist who was working as a male nurse in order to eat and pay his rent. Within minutes, I heard the young man's voice on the other end of the telephone connection and almost wept in relief.

"What do you think it is?" Bill's screams, now muffled by

the sleeve he held to his mouth, continued in the bedroom.

"Delirium tremens, I'd say," came the answer. "The d.t.'s. You've heard of the d.t.'s, Meta."

"Please, please, come over and help me with him."

I stood helplessly over Bill as he made his outcries, saying "Shhhh" to him as a mother would to a child in agony. When I tried to hold him, he lashed out at me with his arms, catching me once on the side of the head. Not only had I never seen Bill in a hallucinatory state; until now, he had not even lifted his voice under the stress of emotion.

My musician friend, husky and strong, arrived and managed to lift Bill to his feet. "Steady there, old fellow," he said. I saw Bill's eyes turn upward in their sockets as he was guided out of the cottage and up the zigzag steps to Sunset Strip. An hour later, the violinist called to tell me where he had taken Bill. He had been given a coffee enema and would be "dried out" until he was sober again.

Bill was waiting for me a few days later when I arrived home from the studio.

"Meta." He smiled lovingly, and I moved into his arms, wasting tears against his tweed jacket with the leather patches at the elbows.

Other drunken states requiring that Bill be treated were to follow, but this was the only one I witnessed in which his fantasy about German planes figured. I was never repulsed; my love for him never wavered. Bill was not a stumbling, slobbering, incoherent drunk; there was always that magnificent dignity, impervious to the end against the onslaughts of the whiskey in his body, so that even as he was led by strong arms to a waiting car, he carried his head erect, carefully placed one foot before the other, and all but bowed to me, his helper, and the world.

The RKO job gave out, there was a series of short assignments, and then his run of luck stopped; there would be nothing for a while.

"Don't go home, Bill, please don't," I begged him.

"What will I do for money?"

I had no answer for him.

"No, Meta, I don't want to wait around. I have to get back to Oxford. You know why."

"Estelle?"

"I've had the most distressing account of her drinking and I'm out of my mind with worry over Jill."

"Oh, Faulkner."

"It's not good. It's not good at all." Seeing my face break up into planes of grief, he took me by the elbows and forced away the hands that had gone to my blinded eyes. "I'll come back, m' honey. Soon as things are straightened out and there's some movie writing for me to do."

The night before he returned to Oxford, he held me to him for an hour or more, as if the slightest relaxation of his arms would cast me into the mouth of a great wave and I would be carried away from him into some terrible, dark boiling sea from which I would not return.

In the early morning (Jack was meeting him at his hotel and they would begin the drive to Oxford before traffic was heavy), he awakened me to say goodbye. The rough tweed of his jacket was like sandpaper against my bare skin as we embraced.

"My poor, sweet honey girl that I can't give one blessed promise to," Bill agonized in my ear. "I'm going to try this time, my beloved, I really am. But I can't say what will happen or whether anything will happen. If you had a grain of sense, you'd get shut of me right here and now, tell me to stay out of your life."

"You know I can't say that to you."

"I don't want to hurt your life, I never wanted to."

"Write me," I called out as he left the cottage. His footfalls on the Normandie Village steps were like blows against my heart.

Thundershowers, sleet, overcast skies, solemn gray light, would have been appropriate to my melancholy, my doloroso spirits. What director first thought of shooting the heroine gazing mournfully out of the window as raindrops slid down the glass? I was Hollywood enough to want the climatic concomitants of grief. But the days that followed Bill's departure were perversely clear, plumed with brilliant light, and the sun swooped at me like a relentless hawk when I emerged, red-eyed, from my cottage every morning. Work was something to push myself through daily, a succession of hours to negotiate.

The second separation should have been easier for me—at least I knew that Bill would be back—but I had sunk into my own black tar pit of depression, caught there, unable to extricate myself. Antediluvian woman. Clinging vine. I apologized to myself for myself. The female in me was in temporary shock, bereft in a cold bed, no more than that. It was simply that I had never been as close to another human being as to Bill in the last weeks. We had lain together, slept enwrapped in each other's arms, reached and clutched in the dark when our bodies separated in sleep's ballet, awakened joyously together. We had been two penned creatures in a snug enclosure whose walls had now given way.

Bill's letters helped a little but not enough. He wrote that the situation in Oxford was no better, but mercifully it had not worsened, as he feared. With all his heart he wanted to tell me that he would soon be free, but he would not allow himself to stray from the hard, cold fact of his marriage, he would not do my young life that injury. He still hoped. Beyond that, he would not commit himself.

Wolfgang Rebner's telephone call came as a jolt.

"Where are you calling from?" My voice was actually quavering. "Are you in Hollywood? Where are you?"

"In San Francisco." He had arrived an hour before and had only just now checked into a hotel room. His bags were still unpacked. He needed a shave and a hot bath. But first, before anything, he had to hear my haunting voice again.

"I have ten days before the concert," he said. "Is it possible that you can come up? This is a great, magnificent city."

"I know." San Francisco, with its quickened tempo and brisk, toning weather, might give me back to myself. I could walk until my shoe leather flapped like a Mack Sennett comedian's, ride the cable cars, lift my face to the oncoming fog, walk wide-eyed into Gump's, ferry to Oakland from the Embarcadero, spend hours on Grant Avenue in Chinatown.

"Then come, please," Wolfgang begged. "I'm always a stranger in cities. Don't let me be a stranger in San Francisco."

I thought of the money it would take for a round trip on the *Lark,* the train that hugged the coastline, and winced. There was barely enough money left from my last paycheck to get me through the rest of the week.

"Wolfgang, it's impossible," I said quickly. "We're about to start *Come and Get It* and Mr. Hawks would not allow me to leave."

"For a weekend—not even for a weekend?"

"Not when we're so close to a start date."

"Then I'll come down and see you. May I?" When I didn't answer at once, he added, "If I don't see you this time, it will be months before I'm back in the United States for our American tour."

I met him at Central Station. He came up from the lower train level with eyes darting left and right, neck craning, for a glimpse of me in the waiting crowd. He seemed taller than I remembered him to be, a handsome, elegant traveler wrapped in a Burberry coat. I lifted my cheek to be kissed, grateful for the boon of this man who had written that he was "obsessed with me," and felt a first outflow of affection for him, as if the dam of my careful resistance had broken in a critical area.

Where before he had been shy and tentative, Wolfgang was now worshipful, adoring, possessive. In the presence of John and Sally, he held my hand for hours, gazed at me with unconcealed love, and spoke endearments in German. Buoyed up by his devotion and by the music he played hours on end for me at the Crown house, John and Sally slipping noiselessly in and out of the room, I emerged from the doldrums, aglow with health again, able to bear my heartache. Wolf-

147

gang gave me none of the quiet strength that emanated from Bill, who had been—and remained—my circus-of-life strong man whose right arm could snatch me from any catastrophe. Wolfgang, however, had the power to stimulate me, take me out of myself, levitate me like a magician.

"I love you," Wolfgang told me over and over. *"Ich liebe dich."*

"You're sweet," I would say. "You're very sweet."

He would count the days left to him in Los Angeles and fume at time's flight. "I'll be gone such a long time. How am I going to get through all those months without you?"

On the day of his departure for San Francisco, he demanded to know where he stood with me.

"Meta, I have to know whether there's a chance for me. I have to know whether I can hope for your love."

It was time to tell him about Faulkner. Now it was his right to know. The intent eyes behind the heavy lenses blinked in chagrin. I reached for his hands, the sacred hands that drew sublime music from the piano.

"Wolfgang, I'm not married to Bill. There's nothing definite." Suddenly I did not want to cut loose from my life this brilliant musician who loved me and whom I could love in return were it not for Bill. The possibility that Bill might never be free of Estelle struck my mind with the force of a hurled rock. I must not close doors, seal passages. "You have to understand," I pleaded. "I'm involved with another man and it happened before I met you."

"He's married," Wolfgang reminded me.

"I know, I know. But there's nothing definite. It could all come to an end—next week, next month."

It was an irony that for the first time in my life I was being self-protective, as Bill had taught me to be, and at the same time letting myself see a future in which Bill would not be a central figure or even a peripheral one.

"It could also be that you will marry him," Wolfgang said bleakly.

"In time, yes." I moved into his arms and let him hold me.

"Wolfgang, I feel the greatest affection for you as a person and the most tremendous admiration for you as an artist."

"But not love."

"I'm not free to love you—not now. But things change. I could be. I might be."

"Yes?" A small involuntary smile. "You mean it?"

"I wouldn't say it if I didn't."

I sent him a telegram wishing him success in San Francisco and he telephoned after the concert to say that it had been a triumphant evening for Feuermann and himself. The next day they left for Valparaiso and other stops in South America.

My letters to Bill were happier. Phil Stone, despite his disapproval of our relationship, remained the faithful courier. A screenwriting assignment had been offered to him, Bill wrote, but his agent was insisting on the four-figure salary that had been established on the RKO job. I said a small prayer over my typewriter for a quick deal and was rapturous when Bill sent word that the contract was being drawn. A short time later came a letter, brief, only a few lines, that shocked and benumbed me. He could no longer leave Jill with Estelle in Oxford, Bill wrote. He was therefore bringing his wife and child with him to Hollywood.

Part Two

Chapter 11

Hollywood was embattled in 1936 and the consensus by late spring was that although more pictures would be made than at any time in the film industry's history, it was going to be one hellishly bad year. There was a rash of court actions—actors against producers, producers against directors, actors against agents. The Internal Revenue Service descended on top money earners and disallowed deductions. Suspensions of actors under contract were an everyday occurrence. Screenwriters, angry over changes made in their scripts by producers, demanded artistic protection (a boon still denied to them today) and agitated militantly for a closed shop. In that period, hundreds of writers were employed by the major studios and the satraps boasted that there was no novelist or playwright who could not be bought, be it Romain Rolland or H. G. Wells, with Hollywood gold. Directors were also up in arms against producers and formed the Screen Directors Guild, of which Howard Hawks was a board member. Shakeups and executive realignments at the top level stunned industry members. Almost everybody picketed at one time or another. The more moderate shook their heads sadly over the resonances of rancor and violence to be discerned beneath the polemics of contending sides, and sometimes, as they worried over strike threats and shutdowns, I was reminded of Delta folk who looked up to the sky each day for portents of fair weather or storm.

The convulsions of the motion-picture industry touched messenger girls and sound-stage floor sweepers more than me, but now, to camouflage the state of uncertainty into which Bill's news had hurled me, I pretended to have joined in the general pessimism. The year was, indeed, shaping itself into a stretch of unremitting blows and jolts and reverses: sandbags were falling everywhere and the stroller could put no trust in cocoanut palms. My mood was not helped by letters from my parents, still shocked at the mysterious death of Thelma Todd. "Come home," they urged. The warnings were sounded so often that I came to half believe that my parents had finally learned the truth about Bill and me, but I could not be sure. One evening, Helen Morgan, on one of the variety radio programs that were in vogue, sang "My Bill" in her small, sad voice. I couldn't hold back the tears over allusions to "his form and face, his manly grace . . ."

The press preview of *The Road to Glory* was held at Grauman's Chinese Theater. When William Faulkner's name flashed on the screen in the main title credits, my eyes blurred with pride, even though Joel Sayre's name was in first position. It was an important credit, Bill's first as a scriptwriter, and it would (I knew that much about Hollywood as a marketplace) get him many more screen assignments. Writing to him that same night, I reported the favorable reaction of the Hollywood press corps, many of whom commented in the lobby that Hawks' new film was a powerful antiwar document and compared it to his earlier *The Dawn Patrol* as a war genre classic. For myself, *The Road to Glory* held little dramatic interest; multiple screenings in studio projection rooms during editing had stripped it for me of any surprise at all. I have since come to admire film makers whose response to their work is the same the hundredth time as the first. They are able, as I have never been, to see their films with fresh eyes each time they are shown and to maintain an objectivity that is almost prodigious. There are, of course, those who will tell you, "I'm too close to it to know whether it's good or bad," but woe to those studio underlings who believe them when they say, "Please tell me exactly what you think."

Howard Hawks began directing *Come and Get It* in June, some four months later than the planned start date, and for the first of what were to be many periods of distress and anxiety in my life, I found a measure of deliverance in the nerve-battering processes of moviemaking. From the moment my employer strode onto the set each morning, tensions began to build and layer until, by late afternoon, the air on the sound stage was thick with strain, indecision, and malevolence. One reason for the pressure that bore in from all sides was that *Come and Get It* was a Samuel Goldwyn production, and Goldwyn, who had been ill for months and had undergone the surgeon's knife, was unable to act on Hawks' complaints and demands. Another was that Hawks was unhappy with the story line of *Come and Get It* and uncomfortable with Edna Ferber's characters. Aggravating the situation was the lawsuit he had instituted against Universal for failing to pay him the money due him on his contract to direct *Sutter's Gold,* which had been turned over to James Cruze. An important factor, too, was Samuel Goldwyn's promise to exhibitors that *Come and Get It* would be ready later in the year. Hawks, who did not like to work at a fast pace, was putting scenes in front of the camera before he was completely satisfied that his players were ready.

Wanting in solid experience as a script girl, I squeezed everything from my mind but the mimeographed pages of the screenplay by Jane Murfin and Jules Furthman in order to achieve a degree of competency. Time enough at night, working on my liner notes for the film editor, to worry about Estelle and to conjecture on what her presence in Hollywood would do to my relationship with Bill.

Edward Arnold and Joel McCrea were the stars of *Come and Get It,* and Goldwyn had borrowed Frances Farmer, a film newcomer, from Paramount for the female lead. Although she was distrait and aloof at times, I ascribed it to her insecurity as an actress, detecting none of the larger vulnerabilities that were to make her a figure of tragedy. Walter Brennan, under contract to Goldwyn, greeted me the first day with a hearty kiss. Hawks had given him the role of a black-eye-patched oldster with false teeth in *Barbary Coast*. As an actor playing at his own age level, Brennan had been on a professional treadmill for years; as Old Atrocity in *Barbary Coast* and in the role of Swan Bostrom in *Come and Get It,* he was so believably ancient that he was cast as an old man for the rest of his career. Joel McCrea, handsome, without affectation, was impervious to the puerilities and jimjams that became endemic on the sound stage by late afternoon. Andrea Leeds, whom Goldwyn had signed out of UCLA, and Mady Christians, recruited from the Broadway stage, were importantly cast. Then there was Edwin Maxwell, a large, florid actor, who beseeched me to have dinner with him, and when reminded that he was a married man and that I had even met his wife, shrugged and said, "But what harm would it really do if you went out with me?" He later gave up acting and dialogue directing to involve himself in church work. Some of *The Road to Glory* company members were with us on *Come and Get It,* among them Gregg Toland, a top-ranking cinematographer under contract to Goldwyn. Gregg was a good and helpful friend to me on the set.

Bill's letters began to hint of more angry collisions with Estelle over her chronic extravagances. She had a special talent, he said, for ferreting out storekeepers who would give her credit in spite of his orders to the contrary. Bill had heard me remark that some of Hollywood's highest-salaried stars and executives, Howard Hawks among them, were considered dubious credit risks and ran into difficulty when they attempted to charge merchandise at department stores. Surely no Los Angeles merchant in his right mind would give Estelle a dime's worth of goods on the strength of her husband's employment at a movie studio. That, at least, would be a blessing. Estelle continued to bring home unpaid-for items and Bill's fury came to a boiling point. Her lack of consideration for their unstable financial situation, he wrote, would force him to disclaim legal responsibility for her or declare bankruptcy. I dismissed it as an act he would think better of and not carry out for the sake of the Faulkner and the Oldham families until Betty Walter came by the Goldwyn Studios weeks later to have lunch with me. She brandished a copy of *Time*.

"Have you seen this issue?" she asked after we had given our orders. When I looked puzzled, she thrust the magazine to me at a dog-eared page. "Read it."

The news item reported that William Faulkner had placed a notice in the classified sections of the Memphis *Commercial Appeal* and the Oxford *Eagle* to the effect that he would not be responsible for his wife's debts and bills. So he had made good his threat! Now not only Oxford and Memphis but the world knew of the Faulkner marital discord. The blood surged to my temples. Was Bill by this initial move finally setting the stage for a divorce? Would I receive a letter tomorrow or the next day telling me that he had reached the end of the line with Estelle and that she would not be coming to Hollywood?

"What does it mean?" Betty asked, her curiosity avid and cutting.

"I don't know," I said. "I really don't. I was aware that it might be coming—he wrote me—but I don't know what bearing it has on Bill and me."

"Men who intend to live with their wives don't go around putting notices like that in newspapers." Betty raised her glass in a mock toast. "Invite me to the wedding."

"Don't, Betty!" I wanted only to obliterate the image she had evoked. I would not be led into vain hope by friends. There had been too much of it in my life. Somehow, I had survived it, but now I was out of the fuel or steam or whatever it took to last another round. "Betty, let's not talk about it, please."

She bent her head forward in unspoken agreement and for the rest of our lunch we discussed the concerts of the Los Angeles Symphony Orchestra for the coming months at the Hollywood Bowl. She and Victor would get tickets for Leopold Stokowski. Did I want them to buy one for me?

Bill made no mention of the classified ad in his next letter. Estelle, he said, had been persuaded of the wisdom of coming to Hollywood and was no longer balking. Jill was playing at packing her suitcase. Although the prospect of Estelle's being in Hollywood filled me with dread, I was careful in my answer not to upset him with my dark misgivings.

"I feel," I wrote, "that it is the only way out. Who knows better than I how disturbed, how anxious, you become out here when things do not seem to be going well at home? I know it cannot be the same as it was before with us with Estelle in Hollywood, but I want you with all my heart to have the money you will earn from the writing deals your film agents are making for you." (William Hawks, Howard's brother and a former director, was now representing Bill.) "If it can be earned only by her being here where you can keep an eye on her, then no matter how it affects us for the time."

Even as I gave Bill assurances—assurances he had not asked for—of my support and steadfastness, I secretly wished in the night's wakefulness or in passing daylight strokes of panic that he would leave his wife behind. Let them argue, slash at each other with accusation and counteraccusation. Let her continue to drink excessively—in locked bathrooms and in the empty rooms of Rowan Oak—and be physically unable to make the long trip. Or, better still—I would shed my quills, swallow my venom—let her suddenly, miraculously, go on the wagon and give Bill back his equanimity. Anything, anything, so long as she stopped being a rusty nail in his head, pushing deeper every day, a hazard to his sanity and his genius.

Bill detailed plans for the departure. He had persuaded Jack Oliver and Narcissus McEwan to be in Los Angeles with them for the entire stay. Jack would drive Estelle and Jill from Oxford, and Bill would precede them in order to find a modest apartment. Estelle was uncomfortable at the idea of arriving without a place ready to move into. We would have a week or so together, that was something, and then we would have to adjust to the new situation. He thanked me for my forbearance. Irrationally, vexed with myself for it, I began to feel threatened for the first time by Estelle Faulkner. She has no glimmering of your existence, I told myself, not by name, not by face. It was pointless to lose sleep that I desperately required for the next day's demands over Estelle. She was in Oxford, not in Hollywood. From Mississippi, she could not send thunderbolts my way, emit poisonous effluvia that would travel the airwaves alongside the voices of Jack Benny and Amos and Andy to seek me out. Then why was my throat constricted, my mouth dry, my concentration on the set less than total? Stop it, I ordered myself, you're thinking like some superstitious Southerner who believes in conjurers and voodoo spells and incantations in the Delta night.

The real predicament I faced was serious enough without investing Estelle, whose photograph I had never seen, who was all mist and vapor in my mind, formless, spectral, with powers to smite. Would I now, with all the moral detritus that had been stuffed into my head as a girl, all those precepts and dictates rattling around in my skull, be able to continue my relationship with Bill? Would my love for him be the same—without shadow and shame, sweetly abandoned? As I fitted myself into his arms, would I think of the wife close by, huddled in her bed, waiting to hear the opening of the front door and the husband's footsteps moving toward his room? Would my knowledge that, in his own words, he did not love this woman who cast an angry, jagged shadow over his life countervail against the doubts beating at my brain? Only in one or two letters since he left for Oxford had Bill alluded to the possibility of gaining his freedom. Now I had to face the likelihood that, having torn Estelle from her place in his household, installed her in a house that was not her own and in a city as foreign to her as Shanghai had been, he could not ask for a divorce for the length of their exile—his voluntary, to earn money in Hollywood and to be close to me, hers forced upon her. We had come to a deadlock.

Sally was sisterly and sympathetic, but I'm afraid she saw an untidiness about my life that put her off as much as would an unswept, littered room. In the past, she had always been the one spinning in the emotional rapids; now it was I who foundered and flailed, and the reversal of our roles troubled her oddly.

"Are you and Wolfgang still corresponding?" Sally asked, the line of her mouth mildly censorial.

"Oh, yes. I had a letter day before yesterday. The tour is a tremendous success."

"John will be so pleased."

"Feuermann isn't well. Wolfgang says that he's in terrible pain and should have an operation."

Sally, who revered the greats of the music world, winced for the ailing cellist and hoped aloud that they had good doctors in Valparaiso, although she doubted it.

"Meta," she said after a moment, "you know that I think Bill is better for you than Wolfgang."

I nodded quickly to make the admission easier for her. Because of John, she had been careful to conceal her reservations about Wolfgang. He was a new species to her with his wild humor and European self-confidence that she mistook for arrogance. Moreover, she was aware that he stood with the Crowns on her unsuitability as a wife for John and it colored her response to him.

"Have you any idea how John feels?" Sally asked. I didn't actually, though I had been puzzled by his uncharacteristic reserve when the four of us were together on Wolfgang's last evening in Los Angeles, his look of dismay at his friend's proprietary air with me. "I can tell you that John has the most serious doubts."

"Why?"

"Because he knows Wolfgang better than you do or maybe even better than Wolfgang himself."

She started to put her hand to her mouth, like a child who too late realizes that he has blurted out a secret, then arrested the gesture in midair.

"You won't say anything to John?" Sally begged. When I promised I wouldn't, she was noticeably relieved.

Henriette, now the wife of Fletcher Martin and happily pregnant, encouraged me to talk out my fears. She had the trained actor's skill of listening and she gave her whole being to it, receiving and absorbing my confidences, sometimes nodding in solemn agreement, again frowning as if it were she herself faced with terrible choices. In the sparsely furnished hilltop house that she shared with her artist husband, she drew the smarts and throbs of my pain into herself and the powerful maternal juices rendered them harmless. The fears I voiced about my love relationship with Bill astounded her.

"But you said he doesn't sleep with his wife."

"I have to believe Bill."

"Then you're not taking anything away from her."

"But will it be the same?"

"If you let it be." She stretched, yawned, scratched, earth mother all the way. "You don't turn sex up or down like an oil lamp. It's a man-woman thing. Stop thinking about it."

Babka, the Doberman that Nathanael West and his Eileen had given the Martins for a wedding present, barked suddenly at a rustle of leaves and shifts of light beyond the undraped windows. Henriette ordered the sleek black animal to be quiet and led me by the hand to show me Fletcher's paintings. There was an unfinished portrait of a film producer on an easel and at least twenty completed canvases were angled against the wall. She had managed, Henriette boasted, to get this and that commission for Fletcher. And did I know anyone whom she could sell on having his portrait painted? She branded herself shameless in approaching people—other writers, employers, friends, friends of friends, neighbors, family members. Fletcher needed the money.

"Howard Hawks," Henriette reminded herself. "Would you ask him for me?"

"No, dear," I said patiently. "For the tenth time, no."

Her vivid eyes caught sunlight from somewhere. "Well, what about Bill Faulkner when he gets here?"

"He wouldn't be interested."

"You talk about him being a writer for the ages. Why not?" Henriette folded her arms blissfully over the bulge above her lap. "There are things a genius owes the world."

"Yes, and there are things Bill owes to the mortgage company and the grocery store and the—"

"He wouldn't have to sit. Fletcher can work from a good photograph."

"*No.*"

"The little girl, then. The daughter. Fletcher's marvelous at painting children. Nobody's better at it."

I made for the door as she named the Hollywood movie executives whose progeny her husband had painted, and when she intercepted me, I looked at her and envied the unquestioning love that had burnished her skin and deepened the color of her eyes to an undersea green.

"All right." Henriette smiled. "I give up. White flag. Are we still friends?"

"Of course."

"Meta, before you go . . ."

I knew what was coming next. Henriette might retreat on using me to get commissions for her husband, but she would never abandon her political proselytism. An undeviating liberal, super bleeding heart, forever tearing strips from her petticoat, in effect, to bandage humanity's wounded and mutilated, she could not fathom my unconcern with the world around me.

A few weeks before, she had urged me to join the Anti-Nazi League of Hollywood for the Defense of American Democracy. Hitler, she reminded me over and over, was terrorizing Jews, Catholics, writers, educators. Under Mussolini, Fascism was a scourge that could destroy freedom everywhere. When I volunteered to discuss it with Bill when he returned, Henriette threw up her hands. From all I had told her about him, she complained, William Faulkner was hopelessly apolitical. My defense of him was quick and even a touch indignant. I invited her to read the last chapter of *Absalom, Absalom!* in which Bill had addressed himself to the subject of miscegenation and the inevitable mixture of the races, then let her tell me whether it could have been written by a man without political awareness. Why, I went on, Bill's whole imagination had been engaged by the history of the South.

Now Henriette, thinking that perhaps my political focus was closer to home, had a new cause for me.

"The lettuce workers in Salinas need you," she said.

"What do I have to do with lettuce workers?"

"Everything. There's a Hollywood group supporting them and I'm in it and you should be too."

"No, Henriette."

"There are some very important people in the group. Robert Montgomery, Fredric March, Jimmy Cagney, Humphrey Bogart, Melvyn Douglas . . ."

She was still exhorting me to join the ranks as I pulled away in my car.

On the day Bill was due to arrive in Los Angeles, I struggled to keep my attention fixed on script, director, camera, and actors. Whenever the telephone rang, I looked up, waiting to hear my name bellowed out by some crew member. I remained on the vast, ghostly sound stage when the company broke for lunch. Finally, in midafternoon, I was summoned to the telephone.

"It's taken me a solid hour to get through to you," Bill fretted. "It kept ringing busy."

"That's because we're shooting. Where are you?"

"The train station." In the background, I could hear voices bouncing and echoing in the vaulted enclosure. "I got off the train and hurried to the nearest pay phone. Meta?"

"Yes."

"You are my dear love, my beautiful."

Crew members were huddled around the coffee urn nearby, exchanging sound-stage inanities. "I can't talk," I whispered. "When will I see you?"

"Not before tomorrow. Not possibly. I have to line up an apartment, meet with agents, and stop by Twentieth Century-Fox to see Nunnally Johnson. I love you."

I picked my way blindly through cables and arc lights back to the camera.

"That was William Faulkner," I said flatly to Howard

Hawks as he glanced up from his director's chair. He studied my face, then turned away to grapple with a difficult scene set against the background of a saloon. Hawks allowed the same license to others as to himself. He would be the last to inquire or censure.

Bill was waiting for me a few hours later when I came home. Chloe growled and Bill came out of the shadows, squinting into the darkness. I rushed into his arms, laughing as the tobacco-pungent mouth met mine. Chloe, catching his scent, went wild with joy.

Inside the cottage, light switch not touched, Bill held me to him; bodies interlocked, we moved across the floor unsteadily, like combatants in a bizarre ritual.

"I thought you weren't coming to see me until tomorrow," I said.

"So did I, only I couldn't tolerate it." I felt the sudden tumescence of him against my body and heard the excitement in his softly whispered "My love, my long-legged, big-mouf gal. I've been too long away from you."

We made love with half our clothes still on our bodies, then slept enwrapped for a time.

"Nothing has changed," Bill muttered. "Nothing."

"No," I agreed.

"We're not to let it."

"Are they—your wife and Jill—on the way?"

Bill nodded gravely. "I didn't want it this way. I was thinking to come back to you soon as the agents made a deal for me. Then everything back home went from bad to worse. It was the last thing I wanted, but I've had to do it."

I broiled bacon and scrambled eggs the way Bill liked them, water fluffed, and he talked about the short stories he was putting together for a book: they would be linked together by personae and read like a novel. Although I tried to conceal my perturbation over Estelle and what her intrusion into our lives would do to us, Bill picked it up.

"Please don't worry your head about her."

"I'm trying not to."

"Nothing can touch us. Nothing outside ourselves."

"It's just that she'll be so near."

"A geographic circumstance." Bill dismissed it and took me firmly by the shoulders. "I am no uxorious husband. I am, plainly and simply, a loving father trying to protect his child. You believe that, don't you?"

"Yes."

It had not occurred to me that Bill was as wanting in real confidence as I about our new situation and that he was buttressing himself even as he was assuring me. Two days before Estelle and Jill were due to arrive, Bill awakened me from sleep. Opening the door, I saw immediately that he was drunk.

"Bill," I said sleepily, protestingly, "it's almost four o'clock. This is no time for you to come here."

The stench of whiskey was overpowering as he stood in the doorway, eyes glazed, body rocking, but shoulders rigidly braced against blackout and phantoms.

"Bill, please," I said and began to close the door, forcing him back. "Bill, please get some sleep. Call me tomorrow."

"Meta . . . I love you."

The door flattened into its frame and the lock clicked. Hearing him walk away, the weight of him crushing dry leaves, once a crash and a muttering under his breath as he veered into a clump of bushes, I thought, What have I done? That's Bill. I've turned Bill away. Oh, dear God. Reason broke through my sleep-numbed brain and I opened the door to call him back. There was no one to be seen along the steep flight of stairs, washed weakly by an occasional overhead light.

It was not until evening that I heard from Bill. Relieved to hear his voice again, I said nothing of my frantic efforts to locate him (I had called his movie agents and the studio) or the dread that quaked through me when I thought of what could happen in the dark morning hours to a drunken writer on the streets of Hollywood. He, in turn, made no mention of his surprise appearance at my door. Could he see me tomorrow? Just now he was a little under the weather.

A messenger arrived on the set with a note from Bill just

before the lunch break the next day. The first part had been written before he reached me at the studio by telephone and he admitted in it that I was "badly" in his blood and bones and life. In the second part, since I had promised that I would see him the next day—who could resist that imploring, soft Southern voice?—he wrote: "Meta, Meta, beloved, precious, sweet beloved, beloved, beloved. I want to say goodnight to you, but I want to put the words into your hands and into your heart both."

I had thought to shut Estelle out on our last night together, but she slipped through our poor defenses to trouble and bedevil us. Bill was nervous, almost irritable at times, and I was unable to throw off a presentiment of doom. He would not be able to see me, Bill said, for four or five days, something like that—but once they were settled and dug in, we would work things out.

"Bear with me, Meta," he implored once again and I kissed him and put up a brave Irene Dunne-Ann Harding face. Hollywood movies of the 1930's were lessons in how to be noble and sacrificial. I would wait, chin upthrust, all smiling and patient.

It was Bill who found it impossible to stay away from me for the time of maximum separation that he had estimated. "I just had to see you," he said. "I'll stay a few minutes, then I'll get back to them at the hotel."

"You thought it wouldn't be until next week."

He laughed the way elderly Southern gentlemen sometimes do. "Let's get some air on Sunset." We walked slowly, not saying anything. As he left me at the entrance to Normandie Village, I clutched at him. "Bill, how are we going to see each other?" My voice was choked. "You with a wife and child to go home to every night from the studio?"

"Meta." Bill turned to look deep into my eyes. A seemingly endless pause, though only a moment really, and then he said, very softly, "I'll work something out, I promise."

I blurted out before I weighed the hurt it would cause

him, "Bill, my hope's leaving me, it's running out of my hands and through my fingers like water," and I hoped the rumble of a passing car had muffled my words, but he had heard me. His mouth opened and he passed his tongue over his lips in great agitation.

"How long do I have to wait for her to let you go?" I asked, unable to stop the rush of impatience. "Or is she going to let you go at all?"

Bill stared at me, then wheeled abruptly and walked to his car. At the door, he looked back, assessing, considering, then moved quickly into the automobile and drove away.

The Faulkners and their Mississippi servants moved into a furnished house in the Pacific Palisades area a few days later. It was one of those expensive rentals that then and now are available to writers, actors, and directors brought to Hollywood under contract. Bill swore at the heavy monthly bite into his earnings, but it had not been easy to find an owner who was willing to rent to a family with a small and therefore destructive child. In any case, the beach was only a short hike for Jill and him, and on a clear day one could see Catalina Island, where he had heard the hunting was good.

Eleven days passed, edgy ones for me, unused to sleeping alone when Bill was in Hollywood, before he could safely manage part of an evening with me. He brought along a bottle of French wine and we drank it in high spirits, glad for even two short hours together. Maybe, Bill speculated, he could, if only it wasn't so damned far from Twentieth Century-Fox, get over to the Goldwyn lot for lunch, or perhaps we could meet at Lucey's on Melrose. It was so far, so good on his screenwriting assignment at Twentieth Century-Fox (I remember it as *The Last Slaver*) and he was grinding out pages at such a fast clip that the producer was taken aback, but they were good pages. Once there had been a cautious allusion to his difficult dialogue, but Bill defended it, arguing that an actor who couldn't speak the lines was lazy or untutored in speech rhythms or both. It was highly playable dialogue, not to be delivered like most of the arid speeches in movie scripts, but as one would Shakespeare, with the proper pauses and inflections.

Drowsy, a little drunk, I surprised Bill with my fervor, my answering fire. I clung to him, clutching, possessive, imprinting myself on him. As he dressed, I asked about Jill. (Cut my tongue out, drop me from the ranks of well-bred Southern ladies who observe all the amenities, I would not inquire after Mrs. Faulkner.)

"All laughing and golden." Bill grinned. "I take her to the ocean and lift her through the waves. One came up and hit us with the rudest slap and Jill said, 'Pappy, I like the creek at home a heap better.'"

"Oh, Bill, I want to see her."

"I'll arrange it. By God, I will."

"Soon?"

"That will be a sight. You two together. You and Jill."

It happened before I could emotionally prepare myself for it. Bill rang me the next Saturday morning, excitation raising his voice to a pitch higher than normal.

"You free, honey?" he wanted to know. "Scot-free and game for anything? Then please get in your car and drive over here to us on El Cerco."

"To the house?" Pacific Palisades had become darkly off limits to me, a forbidden enclave that Estelle Faulkner, though knowing nothing of me, had nevertheless fortified against any assault of mine.

"Yes, ma'am. Listen. Estelle started drinking this morning before any of us were up and could stop her. Now she isn't well and she won't be for many hours. Meta. Dear love. Drive out and pick us up—Jill and me!"

"Jill?"

"We'll have ourselves a time."

The morning was sun-washed and sparkling. On Sunset past the Beverly Hills Hotel, the baronial houses, set far back from the street, were white and pink; after the Bel Air Gate, there was a first hint of ocean air. I was going to see Jill Faulkner for the first time and I would be with her father for a few precious daylight hours. Bingo! Double feature! Bank night! My heart soared with the first foolish gulls straying inland.

Bill had directed me to park on the block behind the house, which was at the end of El Cerco. In seconds, he appeared, running hand in hand with Jill, and laughing with her at the lark they were sharing. I stood waiting beside the car, not knowing what to expect, and in the next moment Bill had hoisted Jill and she was in my arms, still laughing, and Bill was embracing both of us.

"May I kiss you?" I asked and Jill stopped giggling, but only long enough to give her assent and to call my attention to my sunbonnet shading her blue eyes. I breathed in the little-girl fragrance and Renoir-pink loveliness and decided she was the most beguiling child in the world.

At Bill's "Let's get going," I drove back toward Hollywood, not knowing our destination until Jill, at Bill's prompting, announced that she wanted to play with Chloe, the doggie. Sitting between us, she chattered away about her pony back in Oxford, and about her friends and cousins left behind, asked question after question, and once or twice played the game of divide-and-conquer by whispered confidences to each of us.

Bill flung out his hands, palms up, at his progeny's talkativeness. Grinning, he said, "She doesn't get all that from her pappy."

It had been years since I had heard a child speak in the soft, word-blunting vernacular of the Deep South. Enchanted, I fell back into the regional patois, the old tongue and argot coming back to me easily. Bill leaned his head back and puffed on his pipe; when Jill in her loquacity said something that struck him as funny, he laughed silently, shoulders jiggling up and down.

"She will know how to handle her," Bill said when Chloe, unused to children, fled from Small Visitor. "Don't interfere, honey."

I improvised lunch while Jill allayed Chloe's fears. By the

time I had set places at the table, Chloe, fully conquered, was scampering about the room and skidding on the floor as Jill clapped her hands in high glee. The remaining time allotted to us was spent at a pony track, where Jill insisted on a faster mount than the owners recommended for tots of her size and rode to the finish line holding on for dear life, her piquant face radiant with self-satisfaction.

It was the first of many mornings and afternoons spent with Jill. Her father would call me in great distress from his studio office. Mammy had just phoned to say that Estelle was ill again. Could I possibly pick up Jill and devote a few hours to her? It was no good for Jill to see Estelle in that condition, he would add, though Lord knows she had seen her that way often enough. I would hastily cancel appointments, push urgent work aside, open the door for an exuberant, released Chloe, and push my little car to its limit to get to Pacific Palisades. There Mammy, a pleasant, heavy, middle-aged woman, would bring Jill to me, then hurry back to the house to watch over the recumbent Estelle. We found city parks, stingy of trees and greenery, where Jill romped with Chloe until it was time for sandwiches and milk. Since it was the day of Shirley Temple, Jane Withers, Sybil Jason, and other child stars, I wanted to take Jill to see their films, but Bill, knowing that he could not expect his daughter to be silent about posturing, tap-dancing tykes on the silver screen, advised against it.

I had loved Jill on sight and now I came to love her as my own, almost as if Bill had fathered her within me. I longed to bathe and dress her, comb her hair and buy clothes for her. I would be the most loving and giving of all stepmothers once Bill and I were married. It was a disadvantage to be an only child. I would have Bill's children and Jill would grow up as older sister to them.

When Bill left the Pacific Palisades house (he made no excuses, but simply announced to his wife that he was leaving and would not be home for a while, no need for Jack Oliver to drive him), it was a joyous respite for me from night solitude. Now it was I who wanted him to myself, almost greedily—no evenings shared with Sally and John or Betty and Victor, thank you. Hearing his approach, Chloe would whine and wheeze and I would race her to the door; the corporeality of my lover confirmed by excited hands and kisses, I would close the door on the world. Bill was no less aware than I of the sweet intensification of our love. Time had contracted; what was left to us was broken like the springs of a watch. We were living on snatched hours and everything was stark and heightened.

The trouble was that while I accepted the exclusion from Bill's life on his assertion that it was necessary, to be borne with patience, Bill himself began to bridle under it. He had erected the fences in order not to arouse Estelle's suspicions or to inflict isolation upon her in their new surroundings. Dutifully, in the beginning, he had returned to the house from the studio to sit with her until bedtime or to work on the new book. If, arriving home, he found her drunk, he relieved Jack and Mammy as vigil keeper. He even invited Hollywood acquaintances to dinner, thinking it would cheer Estelle and divert her from the bottle. Now the self-imposed strictures began to nettle him. Unable to leave whenever he wished, he became tense and overwrought. He could not, he realized, make Hollywood into Oxford, Mississippi, for himself. What was normal to him in Oxford was untenable in Hollywood, where I was only a half hour's drive away from him.

"Damn it, I'm not seeing you enough," he railed. "I sit there in that house at night thinking of you and wanting you." My hand went to his, knotted and blanched, veins rising. "You are in my blood, dear love, with the red corpuscles and the white corpuscles and everything else."

During the next week, we were not able to see each other at all. There was night shooting on *Come and Get It,* which was having its troubles, and Bill himself became involved with visitors from Oxford. On Monday of the following week, he drove to the Goldwyn Studios to have lunch with me.

"Listen," he said, leaning over so that we would not be

overheard, "on Thursday night I want you to come to the house for dinner. No, don't start objecting, let me finish. I want you to come with Ben Wasson, as his date."

"Oh, Bill, I don't know . . ." As curious as I was about the woman to whom he was married, the thought of a face-to-face encounter petrified me. "Let me think about it."

"I've already told Estelle. All she knows is that you're from the South and a friend of Ben's."

"You're sure you want this?"

"Positive."

"What about Ben?"

"Ben will accommodate me." Bill leaned back, unwavering and confident in his judgment once he had made a decision. "It's settled then. Thursday night."

Members of Samuel Goldwyn's *Dodsworth* company filled nearby tables and Bill asked if I would point out Mary Astor, who was starring with Walter Huston and Ruth Chatterton. The front pages carried daily news of her court battle with her doctor husband and in every account there was a recap of her love affair with George S. Kaufman. I had seen her several times on the Goldwyn lot and felt a strong kinship. What would scandal do to me if my own relationship with William Faulkner came to light—Jimmie Fidler moralizing about it on his radio show, Louella O. Parsons alluding to it in her syndicated column. I would not—of that I was certain—have the resilience of Mary Astor.

Dressing for my first meeting with Estelle Faulkner in her temporary home, it did not once occur to me that what I was about to do was shoddy and contemptible. Bill had asked it of me and therefore it was right. He was the superior being and I, in my blundering artlessness, my incapacity for self-defense, the lesser one. Bill, who loved me deeply, who was wiser in the ways of men and women and their murkier passions than any writer of his time, would never ask me to do anything that was questionable or degrading. I could trust him, follow him, and seas of jagged glass would part, strangler vines would wither as I walked.

It was only in later years that I came to realize what I, her husband's lover, had done to Estelle Faulkner by invading her home. That mindless imposture still has the power, forty years later, Estelle dead and buried, to chill me to the marrow whenever I remember it. Why Bill really wanted it—was it to feed a morbidity in his nature that even he could not fully understand?—was it to compare the two women?—was it to experience a sexual thrill by playing a dangerous game?—I have never decided. But along with my own mean participation in the charade, I am also aware of the enormity of Bill's punitive act against his wife. I cannot exempt Ben Wasson from fault either.

Ben, clean-shaven and neat, called for me and we drove to Pacific Palisades.

"Nervous?" he wanted to know.

"I'm trying my best to control it," I said. "If I can just keep from trembling."

In frozen solemnity, we analyzed our roles. It would not do, we agreed, to overplay them. For Estelle's benefit, we would address each other every now and then as "dear," but moderation was essential. We would not hold hands. Since Ben knew Estelle, he would be at ease with her and I was to take my cues from him if it became necessary to confirm Bill's falsehood that Ben and I were "keepin' company."

As Jack Oliver opened the door for us, no glimmer of recognition on his face, I panicked for an instant. Jill! She would recognize me! Then I realized in a rush of relief that it was almost nine o'clock and Jill would have been sent to bed hours before. As we were ushered into the foyer, Estelle came forward, hand outstretched, Bill following with his drink.

She was a small, gray wren of a woman in a nondescript dress. If she had ever been pretty—and she must have possessed some beauty to have attracted her first husband—she showed little trace of it now. Of the first impressions swirling in my mind, the discovery that she was a pale, sad, wasted creature was the most startling.

"Billy tells me you're originally from the Delta," Estelle

said in a thin voice that was being manipulated into cordiality. "What a small world we live in."

Behind her, Bill (I instantly recoiled from Estelle's "Billy"; William Faulkner a "Billy"!) hardened his face against wink, smile, leer—anything that would give away our roles. I avoided his eyes then and throughout the evening in fear that I might, for a telling second, respond to them with unguarded love.

Bill, a far better actor than Ben or I, mixed drinks with steady hands, as if my presence were of no moment at all. Estelle was limited to a glass of white wine. Ben was talking about a short story of Bill's that had just been accepted by *The Atlantic Monthly* when Jack appeared to announce that dinner was ready.

I was seated across from Ben. Bill was at the head of the table and Estelle faced him at the other end. Although there were two servants, the Faulkners elected to follow the Southern upper-middle-class style of serving. Jack brought the salad to Bill, who dressed it with oil and vinegar. When the roast came, Bill rose from his chair and carved the meat with authority. Mammy appeared with vegetables and plates were passed to each person. I praised the food, but it had hardly been touched when Jack cleared and dessert was offered.

The conversation for the rest of the nightmare evening was unlaggingly mundane, but I tried to project ease and charm from every pore to please my lover. Bill silently lowered the alcohol level in glass after glass, contributing little to the small talk. Once I saw him firmly remove from her hand a fresh drink that his wife had poured for herself, she protesting, "Billy, don't." We talked about the South and people we knew in common, including my Oxford relatives. Looking up, I saw Bill shift his eyes from me to his wife and back again, almost as if measuring us against each other, but it could have been no more than a visual reflex.

My aplomb did not last the full evening. Bidding Estelle a polite good night, I heard her say that it had been a pleasure to meet me. She somehow found it easier to talk to other Southerners. Didn't I, even after all my years out here?

"I hope," she said meekly, "that you and I will see a lot of each other and become good friends."

An embarrassed mumble from me and I turned quickly away, avoiding Bill's face and whatever was written there— irony, pity, contempt, surprise—to hurry to Ben's car. I was in it before he could open the door for me, trying not to see even peripherally the woman waving from the steps, Bill at her side.

For Ben, I suppose, it was no more than a service to a client and friend, something that one man will unhesitatingly do for another when deception will help him bed a woman or deflect a wife's mistrust. (Women, I later discovered, also help each other with lovers and husbands.) The full force and import of the evening's shameful dissemblance would not hit me for years to come, but it left me at the time with an enemy shrunken in size, foreshortened, no longer the commanding, baleful woman whom I had constructed from the clay of imagination. My hatred had been taken from me and without my consent. But friend I would not be to her.

When there was little more than a week to go on *Come and Get It*, Samuel Goldwyn returned to his office at the studio, although still under care of his doctors. Howard Hawks could now make his demands known to the movie kingpin himself, no more dealing with envoys and aides. The meeting, predictably, did not go well. Both Goldwyn and Hawks were strong-willed, arrogant men whose skins all but clanked like battle armor, and they met headlong in obstinacy. Hawks, raw-nerved over his dissatisfaction with *Come and Get It*, was firm in his catalogue of complaints; Goldwyn, still smarting from a lawsuit brought against him by Paramount for allegedly talking Gary Cooper out of signing a contract renewal and from Eddie Cantor walking out on him to join the Twentieth Century-Fox star roster, was implacable. Hawks returned to the sound stage long enough to pick up a few personal possessions from his trailer office, then walked off the set without an explanation. Gathering up my marked script and papers, I followed, leaving actors and other company members mystified.

With Hawks' departure, Goldwyn shut down production to give Jane Murfin, the screenwriter wife of Donald Crisp, a week or so to draft a new ending. William Wyler, under contract to Goldwyn, was brought in to take up where Hawks left off on *Come and Get It*. Although his contribution was fractional, a matter of one week's shooting, he would share screen credit with Hawks. Since I was not a recognized exponent of the craft, another script girl, one who had worked with Wyler before, was hired to finish the picture. Dehyphenated and crushed, a mere secretary once more, first obligations to Howard Hawks, I tried but could not muster the unbothered, relieved air that my employer affected. For weeks, I had been a member of a movie company, gaining authority in my work each day, and now, depressingly, it was all over for me but not for the others. Hawks vanished, leaving me to finish the exhausting task of packing his effects and calling in burly men to move his furniture. Samuel Goldwyn's publicists issued a statement acknowledging the rift with Hawks and attributing it to the failure of the two men to agree on story points. The rupture was far more bitter than that, and the amicability stressed in the news release was blatant fiction.

A benefit unlooked for came with my abrupt separation from the canvas chair on which my name had been imprinted and which had always been placed next to Hawks' leather chair on the set: I could now sometimes slip away in the afternoons to meet Bill at one of the coffee shops near the studios. As a rule, however, we would have cocktails at the workday's end and hold hands under the table, both of us dreading the moment when Bill would have to go home to Estelle.

The sudden death of Irving Thalberg in his mid-thirties shook Hollywood rudely and reminded its denizens that they were as perishable as the film on which they recorded images. Hours before the headline was shouted in extra editions by news vendors along Hollywood and Sunset boulevards, Athol Shearer called to tell me of the demise of her brother-in-law.

She was at the Thalberg house with her sister, who was close to collapse, and their brother, Douglas, a brilliant sound engineer. Would I please let her husband know of the tragedy so that he could return to Hollywood if possible for the funeral? Although it meant giving up precious time with Bill, I made myself useful to Athol, who was with Norma day and night, and at her bedside during the actress's serious illness following Thalberg's burial. I had to find and hire a new washerwoman for the Hawks household. I picked her up on a street corner every Saturday morning at 6:30 to take her to the Benedict Canyon home, where she tackled the accumulation of soiled clothes and linen. In my tiny car, I drove the two boys, Peter (Athol's son by a previous marriage) and David, out for weekend visits with their paternal grandparents in Pasadena and picked them up again at an appointed time. I telephoned long lists of relatives and friends, ordered groceries and meats, answered letters of condolence, and made endless family arrangements. It was a wearying time, but I liked Athol and whatever I undertook was actually within the accepted duties of the personal secretary of that time.

My first encounter with Estelle, I had promised myself, was also to be my last. I could do without multiple images of that small, sad woman to whom Bill Faulkner was married; the one that kept insinuating itself into the corners of my mind was palling enough. The first test of my intention to avoid her assiduously came during an evening when Bill had long overstayed himself.

"Are you going to the Crowns' musicale on Sunday?" he asked as he fumbled for his shoes and socks. He would dress in the dark to spare my eyes the shock of light.

"Yes, I promised them."

"John asked me to bring Estelle."

"Really?"

"She'd enjoy it."

He finished his splashing around in the bathroom and came to the bed to bid me good night.

"Bill," I said, "if you're bringing Estelle, I don't think I should be there."

"Why not?" He kissed my eyelids and my forehead before his mouth found mine. "She'll think it odd if you don't come. She knows that Sally and John are your close friends."

"Bill, this one time—"

He would not allow me escape. "Please be there. I love you. I can look my eyes' fill at you when nobody's watching. Be there in the name of shabby necessity, please."

"Why do I do whatever you ask?" Annoyed with myself and ruffled.

"You are my love is why."

The large room with its Spanish ceiling was packed with close friends and many acquaintances. Before an informal gathering of good friends, John always performed with an extra flair. As Sally turned the pages for him, John closed the program to thunderous applause with the new work of a modern American composer unknown to me. I sat with my head tilted downward to avoid Bill's burning eyes. He was making good his pledge to keep his gaze fixed upon me and endure the music that way, to hell with anybody who caught him looking at the blonde across the room. Next to him, Estelle sat listening with head angled oddly on her neck. In spite of the years she had spent in the Orient, the stamp of a small Mississippi town was upon her—dress lacking in distinction, hair stringy and uncontrollable, the splotch of rouge and layering of powder on her face giving her a pasty look.

What, I wondered, was going through William Faulkner's heated mind as he sat among music lovers stilled to pure listening by John's artistry, even their breathing an intrusion? Was he thinking how to finally break with the woman at his side without bringing irreparable damage to himself? Was he imagining us together once again at the Miramar, time as plentiful as sand grains, to be squandered and flung? Or had members of the Sartoris family taken center stage in his imagination, there to wait while he sent them to their dooms or glories, making note to remember their disposition when he next sat at his desk.

People clustered around John. I made my way through knots of excited music buffs, balancing teacups, to find the Faulkners.

"Hello, Mrs. Faulkner," I said with counterfeit cheeriness, resenting the civility that Bill had thrust upon me but determined to hold up my end of the deception for whatever reasons he had for continuing it.

"Why, Miss Carpenter, how nice to see you again." Estelle put out a thin hand that played dead in mine and then slid away. "Wasn't it a lovely concert?"

I agreed, holding my smile until my jaws ached, then moved on to shake hands with Bill, who offered seething dark eyes while he muttered a restrained greeting. As Sally brought other people to meet the William Faulkners, easily the celebrities of the afternoon, I was edged away, but not so far that I could not overhear Estelle Faulkner. She was talking loudly to gain Bill's attention and there was a strident insistence in everything she said, as if it were a life-and-death matter that Bill recognize her own powers to compel an audience. She was not, I made the judgment, an interesting person. It was also clear from her conversational gambits and responses that she knew little about music, and that for all her vocality, she had nothing of substance or consequence to impart. Let me go home and quickly, I decided.

"Billy," I heard her say, "is going to teach me to write, aren't you, Billy?"

The narrow face fevered suddenly with the audacity of what she had said and entreated her husband to say yes, to grant her the miracle that would transform the dross of herself. Zelda Fitzgerald had written stories and a novel; so then would Estelle Oldham Faulkner in her desperation to achieve parity with the man to whom she was wed; there would be published novels; she would no longer have to skulk in Bill's great, devouring shadow. I caught the suffering on Bill's face before he turned his head from her, chagrined, pretending not to have understood, not to have heard at all.

She was foolish, all pride drowned in whiskey and lovelessness. Perversely, even as I felt Bill's deep humiliation, I was sorry for Estelle. The fissure would widen as the years passed. Let him go, Estelle. I can grow with him. You can't. I'm younger. Prettier. I can hold him, grace his life, keep him from alcohol, slake his passion, calm the volcanic rages.

The last time I saw Estelle Faulkner was at an informal reception I gave after Christmas for my brother and his bride, Laurelle, who had come to California on their honeymoon. Marjorie Williams, whose friendship I had kept since moving from the Studio Club, would not accept a fee for the use of the large room. I would be expected to provide the refreshments and pay the serving and cleanup staff.

It was Bill who suggested that I invite him with Estelle.

"She needs to get out of that house and be with people," he said. "Besides, she's been asking about you."

"All right, Bill, if you think so."

"Will you call her?"

"Of course."

The thought of another meeting with Estelle Faulkner chilled me. Still, I decided, her presence would serve a purpose. Whatever suspicions my parents might have would be dispelled when Ralph and Laurelle reported that I was on friendly terms with Bill's wife. The society editor of the Hollywood *Citizen News* would carry the names of Mr. and Mrs. William Faulkner in her account of the reception; that would unstitch and unseam all the Saturday-afternoon habitués in the back room at Musso & Frank's.

Bill walked into the Studio Club with his wife as if it were for the first time and looked about with the proper air of vagueness, the perfect muddled man who did not quite know whether to go right or left, advance or retreat. Luckily, most of the girls were out for the afternoon and nobody recognized him. My own performance with Estelle was equally without flaw. Most comfortable with Southerners, she sought out Sally and Betty, who kept her engaged with questions about Oxford and Rowan Oak while Bill talked to my brother and his bride. At her request, I took Estelle for a tour, guiding her through rooms where Bill and I had played Ping-Pong, held hands, kissed. It was the least galling of my times with Estelle and I thought as she said goodbye, Good heavens, I'm getting used to her.

It was one of the paradoxes of loving Bill that I knew more about him through his letters from Oxford than through any confidences he granted when he was in Hollywood. As joyous as our reunions were, hearts spinning like great Catherine wheels, I was always disconcerted by the stoppage of communication. The great carapace was impenetrable, even in our most intimate moments, but at a distance there were soft areas. Little by little, I learned to read him by his moods and attitudes, by voice tones and gestures. At rope's end, he would scratch the back of his hands. Outraged, his speech would be measured and deliberate. It was not much to go on and it told me little enough, but it was a barometer, a key of sorts.

Now, I began to intuit, without understanding it, a new boiling up of pressures within him, tensive forces that made his face long and grave and his movements heavy, almost leaden. It could not be laid to his work (one assignment after another), problems with Estelle (the same), the situation in Oxford (his mother and brother were well) or money (he was earning more than ever). No, it was as if he was advancing irresistibly toward something dangerous to himself from which he would not turn back.

"Bill," I would ask, "is anything wrong?"

"I've told you, m' honey," he would say, "I'm fine, just fine."

"You're troubled."

"No'm."

But he was, sorely, and I did not guess that he had finally steeled himself to ask Estelle for a divorce. One step away from it, he was pushed to the edge by a telephone call to me from Wolfgang, in the Midwest, as we half-dozed in each other's arms.

"Thought he was in Brazil or someplace," Bill grumbled.

"No, he's on a long American tour."

"He's persistent."

"Bill, I told you before, it doesn't have anything to do with us."

"You haven't talked about him since that one time."

"No."

"Why not?"

He was strong and adamantine; deal him a blow and he would right himself like an old-fashioned toy figure weighted at the bottom. I did not have to make light of Wolfgang's calls and letters; I did not have to minimize or lie to Bill.

"Wolfgang," I said carefully, "believes that he's in love with me." There was a twitch at one corner of Bill's mouth, no other sign that he was shaken. "I didn't think it fair to tell you. You might have thought I was using it as a threat. I didn't want that."

Bill pondered it for a moment, then reached over and took my hand. "You want me to shut up about it?"

"Yes."

"All right, dear one." Suddenly the eyebrows shot up. "Is he coming to Hollywood?"

"When the tour's over."

He was worried and I felt it through all the webbing, the padding, the chain mail that he wore over his vulnerabilities. His fingers played spastically with my own and there was a faint pulse under one eye and for once he did not want a drink for the road. Framed in the doorway after saying good night, he suddenly pivoted and regarded me in wild conjecture, as if everything had become defocused for him in one instant, and more that was terrible and punishing would overtake him in the next. Alarmed, I called his name and moved toward him, but he put up his hand in mute apology and hurried away.

It must have been that weekend that Bill Faulkner found the courage to broach the subject of final separation and divorce to Estelle and to tell her that he wanted custody of Jill if she would agree. She must realize, as he did, that their life together was empty, meaningless and without substance. It was (probably) then that he saw fit to tell her about me. He confided only what he wanted me to know of the clash between them, little or nothing of her reaction to my name, but there was enough in what he vouchsafed for me to know for myself how he had finally phrased and spoken the words that he had not been able to say before, and how at first she had stood there, inert, paltry, superable, and then, learning that the other woman was I, who had been a guest in her home, who she had hoped would be a friend, became a wraith of iron, transformed by outrage into a screaming, frenzied woman, venting all the compacted meanness within her on this man who would sunder all that held her together, take away her child, give his name to a younger woman. He held her off from him while she, with the unnatural strength of the deranged, struck out at him, fought him, cursed him, then ran up the stairway threatening to ruin him.

For days, they lived under the same roof in the rented Pacific Palisades house, passing each other without nodding or speaking, stiffening themselves to mock civility only in Jill's presence. Mammy and Jack, who adored Bill, went about their tasks with severe faces; inured to the ongoing warfare of the Faulkners, custodians of secrets about both, they waited for Estelle to submerge her woes in alcohol. The gloom would lift when she finally lay insensible in her bedroom. But Estelle, for once, did not resort to boozy forgetfulness. She would make Faulkner cringe, bring him to his knees for sleeping with another woman and for wanting that woman to replace her in his life. The prospect of it heated the blood in her veins like the finest whiskey.

Bill was gray of face, eyes bleared as though he had rubbed them savagely, when he came to my door. He had been drinking. Throwing himself into a chair and putting his head back, like someone submitting to some cosmic dentist's drill, he muttered, "Damn, damn, damn." I poured him a jigger of bourbon and watched as he tossed it down.

"It's Jill, isn't it?" I guessed. "Estelle won't let you have Jill."

"I expected she'd give me a fight over Jill. That I was braced for. What I didn't expect is that she would want to take everything. I didn't dream she'd go that far."

"But, Bill, she knows you're still in debt."

"Estelle doesn't understand what that is. Doesn't want to. Never has wanted to."

I turned out the overhead light, the glare of it raw on his swollen eyes, and cradled myself in his lap. He was trembling violently.

"Bill, try not to worry," I said. "She's reacting the way some women do. Most of them, I guess."

Bill left me as the sky was whitening through the windows. His anger had subsided. He would not give up. He would not let Estelle manipulate him.

He told me later that for days after he had tried to reason with Estelle. She was obdurate. She would never let him have Jill. The alternative for Bill would have been to make Jill a ward of the courts and that he most decidedly did not want.

Estelle was cheated of the sweet pleasure of turning her husband into a defeated man, all arm and leg stumps. Convinced finally that she meant to strip him of everything, pauperize him if it came to a divorce action, he retreated all the way. He would no longer press her for his freedom. He knew that he would never be able to give her the money she would demand, even if he earned twice as much as Hollywood was now paying him. He was still insolvent. Still the supporter of many people. There were grave responsibilities. She was to forget that he had ever spoken of separation and divorce. Things would have to go on as they had—badly.

It was amazing how little she knew at the time of the husband who had once found her flesh irresistible, whose two children—one dead—she had borne, whose mind's peace she had destroyed with her drinking.

William Faulkner in extremity might gamble on Jill's being somehow able to survive in her alcoholic mother's custody. Backed against the wall, he might even give me up. He would not, however, permit Estelle to wipe out the years of

184

serious writing that were left to him, abort the novels and short stories reposited within him, slaughter the Southerners, black and white, who fought with one another for hegemony in his battered mind. To pay that price was unthinkable. He would have to become a movie studio hack, grinding out treatments and screenplays, rewriting the work of his colleagues, hardening himself to the trivialization of his scripts by producers and directors and other writers, and in the end, lose the sacred power that was his gift. Even in his relatively short time as a wage earner in Hollywood, he had seen the system so corrupt novelists of great promise that their new books, if they wrote them at all, were little better than potboilers, scarcely recognizable as the work of the same authors. There were even writers who became so habituated to turning out pages only when the first check was in their hot, greedy hands that they could never again write on speculation. "Whores," Bill said of them.

So Bill flung the bane that would have rendered him impotent into his wife's face and preserved himself and Yoknapatawpha and the gallery of men and women that he was to create. Had he gone the other way, paid the cost of his freedom, *A Fable,* the Snopes trilogy, *The Unvanquished, Requiem for a Nun, Intruder in the Dust,* and the later short stories would never have been written. There would have been forgotten screen credits instead.

"Promise me," Estelle insisted, "that you will never see your Miss Carpenter again."

"No, I will not promise you that," Bill said firmly. "I love her and I will see her."

Estelle turned, ran up the steps. At the door to her bedroom, rage froze her hand on the doorknob and she went back to the top of the stairs, took a dramatic stance, and flung out the words to Bill below.

"This is the twentieth century. You may have Miss Carpenter, but I shall keep your name until the day I die."

Almost a week passed before he felt it safe to leave Estelle, even with Mammy and Jack in the house, to spend a few hours with me at night. The indignities heaped upon him by his wife had leeched him of passion and he wanted only to hold me quietly in his arms. The day before, she had charged a $125 dress, and when Bill protested that he could not afford it, she had taken scissors and cut the dress to shreds before his eyes.

"Always before," Bill said hopelessly, "I've told you I had hope. Now it's gone. I can't get free, Meta. I know now, I can't get free. Not for a long, long time."

I stared at him unbelievingly. "Are you telling me there's no chance for us? No hope that we can be together?"

"None," Bill said quietly. "None, ma'am, at least not until Jill is old enough to go into court and tell a judge whether she prefers to live with her mother or father."

"When will that be, Bill?"

"I would say she'd have to be around twelve or so. By then, she should know her own mind."

"That long?" All the glue that had held me up went to water, the masonry I had built on his hope crumbled. "Good Lord, Bill, that's ten years, or almost."

Dead silence. Interminable. Then, "Yes . . . I know."

"Isn't there any way you can appeal to her reason?"

Bill shook his head with finality. "I called a truce and I have to be careful, not only for Jill and myself, but for you. She would have named you as corespondent."

"Oh, my God!"

"Among other threats and maledictions, she said she would have my Miss Carpenter's name dragged in the mud from here to Memphis."

Bill left me that night in the blind, stubborn expectation that somehow we would go on as before. He would not allow himself to believe otherwise in the state he was in, studio work to be done as usual on the morrow, the mocking wife to face when she chose to come out of her bedroom, and Jill to be shielded from the venomed air in the house. I made no sign that anything had changed, but later as I wrestled with sleeplessness, I knew that I was coming to the end of my love alliance with William Faulkner. The weary spider had exhausted her silk and there was no more to pay out. There were women who in my position would have forced Bill to obtain a divorce and damn the price tag to him in pain. The killer instinct was missing in me, however; I had not an ounce of it. Bill did not care what other people thought of him, but I lacked his magnificent contempt for others' opinions. The possibility of being named corespondent in a divorce case involving William Faulkner, he whose modest disclaimer of responsibility for Estelle's debts made the pages of *Time,* filled me with dread. It would bring shame to my parents, my brother, my beloved aunt, and other members of the family. A product of the South and of my times, I could imagine nothing as damaging. Notoriety, I was certain, would stigmatize me. In the mid-1930's, I trembled like a Victorian lady.

I could no longer cope with the situation. I could not handle subterfuge, play games, deceive, live in the Back Street, as we called it then, of a married man's life. Bill was locked in—and so was I. I could not wait the ten years until Jill might or might not tell a kindly judge that it was her father she chose to live with, not her mother. I would be past my middle thirties, forty only a blink away, and it would be difficult for me, impossible perhaps, to bear healthy children at that age. Bill's close friends would pretend to accept me in Oxford, but I would be an object of disdain for the general community, particularly people sympathetic to Estelle and partial to the Oldham family. Shopkeepers would let me stand at the counter until I understood that they did not wish to sell to me. Women would turn their heads away as I walked around the Courthouse Square and loose-limbed oafs would leer. I had known shy and eccentric women in the South who lived out their lives behind shuttered windows, never venturing outside—a reclusiveness that might have to do with madness, unrequited love, or a skin too white for the merciless sun of Mississippi. Was that to be my lot? We had exhausted our options, Bill and I. Brick walls rose around us.

By morning I had made my decision to break off with Bill.

As I drove to the studio, I beseeched all the angels of heaven to give me the strength to prevail against my love for him. It was not only a matter of terminating our physical relationship, never less than rapturous and binding, but the necessity to lift from his shoulders my dependence on him that he bore so manfully—for emotional fulfillment, friendship, guidance, growth. I would have to put my life back together or I would have no life worth the bother of living.

Because he was bruised and bloodied enough, I said nothing to Bill, but withdrew gradually, gently, from the coil of our love. He counted on me to put him ahead of anything else when he was free to spend an evening with me. Now I began to find other priorities. Night work for Howard Hawks on several projects, none of which would come to fruition. A concert that I could not bear to miss. An old friend from Memphis. When Henriette Martin miscarried and almost died as a consequence, I spent more time with her than was actually necessary. But it was not total severance. There were nights when I could not deny him. I did not know how to make my love for him small and manageable.

As I put space between myself and my need for Bill, I began to open up emotionally to Wolfgang Rebner. Always before I thought of him as the great virtuoso, seated at the piano, fingers flexed for the fire and the beauty he would draw from the keyboard. Now the man himself, all flesh and bone and blood, became a reality. His declarations of love and adoration lifted me like a dancer in an adagio turn. Whole areas of my heart were liberated. For the first time with Wolfgang, I ventured, almost shyly, the first expressions of love. I reached out to him as to a rescuer and preserver, grateful for his ardor and astonished that he loved me in spite of my involvement with another man.

In September, I received my first proposal of marriage from Wolfgang. He wrote that he had applied through the State Department for immigration papers and would seek American citizenship. He would not ask me to live in Germany with him, for the adjustment would be too difficult for me; besides, Germany was a torn and fearful country. But we would honeymoon there and I would meet his family. Would I search my heart and give him my answer?

I had not yet drawn far enough away from Bill and I temporized, not yet sure that I was capable of the final and terrible wrench. My letters to Wolfgang were sweetly affectionate. I now addressed him as "my dearest." He must give me time to decide. There would have to be a profound alteration in my life before I could weigh my feelings toward him, and while even now changes were being wrought, there were still the last emotional thongs to be loosened.

Bill knew, of course, that I was receding from him. Nothing about me went unobserved: the quaver in my voice, the tightening of my throat, the suffusion of blood under my skin. The distance that grew between us saddened him, and more and more, when I could not avoid sleeping with him, he would hold me in his arms, almost as a father a child that would too soon leave to go on his own.

Wolfgang pressed for a decision. In December, I wrote him that yes, I would marry him, and a few days later, having just read my promise, he telephoned to express his joy. Would I give him my parents' address so that he could ask them for my hand? Yes, he knew it would be considered old-fashioned in America in the mid-1930's, but he was a European and that was his way.

When I saw Bill for lunch at Lucey's restaurant, I told him that I had become engaged to Wolfgang, and waited for the earth to shake, the skies to open.

"I should have known it was coming," he said after a stunned moment, "but I just wouldn't let myself admit that it could happen."

"Wish me happiness."

"I do. I want you to always be happy. You know that."

"No question."

"You don't feel that you can wait it out with me?" His eyes seemed to slowly darken, the whites shading into a sick gray.

"Before I know it, I'll be thirty."

"Give us a little more time, dear love."

"For what?"

"I don't know. The great unforeseeable. A lightnin' bolt out of the sky."

"You don't really believe that, Faulkner."

"No, ma'am, I can't say as I do in our case."

"Well, then . . ." My hands went limp and lifeless.

Bill regarded me with a look of strong astonishment. "You don't even know this man very well."

"I do," I protested. "He's a fine person."

"You can't go by letters."

"He cares for me, Bill, and I care for him. I've come to it." I reached for the nicotine-stained hands. "It's going to be a new life for me, Bill. I want it for myself. I can't let it pass me by."

Bill seemed not to have heard. He looked down at my fingers crosshatched on his own, limp and unmoving.

"There has to be a way," he finally said.

"No, Faulkner."

"Something . . ."

"You can't live in Hollywood."

"No, I guess not."

"No more than I can live in Oxford."

He nodded gravely.

"I don't belong there, but you do. To the fields and the sky and your cronies and the Negroes and the hunting—"

"And I belong to you, too, ma'am."

I looked up, taken aback.

"As I feel," he added, "that you belong to me and always will."

He declared it with such endearing simplicity that I was momentarily weakened, almost undone. "You also belong to Jill," I reminded him. "If you lost Jill on my account, I couldn't endure it, Faulkner. I won't be the cause of that. Not that."

"Jill." He passed a hand over his mouth and sighed from the core of his private anguish. Nothing would induce him to give up his daughter, the golden, living child who had come to replace the dead infant. No woman was worth that. Not I, not any woman. There was no longer any hope that he could hold out to me and his temporary disablement confounded him.

"I have to get back to the studio," he said, fumbling for the money to pay the check and refraining from looking directly at me.

In midafternoon, Bill telephoned me at the office. Would I have a drink with him when I finished work? He had been staring at the paper in his typewriter for hours, unable to function. There was nothing he had to say to me. We would just sit quietly and that would calm him. The excuse I had been inventing as he talked came apart. I would meet him, yes.

He rose from our favorite table—he always did when I came in—and pulled out a chair for me. As I sat down, he put his lips to my hair and whispered, "Meta, dear love." For a few minutes, it was as he had promised, a sharing of unspoken thoughts, sweet glances, the communion of hands. Then the bar became crowded and there was raucous laughter at the far end and Bill was unable to hide his irritation.

"Let's go to your place," he said.

"No."

"No?"

"I'm not going to sleep with you anymore."

He looked beseechingly into my eyes.

"I mean it, Bill. I'm engaged to Wolfgang. I'm going to marry him."

"He's off somewhere, a thousand miles or more away."

"That makes no difference."

"I'm here."

"I know you are and that's what makes it difficult for me."

"I think," Bill mused, "that you're in the flush of pure romantic fancy."

"Call it what you will, I'm not going to bed with you."

"Not even one last time?"

"No."

Young women today may find it inconceivable that I would cut myself off sexually, out of moral scruple, from a man I loved. But I could not change myself. My mother had taught me what her own mother had taught her: that a woman must keep herself chaste once she accepted a marriage proposal. It had been a long matriarchal chain, mothers to daughters, and I was compelled by precept and commandment to embrace virtue now that I was Wolfgang's fiancée.

Bill, who had written about Southern women like me and would many times again, tried to absorb his dismissal as a lover, grapple with it, but he could not find a place for it among the new inflictions he was suffering. The cocktail waitress at his signal brought him another drink and he downed it in record time even for him.

"Can we see each other as friends?"

"Of course."

"That's better."

"Not at my place, though."

He forced a grin and kissed my hand and said that I was to go home now; he needed to be solitary for a spell and this—indicating the bar with its cargo of hunched-over men—was as good a place as any for it.

Another drink was placed before him.

"Bill," I begged, "go easy."

"I'm not going to get drunk, if that's what you mean." It was a pledge as he said it, teeth clenched, nostrils flared, and I left him there, rueful over his glass. When I telephoned him the next morning, he was at his typewriter, pleased with a plot turn that had come to him.

Bill patiently played the hobbled lover for a tick over a week, then exploded. The forbearance I demanded of him was too severe. Wolfgang and I were not married yet. Only a married man could be cuckolded, didn't I know that? How could I hold him off this way? He was not a monk. For two days at the studio he had been dry and unproductive. He was combative and fractious. Why wouldn't I let him make love to me again? Why couldn't we go immediately to my place or to a hotel . . . anywhere?

It was then I realized that I must have my Aunt Ione with me until I was married. I appealed to her to take the first train to Los Angeles and I knew she would understand fully when explanations were made.

"If you need me that much, Meta," she said, "then of course I'll come. I'll arrange to be there day after tomorrow."

Bill knew at once why Aunt Ione had appeared on the scene. I had checkmated him and he accepted the move with wry grace. The prohibition against visiting me at Normandie Village was lifted, and he came by frequently to have dinner with us and once or twice brought Jill on weekends. Auntie had only to observe Bill as he looked adoringly at me to know that she had been given the role of protector. Far more worldly and tolerant than my mother, she asked no questions.

Wolfgang wrote that he would be finished with the American tour at the end of March and that Feuermann's illness precluded any further bookings. I could set whatever date I wished for the wedding ceremony and the sooner the better, but please advise him so that he could book steamship passage for us. We could go to London for the coronation if I wished, and then proceed on to Frankfurt am Main.

If I wished!

I informed Howard Hawks, who was just beginning to prepare *Bringing Up Baby* for Katharine Hepburn and Cary Grant, that I would train a new secretary for him. The Wee Kirk o' the Heather was reserved for the wedding. John Crown would attend Wolfgang in the ceremony. With my meager savings swelled by gifts of money from my parents and relatives, I bought a lavish trousseau. Wolfgang Rebner came from a wealthy family and would command top fees as a concert artist. The lean days were over.

My parents came from Kingman, Arizona, two days before the wedding and my godmother flew in from Memphis. I decided to go alone to the railway station to meet my future husband. He was taller by a head than any of the other debarking passengers, handsome and suntanned, and at the sight of me, he moved forward to sweep me into his arms. *"Tierchen,"* he said, *"my Tierchen,"* bestowing the German sobriquet of "little animal."

The small doubts—had I been rash in breaking off with Bill, no matter the impasse we had reached?—were washed away in one great surge. Wolfgang kissed me boldly, possessively, indifferent to the jostling of passengers rushing for trains. I love him, I thought to myself, I really do love him. Everything was going to be all right. I had acted decisively and wisely.

Two days before our wedding, Wolfgang brought me to my door at midnight, kissed me ardently, then left to avoid disturbing Aunt Ione and my godmother. I had no sooner closed the door than Bill was there, haggard in the weak light, livid gashes caked with blood disfiguring his face. "My God, Bill, what happened?" I whispered, drawing him inside while muzzling a frantic Chloe with my hand.

"Estelle's signature." He shrugged. "Do you have anything in the place? I need a drink!"

I poured him what was left of his own bourbon and listened incredulously as he told me of Estelle's assault on him.

"We were riding along," Bill said, "and she began inveighing against you. I said. 'Estelle, she's getting married . . . it's all over with us,' and Estelle said, 'But that doesn't mean you've given her up, or that you don't still want her'— and then she tossed an expensive compact out of the window. I lost my temper—the damned thing had cost twenty-five dollars. Did she think I was writing movies in Hollywood so that she could cut expensive dresses into ribbons and fling away expensive compacts? Before I knew what was happening, she had raked her fingernails down my face. I was driving. She could have killed us both." Bill removed a blood-spotted handkerchief from his jacket sleeve—he had folded it neatly so that the stains were hidden—and pressed it against the still bleeding wounds. "I think she wanted to kill me, if not herself."

My aunt called from the bedroom, "Meta, is everything all right?"

"Yes, Auntie," I answered her. "Go on back to sleep. It's just Bill and he'll be going any minute now."

He drew me to the couch and put his head against my breast. I held him, careful not to touch the lacerated skin, and smoothed his thick hair with my hand.

"I wish you every happiness," Bill said.

"Thank you."

"I'll see you in New York—when you come back from Europe."

"Will you really?"

"You don't think I'm going to let you out of my life?"

Walking down the aisle, my father escorting me past Betty and Victor and Sally and a host of friends gathered to see me joined in marriage to Wolfgang, I visualized Bill Faulkner's torn face for one terrible moment, then joined my husband-to-be at the altar. We spent our wedding night at the Santa Monica home of Ernst Toch, the renowned modern composer, and then left by car for New York, where we would sail for London.

A letter from Henriette Martin reached me months later in Germany. The day of my wedding, she wrote, William Faulkner had gone on a nonstop drinking binge. A few days later, he had been rushed to a Los Angeles hospital in an acute alcoholic state and had been given medical care for six weeks. She had heard that although he was working again, he was skin and bones, and hardly recognizable.

Chapter 12

On the first night in the stately old Riesser house in Frankfurt am Main, I slipped out of the feather bed whose oppressive warmth made me feel like some hibernating creature
existing on its fat and peered out from the lined draperies at
the view from the fourth floor. We had arrived from Holland
the day before with Wolfgang's mother, Paula, only to be
informed by Herr Emig, the butler, that Frau Riesser had
already retired and could not possibly receive us at such a late
hour. Wolfgang and my mother-in-law knew better than to
question the decisions of the ancient lady who lived with her
four servants at Friedrichstrasse 63; her orders were irrevo-
cable. We drove by taxi to the Frankfurter Hof in the glittering heart of the city. In the brightly lighted public rooms,
hotel guests in evening dress moved about in graceful choreography, pairing, grouping, separating, crossing, and recrossing. My husband and my mother-in-law, curiously ill-at-ease,
looked askance at my suggestion that we go downstairs to
mingle. We were all exhausted and needed sleep, I was reminded, and tomorrow morning we were expected by Grossmutter immediately after breakfast.

Below me, the light cast by a sailing moon on elaborate
formal gardens had the quality of new ivory and I could
make out pathways, shaped hedges, intricate shrubbery de-
signs, iron benches, statuary, and a great water-stained foun-

tain. Wolfgang began to snore lightly. In a moment or two, I would crawl back into the German bed and he would, without waking, fling out a long, protective arm into whose crook I would harbor myself. When he made love, he was a healthy, sportive, frolicking male, smiling down at me, the still-shy wife, laughing aloud at my grave face, gathering me to him finally to nestle and whisper boyish endearments. So different from Bill, ravenous, carnal, and female-intoxicated in the act of love.

Was Faulkner back in Oxford? I knew he was not happy, but was he well? Had he stopped drinking? Had he thought of me as I had of him since our last time together? Images slid into my mind without summons or association: Bill blotting his forehead with the clean handkerchief that he wore in his sleeve; Bill looking at me with sad, congested eyes; Bill chewing on his pipe stem.

Wolfgang, used to heavy European bedding, secure in the house that he had known since childhood, made a sudden movement behind me, shuddered, then sank back into the deeper divans of sleep. He had changed drastically. His *joie de vivre* had vanished and in its place had come preoccupation and uneasiness. The closer we came to Europe, the greater his tension. It had actually started before we reached New York. Something—a letter, a news item, a radio broadcast—had become a worriment to him. When I asked what was wrong, he told me not to be concerned; he was mercurial, nothing more. But one morning, more nervous than I had ever seen him, he announced that it was suddenly of the utmost importance that we get to Germany with the least possible delay. Would I mind if we didn't attend the coronation after all?

I had been dreaming of London and great processions of royal personages, pageantry, and drum rolls, but I concealed my disappointment. My husband was not given to whims, that much I knew of him with certainty. Clearly, he had sound reasons for his haste to get to Frankfurt am Main and he would confide them all to me in good time. It had not been easy to change travel plans, for our passage had been booked and paid for from Germany by the executor of the Riesser estate. Finally, Wolfgang telephoning for the greater part of a day, arrangements were made for us to sail on a small steamship to Rotterdam, where we would meet Wolfgang's mother.

"I feel awful not to be able to show you London," Wolfgang apologized once the change had been finalized.

"It will be there next year surely."

"But there won't be another coronation."

"I'm afraid I'd have seen it through Hollywood eyes anyhow. Wranglers in charge of the horses. Western Costume Company supplying royal robes. Extras from Central Casting everywhere. And Cecil B. DeMille, he's so right for it, directing."

"It was something I wanted for you, *Tierchen*."

"Make it up to me." I wrinkled my nose and kissed him.

"I will. I'll do a recital in London at least once a year."

In New York, I met the first of my new in-laws—Edgar Rebner, a smaller version of his brother, with reddish-blond hair and a delicate skin, and his pretty wife, Marjory, from a wealthy Texas family and clearly not Jewish. Neither, I learned from her, was Ingeborg, the wife of the third brother, Ludwig, who lived in Copenhagen. Edgar from the outset was warmly approving of me. But would the European family members accept me as unquestioningly?

One evening before we sailed, there was a party in our honor and I was introduced to an elderly man who wore a monocle and spoke reverentially of the salons at the home of Wolfgang's grandparents and of unforgettable rehearsals of the famous Rebner Quartet at the family house on Schwindtstrasse, a short distance away from the great house on Friedrichstrasse.

"Are you rich?" he asked bluntly.

"Poor," I replied, thinking him a rude old party.

"What a pity! They will be disappointed in Germany that Wolfgang did not marry a woman of great wealth."

"Really?"

"An Astor or a Warburg at least."

"I'm sorry."

"They had counted on it, you know. Wolfgang is the crown prince of the family. The only son with outstanding musical talent. It was a foregone conclusion that he would make a good match."

As it turned out, I need not have wished that I had been born an heiress or trembled so violently on descending the gangplank in Rotterdam to be presented to my mother-in-law that I had to hold on to my husband's arm. Paula Rebner, a trim, lively woman with the same hair and skin coloring as Edgar, embraced me excitedly.

"You have chosen well, Wolfgang," she said, beaming. "Your wife is as gentle as she is lovely. I was so afraid"—turning to me in eye-rolling dread—"that my son would bring home one of those Hollywood platinum blondes."

Paulinchen, as she allowed me to call her, had a separate living arrangement with Wolfgang's father, Adolph Rebner, whom I would not meet until we left Germany for Denmark. The daughter of a steel magnate, she had been reared in luxury and by her own admission could not cook an edible meal, make up a bed, drive a car, or be trusted with domestic chores. All her life, she lamented, others had done for her. Small wonder that she was inept and clumsy.

"I hope Wolfi will do better than I." She sighed. "He, too, has been shielded. His father and his brothers would not let him bother his head about practical matters, and I, myself, am not without blame. It was always, 'Go back to your piano. Do not concern yourself. Practice, practice, practice.' "

"Now, Mother, Meta isn't interested in all that," Wolfgang protested.

"My son cannot drive a nail into a wall or balance a checkbook or boil an egg for himself."

"Mother!"

"It's true," she insisted, ignoring the rebuke in Wolfgang's voice. "You will see, Meta. He has been spoiled and pampered, and I am not sure"—her voice dropping almost inaudibly—"that it was a good thing we did, the way the world is going."

Paulinchen and I not only managed the most harmonious coexistence, but, something very sweet for me, we became extremely good friends. I was often to stoutly defend her when Wolfgang and others in the family found fault with her for failing to do effortfully what the most ordinary women achieved without even trying.

In the few days that we lingered in Holland, I was a neckswiveling, stumbling, gasping American tourist straight out of Henry James. The soil I walked on was European! The canals were real, not water-filled ditches on a movie studio backlot. The endless fields of brilliant, upright tulips had not been painted on glass for cinematic visual effects. Those were really cobblestones on the streets of Haarlem.

A bird—my first nightingale?—trilled in outrageous bel canto in the garden. The branch of a tree scraped against the house in a gust of wind. Wolfgang had not prepared me for the size and grandeur of the Riesser estate. Dressed in my best suit (a copy of an Adrian design), with a small fur cape and a modish hat, for the crucial meeting with Grossmutter, I lost my self-possession at the first sight of the mansion. Herr Emig admitted us through the locked iron gates and guided the three of us to the four-story brick structure and into the grand hallway. We moved up the stairway past the family coat of arms on the wall to a small waiting room with a damask-covered settee. While we waited for the matriarch to make an appearance—even Paulinchen was on ceremony in her mother's home—I was shown the elevator, the first of its kind in the city in a private home, installed by the ailing Eduard Riesser before his death. The marble sink with the gold spigot was for guests who wished to wash their hands before being announced.

Wolfgang took me to an anteroom and indicated, with a flourish, an Italian ceramic toilet. I was to notice the vertical brass bars on the side.

"So my grandfather could raise himself up from the throne," he explained. "Otherwise, he was too arthritic and massive to manage it."

Tapping, a blind beggarman's tattoo on marble, sounded from the living room and Grossmutter called out in a Helen Westley voice, "Meta, is that you?"

Wolfgang opened the living-room door and led me to his grandmother. She was a portly woman with white hair done up in a stately pompadour; a lace collar with stays relieved the severity of her black rustling taffeta dress; the spotted hand that clutched a gold-handled cane trembled slightly. I was kissed, regarded with shrewd, appraising eyes, then rekissed. Paulinchen crowded in for an emotional reunion, then Wolfgang, who had not seen the old woman for two years, rocked back and forth with her as she wept with joy.

Grossmutter seated herself in her favorite chair in the living room with its magnificent furniture, luxurious rugs, a Steinway concert grand, and priceless *objets d'art*.

"In the last few years," she complained in English as faultless as her daughter's, "I have grown heavy, far too heavy. Before the political changes, I used to walk briskly each day to the Palmengarten, where I could watch the children at play and enjoy the flowers. Now I am no longer allowed in the park that my husband helped pay for and establish. I am no longer welcome."

Resting my head against the cool windowpane, breathing the faint air that somehow forced itself through, as stubbornly as weeds through concrete, I remembered the heavy sorrow proportionate to her bulk. I was confused but too timid to ask why the park had been forbidden to her and why she did not at once advance angrily upon city hall or whatever to protest. She was an aristocrat. Wealthy. In the United States she would be regarded as a philanthropist and honored for it. What had she done to be ousted from the Palmengarten? Wolfgang made light of the order; it was an error, he insisted. The prohibition would be rescinded. At lunch Grossmutter wept again to have her daughter, her beloved grandson, and his American wife around her. We toured the garden with its charming gazebo, sunned ourselves in the solarium, and talked endlessly on the cool verandas. There was a sumptuous dinner—the Riessers believed in abundance of food—and I was entranced by the embroidered linen table-cloth and the gleaming silverware.

"Tomorrow," the matriarch said when I admired the place settings and the serving dishes, "I will show you the family china that the German Government forced all Jews to buy as a special levy when marks were needed to replenish the German treasury. No Jews, rich or poor, were exempt. That was many, many years ago—before the present regime. It is very beautiful china but painful to me, so I keep it hidden away."

Jews! It had slipped my mind that I had married into a Jewish family. There had been articles in the Los Angeles newspapers about the terrible treatment of Jews in Germany, but I had barely scanned the lead paragraphs. Nor had I listened with any attention to radio reports about Germany. My eyelids were drooping. I would put it all together tomorrow.

"*Komm schlafen, Metachen,*" Wolfgang muttered thickly from the bed behind me.

In the morning, there was a cautious knock at the door. A lady with a round German face introduced herself to me as Emma. She had been assigned as my maid and would now draw my bath. Her air of being overcome with joy to serve me was offensive; the black servants I had known in my girl-hood went about their tasks without dishonest effusion. When I stepped out of my bath to find Emma waiting with an enormous terry-cloth sheet, I suffered myself to be wrapped in it, but once she had vanished, I told Wolfgang to inform her that although I had grown up in a house attended by servants, I was not accustomed to such highly personal services.

Breakfast over, I left Wolfgang giving an account in German to his mother and grandmother of his tour with Emanuel Feuermann and found stationery to write a short note to William Faulkner.

I hope you have not worried unduly about me. I am in good health and exceedingly happy. I do not think it prudent that we correspond, but I want you to have this word from me. The address at which I can be reached in Germany for the extent of our stay—I do not know how long it will be before we leave for Denmark—follows. If you become ill, if anything untoward befalls you, I want to know. You are please to write me in that case.

In warm affection,
Meta

For the first week, we explored the neighborhood while taking our constitutionals. The Rebner home, which had been sold after the three boys went their separate ways, was located on Schwindtstrasse, within walking distance, and each time we passed it, Wolfgang remembered incidents of his childhood.

When I asked when I was to be shown the sights of the city, my husband exchanged uneasy glances with Grossmutter and Paulinchen.

"I really haven't seen anything," I protested. "My travel book describes historical buildings and museums and Gothic churches and—"

"Sightseeing is so bloody strenuous," Wolfgang interrupted.

"I don't understand why we stay so close to the house, Wolfichen."

Wolfgang closed his eyes wearily. "Frankfurt is hardly Berlin or Paris or Rome."

"I want to see it just the same."

"There's no family car now, *Tierchen*. We would have to go by streetcar and foot."

I was too uninformed about the world around me, too obtuse, to guess what was behind his reluctance or to grasp the reasons for the apprehension on the faces of Grossmutter and Paulinchen.

"Wolfi," I fretted, "this is my first time out of the United States. I'm in a great German city, and except for the first night, I've seen nothing at all."

Grossmutter rapped Wolfgang's knee with her cane. "She's right" came the judgment. "Show her around. Only be careful."

Careful? But there wasn't time to ask any questions. Wolfgang was pushing me toward the elevator with a "No high heels, *bitte*" warning and grumbling that he was the world's worst guide.

Frankfurt am Main unfurled for me like a scroll of dazzling colors and shapes. On the streetcar, Wolfgang whispered to me to keep my voice down as I plied him with questions; when I looked about quickly, expecting to see disapproval on the faces of other passengers, there were only people reading their newspapers or staring straight ahead.

We walked slowly through the winding streets of the old city. I marveled at the storybook architecture, the quaint streetlamps, the ships and barges on the river, and the scrubbed cleanliness, as if the streets and sidewalks were washed hourly with strong soap and water. Der Römer, the medieval city hall surrounded by old buildings, took my breath away.

"*Wunderschön,*" I said over and over, finding pleasure in using German words.

When pedestrians fell in behind us or approached too closely, Wolfgang, gripping my elbow, would veer me away until they passed. Only when we were at a distance from other sightseers did he relax his vigilance. What keyed him to such razor-edged anxiety? Of what was he afraid? I refrained from asking, certain that he would be all the more upset, perhaps enough to cut short our exploration of the city.

We arrived back at Friedrichstrasse 63 late for tea by fifteen minutes. Wolfgang apologized—his watch had stopped, he said—but the fault was mine for tarrying inside an ancient church where Holy Roman emperors had been crowned.

"I am very strict about punctuality," Grossmutter said, clearly not of a mind to invite us to sit down at the tea table. "One must be for tea at the exact hour or not at all. I have come to the time of life when I hold to old forms. It is one of the few things left to me. Tomorrow, you are both certain not to be late and we will have a lovely tea together."

The time came for us to pack for the remainder of our honeymoon. Paulinchen was also making preparations for a return to her beloved Italy, where the climate and the people —"I do not know what has happened to Germans," she lamented—were more to her liking.

Coming down in the elevator for our dinner before departure the next morning, Wolfgang studied my face critically.

"What's the matter, *Liebchen?*" I asked, made uncomfortable by the severity of his gaze.

"I will appreciate it," he said, "if you will not wear quite as much make-up in the future."

I put a guilty hand to my face. "Why?"

"It attracts far too much attention."

"Are German men looking at me?"

"Please don't ask any questions now. I'll talk to you later about it. But just give me your promise."

"Of course," I said, ascribing the ban to a male jealousy I had never known he possessed, and at once both secretly pleased that my husband knew I was desirable to other men and resentful that I, as an American woman, had been given a virtual ultimatum by my husband.

We first journeyed to Hofgastein, in Austria, where great pines spiked the sky and gave off an aromatic, healing spice. Mineral baths of hot water bubbling up from deep inside the earth calmed Wolfgang for a time; the strain vanished from his face and he was more relaxed and amusing. We nodded and smiled at guests and staff members, but my husband would not allow any familiarity. We were on our honeymoon, he reminded me, and strangers, if encouraged, would heartlessly intrude upon our privacy; best to remain aloof and untalkative. It was the same at Bad Ischl, where Franz Lehár had lived and composed, and again at Galspach.

In that picturesque village, Wolfgang underwent treatments for a nervous condition in his right arm and I waited for him on the spa terrace, my German grammar book open on my lap as my eyes were lifted again and again to the great mountain that blocked out the sky. With twilight, the countryside became stilled and peaceful, touched with myth by the dark forms of flowering trees and hills. Belled cows and sheep returned from hill and pasture land. I discovered *Marrillenknödel*, a soufflé of apricots that came out a golden, delectable orange-brown, and it was all I would order at the *Hofbrau* that served it as a specialty. We walked before bedtime every night and slept in fragrant hand-washed linen that had been dried in the sun and lovingly ironed.

Although Wolfgang in Salzburg was once again guarded and tense, the city of Mozart's birth made up for London and a dozen coronations. We were given the considerable honor of occupying Arturo Toscanini's box at a concert in token of the friendship of Wolfgang's father and the renowned conductor. When we weren't in concert halls or at chamber music performances—the only opera we could spare ourselves for was *Jederman*—I dragged Wolfgang, who had seen it all before, to cathedrals and monasteries, and to the Mozarteum to view the composer's piano and memorabilia.

Grossmutter would not have it otherwise on our return to Frankfurt but that we occupy the fourth-floor apartment once again as guests. I looked for a letter from Bill but found none among the mail from my parents, Aunt Ione, Sally, and Henriette. Good. Then he was well. My mind was set at ease and I turned my thoughts to my new life and the experiences that were still ahead before we crossed the Atlantic back to New York.

As the weeks went by, I became listless in the unchanging round of days and my husband himself showed boredom with the regimen imposed upon us—late breakfasts, mornings at the piano (I would sit in a far corner of the salon while he practiced or composed), lunch with Grossmutter, servants fussing over us, walks through the same neighborhood streets, formal dinners with visiting aunts, uncles, cousins, and often, of late, secret conferences in the library with lawyers and businessmen summoned to the house by Grossmutter for reasons that I did not fully understand; uninvited, I sometimes heard snatches of heated debate that I could not follow and over it all Grossmutter's voice addressing everyone, it seemed to me, as Herr Doktor. One afternoon, Wolfgang shut the book he was reading in explosive impatience and asked if, for a change, I would like to go with him to a charming restaurant nearby, one that we passed within a few blocks on our daily walks. A message was left with Herr Emig for Grossmutter, who was having her nap: we would not be home for dinner.

We were a larky pair as we walked arm in arm to the little restaurant. Suddenly Wolfgang broke his gait and pulled me back.

"Look," he said, lowering his voice and indicating a printed white card on the door.

"*Juden,*" I said, puzzled. I had heard the word in the whispered conversations between Grossmutter and Wolfgang and the elderly men who came to the Riesser house for evening conferences.

"It means Jews," Wolfgang said grimly. "Jews are not welcome here."

"Oh, Wolfi." I turned to face him, aghast.

"Let's get away." As we walked quickly from the area, pain and anger contused my husband's face.

"I know the owner," he muttered. "I always liked him. He always liked me."

"Perhaps someone else has taken over."

"By order of the Gestapo." The possibility hadn't occurred to him and now it seemed to alleviate his distress. "Listen, I promised you dinner out and you're going to have it."

We took a streetcar to the neon-shining heart of Frankfurt, where there were sidewalk cafés, restaurants, cabarets, and dives. The streets were thronged with Germans and tourists. The energy of the city at night was like a great revolving belt, propulsive and overpowering. We made our way to a restaurant where, to my relief, there was no sign to chill my husband's heart. A table for two was found for us with great courtesy. I stole glances at the men and women around us and took notes of the garish décor; I would describe it to my parents in my next letter. Wolfgang was telling me about earlier times at the restaurant with musician friends when suddenly his attention was caught by something straight ahead and he went rigid.

As I started to turn my head, he pounded on the table and spoke in unusually loud tones, "Well, have you had enough? Would you like to go now?" In one quick movement, he flung money down and took my arm. "Don't say anything," he whispered commandingly. "Just walk with me."

Then I was being guided through spaces between tables, around knots of standing people and back of waiters at attention at their stations. Before we reached the exit door, I saw two uniformed Nazis edging their way through people toward the table we had just left.

I waited until we were blocks away before I dared ask my husband what had happened.

"You saw the SA men," he said. "First they stared at you, then they started toward our table."

"How can you be sure?"

"I know, *Tierchen*, I know."

"What would they have done?"

"I think they would have made remarks." He bit down on his lip. "You'd have been insulted and I would not have been able to say a word. Do you know why, my precious wife? Because it would have meant my arrest and perhaps arrest for every member of my family."

When we returned to the Riesser house, Grossmutter would not let us go to our room. What had happened? She demanded to be told the truth. Wolfgang calmly recounted the events of the last hour, and when he was finished, Grossmutter tapped the floor indignantly with her cane.

"Barbarians," she said. "They are all turning into barbarians—a whole nation of people."

"I don't understand," I said. "Why should those men want to insult me?"

Grossmutter put her hand on my arm. "Meta, it's because you draw notice with your beautiful American wardrobe," she said uncritically. "You must have observed that German women today wear old clothes. There is no money to buy new ones. Next to them, in their faded and mended dresses, you are far too conspicuous. You are—"

"Why don't we stop hiding the truth from her?" Wolfgang broke in. The old woman cast a look of dismay at him, but he would not be deterred. "You are a gentile, my sweet one," he said in a quiet, even tone. "A gentile married to a Jew. That, in Germany today, is not only dangerous to all of us but to you as well."

I looked to Grossmutter for denial, but she had put a trembling hand over her eyes, as though truth gave off a blinding light.

"We're well known in this city, the Rebners and the Riessers," Wolfgang said. "Those two men recognized me with my Aryan wife. They wanted to make trouble. If they had been able to make me angry, they would have had their Jew."

I suddenly felt ill and weak, nausea hitting me in the pit of my stomach. All this time they had kept from me their horror of what lay behind the iron gates of the mansion and their fear that it would one day move into the garden and from there to the doorways and windows and chimney openings, blocking all escape. They were awaiting siege, unarmed and unprepared, and yet for me they had maintained the illusion of serenity. Why had I been so unknowing? Why hadn't I guessed the reason the muted conversations in the library ceased when I came near? Why had I not seen the pain that showed through them, for all their efforts to conceal it, like light shafts through closed doors? Why hadn't I been perceptive enough to relate them, as Jews, to the political situation of the country of which they had considered themselves patriots?

"You are not to worry, *Tierchen*," Wolfgang said. "You are an American, nothing will happen to you."

"You cannot be sure," Grossmutter corrected him. "One

never knows with these brutes. I do not trust them, not at all."

Wolfgang bent over the old woman sitting rigidly in her chair, lower lip outthrust, and kissed her forehead. "You have not had your dinner. We can talk about all this later."

"Tomorrow, no later than tomorrow," she said, inflexible, not to be humored or coddled. "We will seek advice on how to get money out of the country for you. In any case, you must not stay in Germany much longer. You must have your visit with your brother in Denmark and take Metachen back to America."

The secrecy ended with Grossmutter's pronouncement. Nothing was ever again kept from me. It was as if overnight an intricate set designed to deceive me with optical fallacy had been struck and now the play was being performed on a bare stage, all scarred surfaces visible.

Night after night, Wolfgang's need of money to launch his career in America was discussed in the library with professional and business men from the Jewish community, some of them recognizable from earlier parleys, others strangers to me. The new laws of the Third Reich made it impossible for Jews to take money out of Germany. But it was crucial, Grossmutter reiterated, that a minimum of fifty thousand dollars—it could not be done for less—be made available to Wolfgang in New York to cover the losses of first recitals, to pay for auditoriums, publicity, advertising, road tours. She had one great wish now and that was to finance her grandson's ascent to stardom as a concertizing pianist. He had been assured from childhood that the money would be there when he was ready. Now she was desperate to make good that promise. Could the *Herren* give her a foolproof way for the money to be spirited out of Germany? Surely there must be such a way.

One evening, a non-Jew was brought to the house by a family friend. For an admittedly large fee, he had taken money and jewels from wealthy German Jews into Belgium and Switzerland, leaving the contraband with relatives and friends who would hold it until the rightful owners could claim it. No, he would not name his Jewish clients; that would violate the trust placed in him. Grossmutter thanked the self-styled go-between. She would try to think of people outside of Germany on whom she could rely; if any came to mind, she would consider an arrangement with him. When the man departed, she branded him a transparent crook, a vulture feeding on the desperation of others. She was certain that he would abscond with anything of value turned over to him or sell it for cash within hours.

A tragedy that befell members of another Jewish family at the hands of Hitler's elite SS men convinced Grossmutter a few days later that Wolfgang and I must leave for Denmark immediately. Clearly, there was no solution to the money problem. The schemes that had been suggested were either impractical or dangerous. Well, she would see to it that we would not leave empty-handed. On the marriage removal basis recognized by the government in the case of nonreturning Germans, Wolfgang could take what he wished as household effects. In addition, we were to buy china, linens, silverware—anything that we could use or even sell in New York—at the finest of Frankfurt's stores; Herr Doktor Lewald, executor of her estate, would pay all bills. Everything, including the smaller of the two Steinway grand pianos, would be shipped to us in New York. And, oh, yes, a trustworthy jeweler was at the moment fashioning a heavy bracelet for me from platinum that she had ordered him to buy; if we found ourselves in desperate straits, I was to sell it for a great deal of American money. There was no time to lose. We shopped during the day, making our choices quickly in order to avoid suspicion, and packed by night.

Before we left, I signed papers that entailed the Riesser estate in my name. It was the only way, I was advised by family lawyers at a final conference in the library, that the estate could be saved.

As the taxi arrived to take us to the railroad station, Grossmutter walked slowly with us to the front steps leading to the garden. Aware that she would never see her grandson and his wife again, sensing her imminent death, whether by old age or the hordes that would storm through the iron gates, the old woman sobbed inconsolably. I remember turning my head as the taxi moved off for a last glimpse of Grossmutter. Leaning heavily on her cane, she waved a lace-trimmed handkerchief in a last farewell.

A year later, the matriarch was dead. Emma, the same Emma who had been my maid, hastened to inform the Nazi authorities for the reward she would receive that the Riesser mansion was full of treasures. Uniformed men came as to a fire to remove paintings, all the volumes of the Goethe library, the priceless furniture, the family silver, sculptures, rugs, porcelains, the Limoges china, and the full concert grand that Wolfgang had left behind.

On the train, sharing Wolfgang's panic when Deutsche Pass Kontrolle officials asked to see all passports or when SA men passed through our railway car, the violence within them shafting through narrowed eyes, I began to grasp what Henriette had been saying to me for so long and with such little effect. Suddenly I knew what it was to be a Jew, a Negro, among a majority people who needed scapegoats. Never again would I blindfold myself to the suffering of others. Nothing had happened to me, with the proper skin coloration and correct facial configuration as my talismans in a savage world, yet everything had happened. I had smelled, tasted, and experienced human fear; the people I had been among had given it off like animals herded into the open, pressing together, watching in helplessness the skulking shapes under the trees.

My hand found my husband's whenever we pulled into a station and SA men, heavy thighed in their uniforms, entered our car. I had worn a black dress from which I had stripped all trim, and my long blond hair was gathered under a small, plain hat. The train passed great factories belching furious smoke—"Munitions," Wolfgang whispered—then rolled into open country. I looked out at the terrible land and asked my plain-young-woman reflection in the window how I could have been so unaware of the dooms imposed upon the weak by the strong. As a child, I had wept when Mammy, overcome by thirst, could not drink water from the water fountain marked "Whites Only" at the depot and had to ride separately from the family in a coach for blacks. Why had I lost that early concern for the disfranchised?

Arrangements had been made for us to spend the night in a safe, inexpensive Berlin hotel. We paid in advance from our small fund of marks and were left enough to maintain us until train time the next day. Everywhere we looked in the vast railroad station as we waited for the train to Copenhagen to be announced, there were Nazis in brown or black uniforms. Hordes of men and women who worked in Berlin and lived in surrounding towns rushed past us to their trains. We walked, instinctively, at a steady, unhurried pace to lessen our visibility. Wolfgang carried our luggage; I, a traveling blanket, pillow, and purse. Approaching our car, I felt someone push against me from the side, but when I looked around, there were only other passengers moving toward the car. It was when I held up an arm to protect my face in the crush of boarding travelers that I discovered my purse was gone, cut off from the strap by a thief. Inside it were not only our tickets and my American passport, but our pitiful trove of American dollars and a handful of German marks.

"Don't panic," Wolfgang said at once. "Don't let on that anything's happened." We had squeezed our way back through the crowd to the platform. Dazedly, we watched the train pull out of the station.

With only the money that Wolfgang carried loose in his pocket—twelve paltry German marks—we returned to the hotel where we had spent the night. Wolfgang immediately telephoned Herr Lewald for supplementary funds to help us out of our dilemma and for advice on my situation. We would have to go to the *Polizei*, he told us, and report the robbery and the loss of my passport. There was no other option under the circumstances.

At the police station, I saw my husband go gray-faced as men and women in line ahead of us stepped up to the sergeant in charge, raised their arms, and gave the prescribed "Heil Hitler" salute.

"Wolfi, will you have to—" I began.

"Yes. Yes." He gritted his teeth angrily.

"But how can you?"

"I must."

"Will they expect me to say it?"

"Yes. It's protocol."

I thought of Bill as we moved nearer to the desk. Faulkner, Faulkner, I called out to him silently across the land masses and the vast ocean that separated us, what's happening to me? What does it all mean? Then Wolfgang was wrestling down his pride and making the hated gesture and saying the words. Suddenly everyone in the room was staring at me. It was my turn.

"Heil Hitler," I said in a dry, choked voice. A month ago, it would have meant little or nothing. Now it sickened me.

We filled out many forms and answered endless questions. A description of us, with a detailed report on what had been stolen, was teletyped through the city, and we were ordered to report daily to the police station until the U.S. State Department confirmed that a passport had been issued to me.

For the next two weeks, we were shrunken by humiliation, dread, and mistrust. We kept to ourselves in our hotel room until the ordeal could not be put off a moment longer and we must make our way to the *Polizei*—again to raise the arm, again to repeat the salute, again to state that the contents of my stolen purse had not been retrieved and that my passport had not been found. Wolfgang stoically accepted the abuse of the police officials, holding his head erect and speaking only when answers were demanded of him.

When financial help arrived from Herr Lewald, we paid our hotel bill and treated ourselves to our first substantial meal in days. Did I want to be shown about the Unter den Linden or stroll in the Tiergarten? Wolfgang asked. One look at my stunned face gave him his answer. I had seen enough of apocalyptic Berlin—bearded old Jews being taunted by uniformed bullies, furniture piled in the gutter as Jewish families were forced out of their apartments, and on the countenances of ordinary Berliners themselves the inescapable evidence of hunger and despair. Day and night I wore the platinum bracelet on my upper arm, reluctant to remove it even when bathing. When we returned to our hotel room after our daily appearance before the police, Wolfgang opened the door cautiously, never certain whether the room was being ransacked or we would find our belongings intact.

When my passport was finally confirmed and a new one was issued at the German Embassy, it was all I could do in my enormous relief to stammer *"Danke."* I belonged to a country. I was no longer stateless. Within the time frame of a few weeks, I had come to know the blessing of citizenship. My heart went out to Paulinchen, whose Italian passport was marked on the inside with a yellow J, indicating that she was of Jewish origin and stateless.

By dusk, we were on a train to Denmark, Wolfgang relaxed and unworried for the first time in months. Crossing the German border, he turned his head to hide the wrenching sorrow of leaving, perhaps forever, the country he had dearly loved, whose substance was part of him, his bones and tissue, his hands, his tongue.

My husband had promised that Copenhagen and his well-to-do older brother's hospitality would restore and rally us. The terrible ordeal of Berlin would recede in memory. Our nerves would be stronger when the time came to leave for New York. Instead, we were thrown into bitter family discord. Ludwig Rebner, a chill, humorless man, darker than Edgar and of medium height, lost no time in making it clear to us that our marriage was a ghastly mistake; if I cared for Wolfgang at all, I would cease being a hindrance to his career by giving him an immediate divorce.

"You are not to say that! She is my wife!" Wolfgang flung

out at him. "I love her and I intend to spend the rest of my life with her."

I begged him to move us from the comfortable two-story house, efficiently run by Ludwig's charming wife, Ingeborg, but he had been too long under his elder brother's domination to defy him to that extent.

One morning when we were at the breakfast table alone, Ludwig walked in, scowling. Wolfgang, he said sternly, was to go to the piano immediately and begin practicing.

In conditioned reflex, my husband started to rise from the table, but I placed my hand restrainingly over his.

"Ludwig," I said quietly, "Wolfgang will do what he pleases, when he pleases, as he pleases." William Faulkner had taught me to recognize tyranny in all its subtle forms.

Ludwig spun about and walked away in smoldering anger. From the doorway, Ingeborg looked at me in astonishment. She had never dared raise her voice to her husband and she had never known a woman who dared stand up to him.

The strain was further excoriated by the matter of Wolfgang's earnings, invested with Ludwig over a period of years. When Wolfgang asked for an accounting, Ludwig refused point-blank to return the money.

What was to have been a joyous family reunion when Peperl, Edgar, and Marjory arrived in Copenhagen a short time later became a series of clashes with Wolfgang and Edgar on one side and the obdurate Ludwig on the other. At Edgar's insistence, Wolfgang found a room for us in a nearby hotel.

I took long walks with Ingeborg and Marjory and Peperl. My father-in-law was a dignified, inquisitive man with graying hair. If he shared Ludwig's conviction that I was a nonentity, an obstruction to his gifted son's career, he did not show it. Because his English was not as fluent as that of the other members of his family, he spoke French and German, and was a charmer of the first water around women.

The investment money was finally turned back to Wolfgang, but not until I threatened, as a wife entitled to a share of her husband's estate, to complain to the American Embassy and the two brothers almost came to physical blows.

It was fall when we left for New York and a new life. Standing on the deck of the ship the first night out, the sea wind leaving an oily sheen on my face, I looked at Wolfgang in dark profile, his mind hurtling ahead in time to what lay before us. Germany had been one long *Walpurgisnacht;* Denmark, an emotional battleground. Nothing must ever again demean or scourge this man whom I had married. Nobody would be allowed to make him afraid again. The damage to his proud spirit would lift away. Music would pour purely from him once again. I would stand, a strong, nononsense, protective woman, between my husband and the world.

Chapter 13

We are in New York, living in a small apartment in a building over a Horn & Hardart (the Automat) restaurant at Broadway and 72nd Street. A far cry from Memphis and the Delta and Normandie Village. Wolfi hopes to find a booking agent who will set up a concert tour for him and then we will both be more sanguine about the future. There are also many influential people here to whom we have access through his family. When next you come to New York to see your publishers, please save a day for us. Wolfi is anxious to meet you—he has read some of your books—and I long, dear friend, to see you again.

My letter to Bill was written after we had been in New York a little more than a month. I would look out the splotched, dusty windows of our tiny fourth-floor apartment—we could afford nothing more commodious—at the ant hill of humanity below, people moving in and out of the subway station as if mounted on invisible tracks and sentenced to endless in-and-out revolutions, and I would wonder whether William Faulkner, by chance, was among them—one hundred steps, two hundred steps, and a wall away from me. Once, possessed by the certainty that he was somewhere in New York, a part of my mind picking up what I thought to be his nearness, I telephoned Random House to ask whether William Faulkner, the author, might possibly be in town; then, at the moment the connection was made with the publisher's switchboard, I hung up.

"I go with you to these affairs, Wolfichen, but honestly, I don't like them," I complained one evening when we had returned from another of the endless parties to which we were invited by wealthy friends of the Riesser family and music-world people who knew Adolph and Paula Rebner. "I try to smile and observe the pleasantries, but I'm uncomfortable with people whom neither of us know."

"You are a silly *Tierchen* if you think I am any more charmed by any of them than you." Wolfgang unloosened his starched tuxedo shirt collar and sighed pleasurably. "But they are people of influence, *mit* much moola, as you say here, and one of them may be *my* oil well, gushing inexhaustibly. Who knows? You may find a sympathetic soul among them one day."

"They're rich, but I don't find them warm."

"I'm looking for work, *Liebchen*. I need them as contacts."

"I'm beginning not to like that word—'contacts.' "

"If one doesn't have a great deal of money—and ours is running out fast—then one must accept all invitations and hope for influence and push."

"But nothing has come from these people. Nothing has happened so far."

"It does seem to be taking a hellishly long time."

"They invite us and we can't reciprocate. That's very disturbing."

"No matter." He threw himself on the bed and pulled me to him. "I must say you looked like a Delta goddess tonight. All the elderly boychicks were looking at your gracile figure."

"Gracile?"

"It's in the dictionary, *Liebchen*." I unlaced his shoes and they clomped heavily to the floor. "But really, we must cultivate our beautiful garden of connections. If not for us, then for Paulinchen and Peperl, who must have affidavits of support if we are to get them out of Europe. Edgar and Marjory are trying in all directions and we must also."

"Wolfi"—taking off his socks and watching him wiggle his toes—"I'd like to see Faulkner again."

"Faulkner?"

"As a friend."

"Is he in town?"

"I don't know. But from time to time, he comes up from Oxford to see his publisher."

"I remember that in London it was always said that one came down from Oxford."

"Wolfi . . ."

"Yes, my blessing."

"I would be happy if you and Bill became friends."

"My hand is as good as extended. *Mit* a click of the heels."

"You don't mind?"

He raised his eyebrows in mild astonishment at the question and I saw only acceptance and trust in his face. He was a worldly, sophisticated European (I kept forgetting that), accustomed in the world of music to unconventional relationships and casual liaisons. It was a matter of supreme indifference to him, as my husband, that Bill had been my lover. One loved for a time and then it was over. Ex-lovers found themselves singing in the same operas, playing side by side in symphony orchestras. The pianist went on accompanying the diva long after both agreed that the passion that flared on the road tour was down to the sparks produced by a faulty cigarette lighter.

A few weeks later, the telephone rang as we were leaving our apartment in a rush for Town Hall. As a virtuoso musician, Wolfgang was on the free ducats list of most New York impresarios and managers forced to paper concert halls.

"Meta, it's Faulkner. Bill Faulkner." The voice, soft with wonder and love, still had the power to instantly pull me into it.

"Bill." In a joyous outburst, I turned to Wolfgang, glowering in the doorway, all German punctuality, impatient to be off. "It's Bill Faulkner! Wait!" My throat threatened to close in surging excitement.

"Bill, where are you?"

"Here, in New York."

"Are you all right?"

"I will be, soon as I see you. Carpenter?"

"Yes?"

"Where's our puppy? Where's Chloe?"

I signaled to Wolfgang that I needed another minute or two. "Didn't I tell you? She's with my brother and his wife in San Francisco. I'll have her with me soon."

"When am I going to see you?"

It was Wolfgang's suggestion that Bill meet us outside Town Hall when the recital was over. On the subway that thundered us to Times Square, I wondered how I would look to him after all the months that had passed. Had the stress of my European experiences, my gathering panic over the rapid depletion of our funds, like grain flowing from a sack gnawed into by rats, added lines of worry to my face? I tried to lose myself in the music and the performance of the violinist, peering at the program in the dark when my attention strayed, shifting in my seat, but I could think only of Bill. When the last encore was played, I rose from my seat, half a hundred pulses going in me like clocks, and moved like a robot into the aisle, Wolfgang behind me.

It was only when the crowd awaiting limousines and taxis began to thin out that I saw Bill, jauntily Tyrol-hatted, a V-necked sweater under his tweed jacket, pipe clamped between his teeth. I called out to him against the stridency of automobile horns, unable to move forward because of the crunch of people, and suddenly he wheeled about, disoriented until recognition broke across his face. We inched toward each other, and it was as if I were coming out of the sea, my lungs bursting for oxygen. Then I was in Bill's bear hug, and Wolfgang, a foot taller, was shaking his free hand.

Bill was sparing of conversation at a nearby restaurant where we were shown to a table, but he responded readily to Wolfgang's wit and erudition, as he had that first day on the Miramar beach to John Crown. Since he himself used the colloquial to inspirit and color language, he nodded his head appreciatively at the Germanisms that my husband sprinkled into his conversation for the outrageous humor of them in juxtaposition with English. Although he listened attentively to the man who had taken me from him, drawing him out on his travels and his music, even conversing in French with him, he would from time to time, as if not wholly able to discipline himself, slide his great mournful gaze over my face; his eyes, burning into mine, had in them the interest, the surprise, and the animal guardedness of one who raises his head to discover that he is being stared at by a total stranger. When Wolfgang, turning to me for approval, accepted Bill's invitation to us to have dinner with him the following evening, I knew with certainty and piercing pride that the two men in my life genuinely liked each other. Neither was capable of feigning for more than a few seconds, whatever the end gain, receptivity to people for whom they felt only strong aversion. Wolfgang rudely walked away from bores, fools, and mediocrities, and Faulkner, with equal disdain, turned his back on them. The sense of smarting loss that had weighed on me for months was lifted. Now there was the possibility that Faulkner, who had said that we belonged to each other, whose love for me had not been soured by my marriage, could come back into my life—my loyal friend, my mentor, my alter ego.

"He'd been drinking, you know," Wolfgang observed later as we waited for the subway.

"No!" I thought back to Bill's face in the crowd and to our hour or more together over coffee, and I could not recall one slurred speech, one physical movement, that was not perfectly normal and controlled.

"Maybe for days," Wolfgang said. "Quietly and steadily."

We were to meet Faulkner in the lobby of the Algonquin Hotel, where he preferred to put up on his trips to New York. The rooms were old-fashioned but comfortable, the rates reasonable for midtown, and he liked Frank Case, the affable, witty boniface; moreover, when he wasn't making the claim that he was not a literary man, there were a number of writers in residence with whom he enjoyed drinking. After thirty minutes had passed and there was no sign of our host, I began to worry.

"It's not like Bill to be late," I said, puzzled. "He's always been prompt."

"He may have forgotten."

"No, I don't think so. Not Bill. Not when he cares about people."

"Perhaps he's held up somewhere."

"Then he'd have us paged."

I prevailed upon my husband, who was not built for patient waiting with his long, restless legs and finger-tapping hands, to give it another fifteen minutes. When no Bill Faulkner came through the entrance, I called his room on the house phone. No answer. Outside we scanned West 44th Street in both directions, then began to walk toward Broadway,

"I told you he'd been drinking," Wolfgang reminded me.

Foreboding trickled across my mind. I insisted on going back to the Algonquin, disregarding Wolfgang's grumbles. The desk clerk looked up when I asked if he could give me any information about Mr. Faulkner.

"Mr. Faulkner is ill," he said disinterestedly, "and is not seeing anyone."

I chose not to heed the prohibition and hurried to the elevator with Wolfgang in tow, obviously not happy about the situation. At the door to Bill's room, my husband rapped repeatedly but with no success. Hotel guests leaving their rooms cast stares of distrust at us. A chambermaid watched from behind her cart.

"Shall I batter down the door for you like Clark Gable?" Wolfgang asked.

I turned the knob and the door yielded to my pressure. From the hallway, I could see Bill lying naked on the bed, genitals in full evidence. Wolfgang drew in a shocked breath. I called Bill's name, and when there was no response, I moved quickly to his bedside, blood pounding in my ears, and saw with relief the rise and fall of his chest.

"Bill, what on earth is wrong?" I gasped. The acrid smell of medication overspread the room.

"Carpenter?" Bill groaned. "Carpenter?" His voice seemed to be coming from far away. "Is it you?"

"Bill, I'm here. Wolfi's with me."

"The dinner—I'm sorry."

"Bill, what happened?" I asked. "Tell me so I can help you."

"Drinking," he mumbled. "Went to bathroom. On toilet and fell against hot-water pipe."

"Oh, Bill."

"Burned. Couldn't move. Couldn't get off the damn pipe."

"How bad is it?

"Bad. Devine—you don't know him—Devine came in, got me a doctor."

"What did he say?"

"Third-degree burn." He winced and made an "eeeee" whine of anguish. "Carpenter?"

Drops of sweat covered his forehead. I asked Wolfgang to get a cloth dampened with cool water from the bathroom. While he was gone, Bill turned toward me.

"I started drinking." He slowly pulled out the words. "You know why?"

"Yes, Bill. I think I do."

"Last night I was all right." His breathing was raspy and dry. "This morning, thinking of seeing you tonight . . . belonging to someone else—"

"Bill, dear one. You mustn't. Please."

"Yes'm. You're right. Mustn't say . . . mustn't . . ."

Wolfgang returned with a wet towel and I gently sponged Bill's damp face. He was so heavily sedated that I could not be sure to what extent he was aware of our presence. He mumbled that tomorrow he would be better. Now we should go and let him sleep. We turned off the lights and left him. The burn was deeper, I later found out, than anyone had thought, penetrating almost to his spine. It was to trouble William Faulkner for the rest of his life, particularly in damp weather.

The next day he was able to answer the telephone. Everything was being done for him, no need for us to worry. In a bit, he would have some tea and toast and perhaps a scrambled egg. It would be a while before he could leave his room.

"I can't wear any clothes over the burn just yet," Bill apologized, "but will you and your husband join me for dinner in my room tonight?"

"Bill, it's too soon," I objected. "You don't have to do this for us."

"No. No. I want to. I want to see you . . . see you both."

We were met at the door by Bill in white shorts, nothing else on his body. A table with flowers had been set for three. Almost immediately a room-service waiter wheeled in a cart. With all the aplomb of a man entertaining in his own home, Bill served the soup course. As we brought our spoons to our mouths, I could see that our host, for all the valiant effort to conceal it from us, was still in severe physical agony. He was careful to avoid contact of his naked back with the chair on which he was seated, and he moved stiffly, almost arthritically.

I exchanged a pitying glance with Wolfgang.

"You're in pain, Bill. Wolfi and I don't want you to go on with this."

"But the dinner . . ." He gestured toward the cart.

"Another time. Please."

Within a week, Bill was healing and able to get about again, though not in the Manhattan sense of hurry and dash; he was a Southerner and the burn troubled him, so he moved at his own pace, a stubborn snail of a man, sauntering quietly while all of New York rushed past him. There were days when we would not see him and days when he seemed to prefer our company to anyone else's. Through him we met people who became my own friends from then on—Bil Baird and, until she died, his wife, Cora, puppeteers extraordinary, and as close to Faulkner as anyone I knew; Buckminster Fuller, who, at his office, showed us his design for the Dymaxion House, all metal and prefabricated; and Jim Devine, a writer. One evening at the Bairds'—their apartment bespoke a hand-to-mouth existence at the time; they had even painted a headboard on the wall for their secondhand day bed—Bil Baird spoke humorously of his recent abdominal surgery, inspiring a ditty. We sat on the floor as Cora sang it:

> Won't you come over to my house?
> Won't you come over and play?
> Under my britches, I've got fancy stitches,
> Come over, I live 'cross the way,
> And I'll show you my operation—
> It's bad but it could have been worse.
> Oh, won't you come over to my house.
> I'll play that I'm your little nurse.

The whiskey in our insides cauterized our private woes and the camaraderie warmed our hearts. We whooped with laughter over Faulkner's country yarns, the most hilarious of which was a concise account of Buck Smeeger's mistake:

"During a baseball game in Charlie Meager's cow pasture," Bill said wryly, "Buck Smeegers slid into what he thought was second base . . ."

Cora and I dropped out of competition in a game in which one member of the group gave the first line of a limerick and everyone else, by turn, was required to supply the next line in so many seconds. Faulkner, Wolfgang, and Bil Baird were never at a loss for invention, whimsical and ribald, and we shook with laughter.

Once Bill asked if he might sit in on one of Wolfgang's practice sessions. Pleased, Wolfgang took him along to a studio in the basement of Steinway Hall and played for almost two hours, wresting great washes of color and billows of exquisite sound from the piano. Not a word was spoken. Bill sat upright in an uncomfortable chair, listening in hard concentration, as if he were in the Mississippi woods straining to hear an animal moving through the brush or on a riverbank waiting for the call of wild ducks in flight. When I asked him about the afternoon he would say only, "Wolfi has a *fine* left hand."

The two men saw each other many times after that and often Bucky Fuller joined them for lunch or dinner at Christ Cella Restaurant on East 46th Street. There was no objection from Wolfgang when I began to meet Bill without him when he was busy contacting impresarios and managers. In his friendship with Faulkner, my husband had altered our personal history to expunge him from it as my former lover.

"I trust you and Wilhelm the Faulkner," he said the first time I was to see Bill alone.

Faulkner, in turn, had gone from a knifing awareness of my married state to a total disregard of it. More than once, I had the feeling that, saying good night to us in front of the building where we lived, he thought of us going chastely to our separate rooms. Although I knew that his desire for me was as great as ever, he never attempted to maneuver me to his hotel room. The opportunity was there one day when, after lunching together, Bill suggested that we could talk better in the quiet of the Algonquin lobby; if the idea of love-making occurred to him, he resisted it. One did not, if one was a Southern gentleman, seduce a married woman, not even one with whom he had slept when she was single.

On the day he was to return to Oxford, we walked along Fifth Avenue. In the late 1930's, New York was a magical, revivifying city, scarred at its edges by slums and grinding poverty, but as immaculate as stainless steel at its center. The blight and canker that were to overtake it were not yet detectable. Panhandlers abounded, but I could walk from West 72nd or ride the subway at any hour without fear of being beaten, raped, or robbed. We could not, in any case, afford taxis. As for Bill, the city conferred blessed anonymity upon him from the moment he arrived at Pennsylvania Station; he was far more relaxed in New York than in Hollywood. Only his few close friends, his agent, and his publishers knew that he was in the city. Nobody pressed in on him, nobody tried to lionize him, and there were no producers' or directors' wives to make outrageous social demands on him as a Southern literary celebrity.

On a bench in Central Park, Bill and I watched the swans, geese, and ducks as they waddled up from the lake for offerings of bread crumbs and grain. I told him of our precarious financial position. The platinum bracelet had been sold for a little over twelve hundred dollars, a fraction of its worth, and unless our prospects improved, Wolfgang would be forced to sell the small Steinway grand piano. I was accustomed to living on very little, as Bill knew, but to Wolfgang, who had always had money, his shrinking bank balance and professional reverses were great, horrendous tragedies.

"Please let me give you some money," Bill offered.

"Oh, no." I was nonplused. Had he misinterpreted my need to unburden myself as a hint for financial help? "No, Bill, we couldn't take anything from you."

"Lend it to you then. For once in my life, I have a little extra that I can spare."

"We don't need it. There's still a little left in the bank. And in a pinch, we can always turn to Wolfgang's brother."

"You're sure?"

I nodded and pressed his hand in gratitude. Sparrows darted between webfooted birds for their share of food. Bill looked at his watch to check the time that was left to him before his train departed.

"Bill," I asked, "are you happy? Is it any better for you—with Estelle?"

"Not to speak of."

"Is she still drinking as much?"

"She can't seem to cut down."

"I wish it could be different for you."

"We have a kind of truce going since all the unpleasantness in Hollywood. That's something."

228

"Jill?"

"The apple of my eye." Bill clapped his hands together suddenly to distract a bullying goose pecking at a small duck. "You know, she asks about you."

"You tell her that I think of her, too—often."

"Carpenter?" Not looking at me at all. "Are you happy?"

"Except for the hard times we're having."

"They go away."

"Bill, I always tell you everything." He bobbed his head in agreement. "I love Wolfgang very much. I can say that to you, can't I?"

"Yes, ma'am."

"I love being in his world. In the center of everything that's exciting to me. Bill, you've no idea how many great artists I've been privileged to hear. Some weeks we go to concerts every night. Chamber music. Opera. Ballet. And you know I never tire of music."

"No, ma'am, you sure don't." He suppressed a grin that threatened to widen out. "Not you."

I studied the strong, humorous face in all its aspects—full, in sharp profile, half turned from me. He had more than loved me; he had cherished me. From the first, he had made me feel that I was important to him, precious to him. I need even now only touch his hand lightly with my fingers to arouse him, to make him want me as fiercely as ever, yet he had loved me as equally for what I was inside—for what he felt I could be inside—as for what outer beauty I possessed that stirred his passion.

Wolfgang loved me, but he was not concerned with my interior being as Faulkner had been—with what I was thinking, with how I was growing, with what had become meaningful to me. But then I had come to my husband as a relatively complete woman, out of a salvaging love affair, and to Faulkner as a girl-woman, shallow and stunted. I could not expect to have Wolfgang's interest and solicitude as I had had Bill's.

"It's fine with us," I said. "It really is."

"Then I won't worry about you when I'm down home."

"If you were thinking that it wasn't going well—"

"Meta." He took my hand and a bolt of his great male energy coursed through me. It had been that way from the first. He was like one of the traveling evangelists of my Southern childhood who performed miracles within faded, patched tents crowded with the sick and the lame. He could have healed me of all the ailments and plagues of the world with those small, powerful hands. "Meta, one of my characters has said, 'Between grief and nothing I will take grief.' " He studied my face as he would a map that confused him with its dim, indistinct iconography. "It's getting late and I have to catch a train. I'll be back in New York before long. And not just because of the book. You know that, don't you?"

When *The Wild Palms* was published in 1939, Bill sent a copy to me from Oxford. Reading it avidly, I gasped when I came to a line that seemed to leap from the printed page and salt my eyes.

"What's wrong?" Wolfgang asked.

"Oh, something that one of Bill's characters says," I said, reading aloud, " 'Between grief and nothing I will take grief.' "

"Very good." Wolfgang went back to his music score.

Bill came to New York often in 1938 and 1939. He would suddenly appear at our door and it was as if he had never left and there would be riotous evenings together at the Bairds' or with Bucky Fuller and Jim Devine.

I gave Cora Baird beginning piano lessons. It was a good period for Bill. He was deeply engrossed in *The Wild Palms*, as he had been in Hollywood, and he still thought it would be his finest and most significant novel. He was particularly proud of the "Old Man" chapters.

Wolfgang all but stopped hoping for a concert career to open for him. The times were all askew. It was as Paulinchen had said: Nowhere in the world could a virtuoso ascend to stellar importance without a financial base or backers.

Claudio Arrau and Rudolf Serkin, I had been told, had powerful patrons behind them. Now Wolfgang concentrated on finding engagements as an accompanist. With the European situation worsening each day as Hitler's Germany moved on Austria, and Czechoslovakia prepared against an invasion of its borders, the United States became a haven for hundreds of concertizing artists and musicians. It was a curious manifestation of the artistic ethos in those days that actors, musicians, dancers, and entertainers were among the first to leave the countries threatened by Hitler; one may rationalize that somehow one will live under tyranny, but to be stripped of one's art, not to be allowed to function as an artist—that is death! Suddenly New York teemed with refugee pianists, many of them concert artists in Europe, who competed for jobs as accompanists to musical luminaries with established reputations in the United States. Wolfgang made the rounds of all the managers he had appealed to earlier, this time for the opportunity to be heard as an accompanist for the stars they represented or as a substitute for ailing pianists in chamber groups. He would rush to the piers whenever a ship arrived with artists scheduled for American tours, but so would every other unemployed piano accompanist.

It was a humbling reversal for Wolfgang. He had been far more than an accompanist for Emanuel Feuermann; he had been a collaborator, a partner with strong musical gifts and convictions, understood, used, and appreciated by the great cellist. Now he would approach performing artists who were fully aware of his stature and plead for a tour with them. A price per concert would be set, usually a nominal one (concert stars were not known for their generosity to accompanists in that period) ; sometimes the verbal agreement held, but other times it collapsed when rival pianists would get to the artist and offer, as once did Jesús Maria Sanroma, a well-known recording artist, to work for ten dollars less per concert.

Erica Morini, a famous violinist who had been helped early in her career by the Rebner family in Austria, arrived in New York to begin a tour. Thinking that she would engage him without question, since she knew of his European reputation and of his long association with Feuermann, Wolfgang contacted her. To his dismay, he was told that he would have to audition for the job. Subjugating his pride, Wolfi went to the audition, confident of his knowledge of chamber music and solo repertoire. The following day, Morini's secretary called to announce that he had won over all the other desperate contestants and that he would be paid forty dollars for each concert. Mortified, Wolfgang sat down with me to figure whether that pittance would allow him to save money; there would be traveling expenses, hotel bills, three meals a day, a dinner jacket to be cleaned, a fresh white formal shirt for every concert, and incidentals. We sent word to the violinist that Wolfgang declined the offer. Within a few days, he was engaged by Virovai at fifty dollars a performance.

Many months later, I found myself in a supper buffet line with Erica Morini at the home of Diane Hearst, of the Columbia Concert Bureau. With Wolfgang away on tour, I was escorted by his uncle, Guido Ansbacher. When Morini commented that Wolfgang had been a very foolish man not to have accepted her offer, I suppressed an unladylike riposte that came to mind.

"I'm sorry," I said frostily, "but I never discuss my husband's business affairs."

It was an inadequate parry. Would I ever learn to be one of those wives who slashed and clawed to help the artists to whom they were married? The instinct for it seemed hopelessly beyond my grasp.

Tours, when Wolfgang could find them—he was accompanying Kirsten Flagstad, Isaac Stern, Garbusova, Ezio Pinza, Ruggiero Ricci, among others—were exhausting. There would generally be between twelve and eighteen concerts in as many cities. Rarely if ever was Wolfgang's name listed in the program notes. Travel and hotel arrangements for him were second- and third-rate. Often pianos were untuned. Although he received a fraction of the stipend that the concert star collected, Wolfgang would have to rehearse for as long— and sometimes longer.

In New York, almost daily, there was depressing news from arriving refugees. Several members of Wolfgang's immediate family had committed suicide in Vienna. A musician friend had been beaten to death by storm troopers. A Russian-born flautist had been taken from his apartment in the early-morning hours and no one knew what had happened to him. Wolfgang and his brother Edgar intensified their campaign to secure affidavits of support guaranteeing that their parents would not become wards of New York or the United States. For a time, we had stopped accepting invitations from the wealthy, but now we never dared miss a function where we might stumble into someone who would sponsor Paulinchen and Peperl. The fact that we could not return the hospitality of our hosts in our dreary, cramped apartment no longer bothered me. Hitler's shadow was lengthening. Time was running out. If Peperl and Paulinchen were to be saved, we must manage to get them out of Europe quickly.

"You know my father's contribution to the music world," Wolfgang would begin. "We so desperately need affidavits of support for my . . ."

"Oh, we regret very much, but we have already given as many affidavits as we are able."

Or "If they were younger, then possibly, but we cannot take the chance of sponsoring people of their age."

Or "The government asks too many questions in the affidavit forms. We do not care to disclose business earnings and what property we own or our stocks and bonds."

Other than carefree times with Faulkner, we enjoyed most the simple evenings at our apartment with American and German-Jewish musicians and other friends from the music world, most of whom were as poor as we. Many of them, like Wolfgang, were attempting to bring over family members from Germany and Austria, and there was some comfort for him in accounts of refugees who had found sponsors. The chairs would seldom accommodate all our guests, but the *Gemütlichkeit* of artists gathered together was so pervasive that even Dagmar Godowsky and a few music critics were not averse to sitting on the floor, ignoring smells of food wafted up from the Automat below. I served Jell-O and home-baked cookies, cheaper than the pastries offered in the stores along Broadway, and there was always coffee or tea.

Evenings at the Rebners' were noisy and spirited. Shades drawn, the apartment, with furniture shipped from Germany, breathed an ambience more Berlin, Munich, and Vienna than New York. The musicians and composers who came to us were happier in our shabby gentility than at the glossy receptions to which they, too, were invited. Pipes could be smoked, shoes removed, jackets shed, collars loosened; the rejections of the day went up with tobacco smoke as they talked about music, philosophy and history, books and paintings and the dance. The poetry of Goethe and Heine was recited as men and women listened enraptured, eyes closed to receive the imagery. The novels of Mann, Feuchtwanger, the Zweigs, Werfel, Hauptmann, and Wassermann were discussed reverently.

I sat close to Wolfgang when I wasn't serving or emptying ashtrays and absorbed it all in a transport of excitement, stimulated mentally as never before. William Faulkner had unlocked a mind constricted by a Southern finishing-school education; now in our modest salon over Horn & Hardart's, it expanded until I thought it would burst with the weight and wonder of new knowledge, new insights, new breadth.

"Speak English, please—*bitte*," I would cry out when they slipped into German, fretful to be left out of it, crestfallen when I could not follow a play on words that provoked gales of laughter.

The strain of scrabbling for work, playing for ungenerous virtuosi, trying to save his parents from certain death, and fighting to be admitted to the musicians' union made Wolfgang tense and often belligerent. Having spent almost twenty-five years sitting at a piano, with others editing out all the unpleasantness of life for him, he could not easily adjust to failure.

The money Wolfgang earned, even when he occasionally commanded sixty dollars a performance, was never enough. What he saved while on tour would last only a few weeks at the most. Unless by some felicitous stroke of good luck he quickly found another accompanist assignment, we would have to borrow from his brother Edgar to get by. I learned where to buy meat and vegetables and fruit cheaply. One day, with only a few cents to make purchases, I made a mixture of stewed tomatoes, bread, onions, and parsley that I remembered Mammy preparing in my childhood. Wolfgang, a gourmand accustomed to the best, tasted it and, looking up at me, said disdainfully, "What is this slop?"

At the outset, when we were given tickets to concerts, we had enough money to pay our way at receptions that followed at the Beethoven Club Association or the Russian Tea Room. Now, Wolfgang in his tuxedo, I in my worn evening dresses, would plead an early-morning rehearsal for Wolfgang, visitors, headaches, colds—anything to avoid the embarrassment of a check that we would not have the cash to cover. Alibi accepted, we caught the subway or bus back to 72nd Street from Town Hall, Carnegie Hall, the Metropolitan Opera, or the Washington Square High School at the foot of Fifth Avenue.

The only blacks with whom I had come in contact in Hollywood were actors who worked at the studios. Sometimes, passing the weary housemaids waiting at Beverly Hills bus stops at day's end for transportation to their ghettos, I longed to be able to talk to them; there were faces that recalled black people dear to me in the South. In New York, accorded full rights in public places, they were everywhere, but I was stunned to discover that prejudice against them existed among Northern whites; it was all I could do to curb my anger when I saw a white couple instantly move away when blacks sat next to them in a theater. There were a number of brilliant black musicians and singers whom we met as our circle of friends increased. One night at a party given by Adele Strycker, then secretary of the Beethoven Club Association, I was introduced to Dorothy Maynor, whom I greatly admired. She told of an unlikely experience that had occurred earlier in the evening when, due for rehearsal, she decided to have dinner at the Pennsylvania Hotel coffee shop—hardly one of New York's finer restaurants. Waiting for her order to be taken, she studied her score intently. After some twenty minutes had passed and no waiter had approached, she looked up, saw that the restaurant was crowded, and went back to her score. Suddenly she realized that she was being deliberately ignored and looked up again. This time, while she had been distracted, a screen had been placed around her table, sparing white patrons the sight of her black skin.

Wolfgang's temper became more and more difficult to deal with as bills piled up. "Does it have to come every month?" he would ask exasperatedly when I handed him the gas bill. He had never had to cope with invoices and statements. Why was he now thrust into this galling position? My own placid acceptance of a marginal existence only added fuel to his ire. What if I had faced privation before? How could he be expected to endure my monumental passivity? Why should the mere act of getting from one day to the next seem to me a small triumph? His flare-ups became more frequent. Our clashes were all flying knives and jagged glass.

When next Faulkner showed up in New York, Wolfgang was away on a brief tour and probably relieved to be out of the storm center with me. I agreed to meet Bill for lunch, thought of backing out, then decided that I had never needed his strength more. My face in the mirror was blade-thin, blotchy, and wan. The shine had gone out of my eyes. Every dress I owned was worn and shabby. Somehow I forced myself out of the apartment and walked to the bus stop, carefully avoiding telling reflections of myself in plate-glass windows.

Bill wanted to take joy in me, but I had only melancholy to offer. I heaped my inventory of conjugal miseries upon him. It was not only that we were living a hand-to-mouth existence, oppressed by debts, but that our vicissitudes, instead of binding us together, had wrenched us apart. The worst of it was that I was beginning to believe that Ludwig was justified in saying that I was the wrong woman for Wolfgang. I had not brought him money or connections. I had not applied myself to learning German and so felt closed out when Wolfgang and his friends opted not to speak English. On a number of occasions, when a more worldly wife would have helped his career, I had been at a complete loss. I also complained that Wolfgang, with his superior academic training, had of late belittled me for my own lack of knowledge.

"Bill," I said in childish vexation, "he actually called me 'ignorant' and 'stupid.' "

Downing his whiskey neat, Bill clucked his tongue at me in reproval.

" 'Ignorant' means a lack of knowledge. You may be ignorant about many things that Wolfi knows as he does the back of his hand, but you are not stupid. You are a bright woman with a flowering mind and you are not"—he put his glass down sharply for emphasis—"to think otherwise."

He was due at Random House and I insisted on walking to the beautiful old building with him.

At East 44th Street, I began to weep, tears streaming down my face, sour tears for the hopelessness of my lot and for the bright promise eaten by rust.

Bill stopped abruptly. I walked on a few blind steps, head downcast, then turned to face him.

"Buck up, Carpenter," he said harshly. "I've never seen you like this."

It was a rebuke from a man who loved me and had never before found fault with me. I was stung and burned by it, as if I had been splattered by boiling lye. Then he was hailing a taxi and paying for my fare back to West 72nd Street; censure was in his face, irritation in his voice. I had lessened myself in his sight. God, I thought, where is my strength that I have let myself become this whining woman, this self-pitying complainer? Where is my pride that I allowed Bill to see me devoid of the gallantry and courage that he loved in me?

I awoke the next morning as if recovering from an illness, every nerve in my body alive and singing. Bless Bill Faulkner. His reprimand had brought me back to my senses. I would see him today and I would be myself again.

He did not appear unduly surprised at the beaming face I presented or my positive attitude. It was almost as though he had manipulated me as he would have a character in one of his books.

"Bill," I said confidently, no hesitation, "I want you to please help my husband."

"How?" He blinked his eyes, bemused.

"You know influential people in New York. Talk to them for Wolfi. He needs a push."

"I see."

"It's demoralizing him that he's not on a recital basis in this country. He had such hopes. You know how you feel when you work in Hollywood? That's how Wolfi feels when he has to grovel for work as an accompanist."

Bill nodded his head, understanding, closing in on it. He arranged for me to meet Bennett Cerf and his good friend Hal Smith at Random House. I reminded myself of Henriette Martin as I faced each man and detailed Wolfgang's background, his training, his accomplishments. Nothing mattered but that my husband overcome the terrible reverses that had ground him down. Now I had fortitude again. I would not think of what it had cost me in the coinage of pride to go to the man who loved me, who still loved me, to ask for help for the man who was to have given me a far better life than I had known with him.

While I was shedding all pretensions, I also wrote my parents that we were in serious financial straits. Could my father help us pay the rent for a few months? It would greatly relieve the pressures on us. By return mail, my generous parents sent a check to cover our rent and pledged to continue the aid for a year.

Then a miracle. A wealthy American of German ancestry

to whom we had appealed on behalf of Paulinchen and Peperl decided to back them as new immigrants. He had our promise that he would not be held to guarantees, that the Rebners would never turn to New York State or to the U.S. government for aid. Legal documents were executed and signed in great haste, opening the way for them to come to America. Paulinchen arrived first, living with us until Edgar found her a small apartment of her own; Peperl came later. Fear had incised its gash marks on their faces. They had aged shockingly since I had last seen them.

At last our luck seemed to be bending away from the poles of failure and disappointment. There were more engagements for Wolfgang, tours with Nathan Milstein and Ricci among them. We were able to repay Marjory and Edgar money we had borrowed. Then, as if a rope holding us securely had snapped, I became ill. After a series of tests, I was told that I had a fibroid tumor and must undergo surgery at once. I came out of the Lexington Hospital weak and depressed. What money Wolfgang was earning went to pay surgeons, anesthesiologists, and hospital costs.

Convalescing slowly, so debilitated that I went about in my dressing gown most of the time, I answered the door one morning and was asked by a woman who had seen our nameplate on the door if I was Mrs. Rebner and if I would show her through our apartment.

"I understand it's just like the one for rent on the floor above," she said. "Since it's locked, I can at least get an idea of the rooms from your place."

"I'm sorry," I apologized, "but I can't help you. I've just had surgery and I'm not well."

The woman curled her lips in disdain. "Well," she snarled, "what else can you expect from a Jew?" It was my first real encounter with anti-Semitism in my own country and for weeks I was devastated by it.

Appalled by the untidiness of our apartment, unhappy with myself for my loss of energy, I tried one day to put things in order. After I had finished with the living room, I dropped down on my knees to scrub the kitchen floor. Minutes later, the top of my incision opened. The pain was excruciating and I was more frightened than I had ever been in my life. When Wolfgang came home, I stammered an account of my mishap.

"Good Lord!" he interrupted, screaming at me. "Don't you know you'll have to go to the hospital again? That's going to cost us money we haven't got. What is the matter with you? What are you trying to do to me?"

It was the outburst of a man who should have learned in childhood to accept the affronts, the chafes, the blows, but he had been kept from falling down, kept from cutting his knees on glass, kept from all ugliness. Family members and servants formed a protective ring around him. All was made clean and pure for him. Now misery was blowing in like weed spores. He was all head lumps and bruises.

Wolfgang, stranger in a surreal world of trapdoors, banana peels, buzz saws, and ground snares, flailed his arms in bitter protest and screamed his primal rage. He needed someone to blame. Suddenly I was not his wife, sharing the adversities, drinking from the cup of exclusion with him, but his enemy, close enough at hand to heap abuse upon. The storm of vituperation followed me wherever I fled in the small apartment and finally I raged back at him. I was an American woman, not a European female to be trod upon by a man; I would not be tied to a post and lashed for the slippage in his career. We hurled ugly words and threats at each other like knife throwers on a vaudeville stage. Exhausted, throats dry and hurting, we backed off and stood glaring at each other from opposite ends of the room.

"*Gott in Himmel!*" Wolfgang muttered as he sought to control his agitated breathing. "I must get you to a hospital."

Although I was still ill and weighed only 102 pounds, I found a job as a model with a Garment Center manufacturing firm. I knew the first day that it could not last. I was not strong enough to be on my feet all day long. A friend who was working for James Roosevelt at Samuel Goldwyn's New York office advised me to apply for the position of receptionist and I was hired on the strength of my Hollywood experience. The money helped us keep our heads above water but it did not save our marriage. We quarreled incessantly and the furious bickering undermined what little health I had left.

"Wolfgang," I said to my husband one evening after a bitter argument, "I can't go on this way. I can't stand any more."

He raised his shoulders unconcernedly, his gaze fixed on the pages of the *Musical Courier*.

"Do what you must," he said. "I can't stop you."

"No, you can't."

"Where will you go?"

"To my parents in Arizona."

"There's no money to buy a train ticket."

"I'll get it from my father."

Instead I wired Bill that my marriage was over and asked for a loan to cover my one-way fare to Kingman. The money, more than I needed, arrived the next day by Western Union; there was also a message asking me to route myself through Mississippi and to break my trip near the Louisiana border.

It was night when the train pulled in at the depot. The lights of a town shone dimly through a screen of pelting rain like luminous fish through the sea, and all at once I saw from the step that the conductor put down for me William Faulkner, face and hair wet, hurrying toward the train with an open umbrella. I clung to him as he directed a black youth in the transfer of my bags to his automobile, unwilling to ever let him go again. The storm's violence increased as we drove into Louisiana through a veritable deluge. I slept on his shoulder for a few hours, waking when he stopped to get hot coffee. It was odd that in Hollywood Bill had been reluctant to drive, but on a two-lane road in Louisiana under storm conditions, he handled the wheel with absolute confidence. I was too ill to spell him and he did not want to rest.

We arrived in New Orleans shortly before midnight and checked into a hotel in the Vieux Carré. It was another rare manifestation of the romantic impulse in William Faulkner, a genetic legacy from some dashing ancestor, that he would brave one of the season's worst storms to be with the woman he loved in the beautiful city of his first youthful amours, the city where he had written *Soldiers' Pay*.

The rain had seeped through my shoes and dress and I had absorbed dampness from his own soaked clothes. By the time we undressed, I was running a slight fever. He gave me raw whiskey to kill my cold, great swallows of it, then he kissed the furnace of my mouth and the length of my fevered body and with his own burning skin kept the first chills from racking me.

I knew from his sexual excitement that he had not been with a woman for a long time, perhaps not since we had lain together. His limbs shook, the great heart was a wild bell in his chest. "Sweet beloved," he whispered in his passion, "it's always this way with you—with you and no one else."

"And I with you."

"You are my beautiful dear love."

Confident that my marriage was a shambles, certain that divorce was the only solution, I felt no guilt. I had come straight to Faulkner because I needed him. He was my best friend, the lover who exalted me, the teacher who gave me wisdom, the source from whom I drew strength.

We slept until noon. Bill put his mouth to my forehead and pronounced it as cool as churned butter in the creek, the fever gone.

"Good whiskey." He grinned. "And Mr. Bowen."

I saw him watching me, mischief in his eyes, as I came from the bathroom. "I love seeing a beautiful woman slip out of bed," he said. "Front and back, it's a wondrous sight to behold." He cradled me in his arms.

"Don't go to Arizona. Stay here."

"In New Orleans?"

"I'll come down when I can."

"Bill, I'm not well. I'm run-down. Anemic. Skin and bones. I need to rest. To think."

"After, then?"

It was romantic extravagance, like the gardenias pinned to my pillow, the poems, the outpourings of amorous hyperbole when he made love. I gave no answer, knowing that he couldn't mean it. He was a writer who was most inspired when he was in Oxford. He was fanatically slavish to the books and short stories that clogged his imagination. He was a farmer, with cotton and hay crops to bring in.

We strolled, his arm around my waist, through the French Quarter. It had been years since I had wandered through the picturesque streets and peered into courtyards. Bill knew the Quarter brick by brick, plank by plank. Here there was a tree that he remembered, there a Jackson Square bench on which he had composed one of the poems in *The Marble Faun*. I was to note the texture of that old wall, the grace of iron grillwork yonder.

In the beginning, it was he who had been the one to leave. Now, for the second time, I was leaving him. He kissed me with great sadness, giving me absolution for slipping out of his life again. My train lurched forward and he was out of sight range, merged with praline vendors and black porters and old men sweeping.

Blandished in Kingman by my parents and aunt, healing in the felicity of a temperate sun and dry desert air, reading Wolfgang's daily letters of self-reproach, I decided to return to New York and try to salvage what remained of my marriage, put it together again if I could. We were both victims of a terrible time in the world, and beneath the ruins of our union there was a love worth saving.

Wolfgang and I celebrated our reconciliation with lobster and champagne—a fig for the restaurant bill.

In August, John and Sally were married in Los Angeles. We were too poor to afford the trip to California or to buy a wedding present. There was other news from Hollywood. Henriette Martin, writing under the nom de plume of Hilary Lynn, was on her way to becoming a top-salaried screenwriter following the success of her first film, *Hollywood Cavalcade*. And Betty Walter, who had broken up with Victor Kilian to marry labor organizer Ed Royce after only a week of courtship, was now the mother of a baby boy.

I had written Bill of our reconciliation but heard nothing from him until a letter arrived with the Oxford postmark in mid-August.

Although he was short of money, he would come to New York about October 15 and try to find a cheap place at which to stay. He protested that he didn't see me enough and that it was bad, physically, to live as he was now. He knew that he should find a girl ("a physical spittoon," he phrased it), but although he had tried, he was unable to.

"I simply won't rise," he wrote. "That's strange, isn't it? After what I know and don't ever seem to stop remembering very long, all else is just meat."

The next month, Hitler's armed forces invaded Poland. Wolfgang and I, walking in the Broadway sunlight that morning, looked at each other in disbelief as we heard news vendors bellow the black headlines. Wolfgang quickly bought a newspaper, scanned the first paragraph, then leaned his head against a rough concrete wall and wept silently for the Europe he had fled.

Chapter 14

Winter set in. We moved to a cheap apartment in Riverdale and huddled by the radiator for its feeble warmth. When Wolfgang attempted to practice or compose, irate tenants pounded on our walls, shouting imprecations in Italian and Yiddish. We stumbled from the subway, spine-bent and listless, after the long, grinding ride to Manhattan and back. We trudged through dirty snow to our doorway.

I wrote Faulkner early in 1940 that we were moving to Hollywood. We would not be in New York when he came up from Oxford again. Wolfgang was weary of competing with other refugee pianists for accompanist work. In Hollywood he would play in the studio orchestras assembled for background music. New York had been unlucky for us. Another year of it and the spirit would be driven from our lives.

With the meager money for which Wolfgang sold his piano, we bought a secondhand Oldsmobile and drove westward with Chloe. The car had long passed the obsolescence for which it was timed. Like our marriage, it held together mysteriously, metal atoms unwilling to grant death to their rusty, battered container. The motor wheezed, sputtered, and failed across America. Great holes erupted like pox in thin, worn tires. One morning the battery was lifeless; a garage mechanic dissolved the corrosive white acid that had formed over it with Coca-Cola as Wolfgang watched in disbelief.

Somewhere in Texas the wiring system had to be partly replaced. My father had authorized me to charge repairs and parts to his account. By the time we clattered into Hollywood, the bills amounted to several hundred dollars.

Settled in a hillside court bungalow overlooking Cahuenga Boulevard as it thrust, prefreeway, into the San Fernando Valley, we allowed ourselves to think that the bad times had been outwitted, left gasping for air in one of the cheap motel rooms that we had vacated before sunrise each day.

Neighbors in other boxes boasted that we were but a stone's throw from Rudolph Valentino's Falcon's Lair; we took their word for it and envied them the jobs for which they left in the mornings and from which they returned at night. Wolfgang came back from a first appointment at Musicians Local 47 headquarters with a face numbed by disappointment; it would be six months before he could obtain a union card. The same pianists were hired over and over by studio music department heads. Composers who conducted their own scores also had favorites. Had we made a mistake in leaving New York? Where in Hollywood would he find concert artists to accompany?

Music—concertizing, arranging, accompanying, conducting —was all that Wolfgang knew or cared about. Untrained for anything else, he would have been incompetent at a desk job, miserable in sales, all thumbs at manual labor. Still of frail health, quick to tire, I looked out a window at the spread of Hollywood below and decided that I would try to find work.

At the Script Clerks Guild headquarters, I begged the business agent to appeal to the board of directors to qualify me for membership on the basis of my records on *Barbary Coast, The Road to Glory,* and most of *Come and Get It.* Somehow I squeezed in, a membership card was issued to me, and my name was placed at the bottom of the roster of the unemployed. Weeks passed and no call came through for me. My prospects, I now recognized, were no better than Wolfgang's. I had been away too long. I was not known in the industry. I thought of Howard Hawks, who always had a number of film projects going, but I could not force myself to call him. My voice would quaver. I would stammer. I might weep. Howard was uncomfortable with desperate people. Better not. So I marched forth each day to track down leads supplied by other script clerks and friends. When I could not get past studio guards, I telephoned people with whom I had worked in years past—secretaries, art directors, set decorators, property masters, camera operators, sound mixers—and shamelessly persuaded them to leave passes for me to enter the studio; once inside, heart beating criminally, I made my way to offices of producers and directors preparing new films. I was a script clerk, conscientious and methodical; I needed a job; would they hire me?

Wolfgang struck it lucky first. Approached by Teddy Saidenberg to join him in a duo piano act at Bill Jordan's Bar of Music, he accepted at once, overjoyed to play for audiences once more. Over a period of weeks, the two musicians wrote intricate classical arrangements of popular themes and light or semiclassical works. We borrowed ninety dollars to buy an elegant light-gray suit for Wolfgang, who had also agreed to serve as master of ceremonies. On opening night, the music rippled and soared, and the two pianists were brought back for encore after encore.

He had little hope anymore, Faulkner wrote in answer to one of my letters, of getting a writing assignment in Hollywood. Agents were unable to sell him to the studios. Lord knows, he wanted to see me again, badly; a few months of movie money would also help him out of the money troubles in which he was again mired. He, too, was distraught over the war in Europe. The German air raids on London and Coventry left him shaken.

He did not like to think of me working at all. Hollywood sound stages, he remembered all too well, were stifling hot in the summer, tomb-cold and drafty in the winter. I must not forget that I had undergone serious surgery in New York and that I had never, in the first place, been blessed with great vitality and resistance. Even when I worked for Howard

Hawks, he recalled, I had fought for health and stamina, had pushed myself to get through difficult days. Although I needed to earn money, I was not to be exploited; I was not to let them work me from dawn to midnight.

The letter ended with a reminder that he loved me deeply, that he had not forgotten anything and never would. The constraints he had placed on himself when I married fell away after New Orleans. He had need to say that he loved me. Having forfeited my right to ask silence of him, I made no protest. He had never been one for spoken sentiment out of bed, distrusting the flatness of the spoken word, resorting to French endearments when the playback of his own voice offended his ears. I knew he loved me by looks, by touch, by the poems and the letters, only seldom by what he said to me.

After a half year of unflagging effort to find a job as a script clerk, one fell, unsolicited, into my lap. It was on a poverty-row Western filmed at Vasquez Rocks. Every morning the alarm-clock bell rang shrilly at the hour of four and I would scramble an hour later down the steep hillside steps to a corner on Cahuenga to be picked up by the company bus. If I missed it, there would be a thirty-minute wait before the next car, with the assistant director and the make-up artist, came along, usually crowded with actors and last-minute props. My limbs froze on location as we waited for the sun to come up for the first shot of the day. At noon the temperature soared and I sweltered in the heat. I wore pants and boots to protect myself against rattlesnakes and poison oak as I followed the director through dense underbrush. Script clutched under my arm, I climbed great boulders. Horses reared with their stunt-men riders and sometimes the hoofs missed me by inches. It was the day before the motorized honey-wagon, as it is now called, and I remember asking the assistant director on the first day of shooting where there was a toilet.

"There are some bushes out there." He gesticulated vaguely. "You'll have to manage that way, just like the rest of us."

By the end of the week, I knew that Bill had correctly gauged the gap between my poor energies and the physical demands of the job. Lowering my aching bones onto my bed, I wished myself a woman with pile-driver shoulders, massive haunches, and Amazonian legs. Where was I going to find the strength to finish the picture? How to draw on reserves of energy that I had never possessed? Well, I would do what I had always done. I would bluff my way through, stretch my mouth in a smile when I was fighting for breath, hold myself up by some gravity of the will when my legs threatened to telescope into my feet, and nobody would be the wiser—not producer, director, or assistant director. If I wasn't one of those manipulative women born to manage a husband's career, I could still earn money to help Wolfgang get a start as a concert pianist. What I could do within my limitations, I would. It had become a commitment.

Urgency turned me like a powerful motor. So crucial to Wolfgang's future was this job of mine, wanted by no other script clerk, that my sleep was riddled by deliria in which, having overslept and missed the last connection, I was summarily fired.

"I get home from my job just as my wife gets up to go to work," Wolfgang complained. "We are like two Russian collective farm workers who warm the bed for each other."

In the Hollywood of the 1930's, miracles of discovery occurred daily. The pretty girl spotted at the prize fights was signed to an exclusive long-term contract. A men's room attendant told his idea for a movie to a producer and found himself in an office with a secretary a few days later. The hope that a powerful film executive would drop into the Bar of Music and almost immediately recognize Wolfgang's genius never deserted me.

One morning my husband awakened me from sleep. *"Tierchen,* I have a movie job."

"Wunderbar," I said happily. "Playing in an orchestra? Composing?"

"No. A casting director came in tonight."

"A casting director?"

"Let me finish. He liked my hands."

"Your hands?"

"He thinks they're the right size to double for the hands of the star in a movie about some composer."

"Oh, God, Wolfi," I cried angrily. "You said no, of course?"

"I said yes. The music on the sound track will be my music. It's more than a week's work, *Tierchen*. We need the money."

Two days after the last rustler had his comeuppance, I was called to report to Warner Brothers Studios for postproduction on a feature film. As actors crawled into fighter planes to be photographed, I kept minute records of all the interlocking pieces, matching each scene with aerial photography obtained weeks before. It was the beginning, although I didn't guess it, of what was to be a quarter of a century as a script supervisor on the vast Burbank lot. The reigning stars were Humphrey Bogart, James Cagney, Ann Sheridan, Jane Wyman, Edward G. Robinson, Ronald Reagan, Alexis Smith, Jeffrey Lynn, Wayne Morris, Errol Flynn, George Brent, John Garfield, Pat O'Brien, Bette Davis, Olivia de Havilland, Dennis Morgan, Ida Lupino, Jack Carson, Brenda Marshall, and Barbara Stanwyck; the directors, Michael Curtiz, Lloyd Bacon, John Huston, Lewis Seiler, Edmund Goulding, William K. Howard, Ray Enright, Vincent Sherman, William Keighley, William Wyler, Anatole Litvak, and Raoul Walsh; the producers, Hal B. Wallis, Henry Blanke, Mark Hellinger, who had been a columnist in New York, Jerry Wald, and Robert Buckner. Every sound stage was in use when I entered the studio gates, though within a short time, as Germany occupied country after country, production would be sharply curtailed for a brief period.

It was a Hollywood markedly different from the one I had left three years before. The European war had shocked the motion-picture industry out of its geographical isolation and its full-time preoccupation with moving enlarged images. Where before the events of the outside world had fallen upon the movie capital with all the impact of feathers shaken from a pillow, everyone was now acutely aware of the war across the Atlantic. Insecurity and raw ambition would never be entirely absent from executive corridors, but for once blatant egoism was offensive. In Europe, people huddled in air raid shelters; cities were blacked out at night; bombs were dropped. Late editions of newspapers were read as sets were lighted and cameras were reloaded. Radios blared from film editors' cubicles. Company offices were closed in country after country as Hitler's armies rolled across borders.

British actors, directors, and writers sold their Brentwood and Bel Air homes to stand with their countrymen as air raids mounted in fury. A top American star drove an ambulance behind front lines. A well-known director joined the British Navy. The question of whether to preserve our isolation or to continue to give help split the film industry. Willkie supporters and Roosevelt partisans quarreled on studio streets. It was fashionable to see *Meet the People,* a political musical revue, at the Hollywood Playhouse. Funds were collected for the Red Cross, British War Relief, Greek War Relief. The Germans were murdering millions of Russians. Out of admiration for the valiant Soviet fighters who resisted panzer divisions, Wolfgang and I joined the Russian-American Art Club. So did almost everyone else in Hollywood. One could have drinks there and be jostled by movie royalty. On the other side of the coin, there were people who considered Communism a greater threat than Fascism, and there were some obsessed by the notion that a fifth column would rise overnight.

Wolfgang and I were with John and Sally and Henriette when confirmation of the fall of Paris came over the radio; the French wine we were drinking became acrid. Shaken, Henriette left early to work on her screenplay of *The Great Profile* for John Barrymore. She was still "torching"—that was the word we used then—for Fletcher Martin. Their marriage had collapsed, leaving her dejected and purposeless.

"I can't forgive him," she told me tearfully, cataloguing

the wounds of all sizes that had been inflicted upon her, tallying the large checks she had sent to her husband in New York for his one-man show. "I can't sleep at night. My health is being undermined. I'm behind on the screenplay. I've missed one deadline after another. The studio is furious with me."

"But you can't stop talking about Fletcher."

Henriette looked at me in uncertain surprise.

"You can't," I repeated, awed by the human heart's insensitivity to reason once it has fixed itself to another being. "If he walked through that door now, you would take him back. You would be in his arms."

I owed her the truth that she was unable to discern for herself. Small payment for disabusing me years before of Southern notions of virtue that cluttered my head, it might shock her into self-discipline as a screenwriter. Years would actually pass before she would cease being obsessed by Fletcher Martin. Even on the march with other Hollywood liberals, denouncing William Dudley Pelley and Father Coughlin and McCarthyism, defending the Unfriendly Ten and the Rosenbergs, she would be thinking of him. She was one of those women of the era of whom songwriters made capital; she was "True Blue Lou" and all her Tin Pan Alley sisters of whom Fannie Brice, Libby Holman, and Edith Piaf sang; female partner in the vaudeville apache dance who crawled back to the cruel, swaggering male for another head-to-head round of dancing.

I was not of that female stripe, much admired by both men and women, though I might have come close to it if I had married William Faulkner. He was not a sadistic man, but his unwillingness to communicate, his moods, and his drinking were in themselves a kind of cruelty. I clung to Wolfgang for the adversities through which we had come, for the Joseph's portion that had been denied him, and for a love that had in it a strong admixture of the maternal. But I was not forgiving of his piques and rages or his occasional belittlements of me. I stood my ground, parried, defended myself, turned my back on him. The compromises, when they were made, were mutual and reasonably proportionate; at the halfway point, I waited for my husband to come the remaining distance.

Our marriage, I now realized, would never be on high ground. Setbacks blew and battered and whipped at it. Wolfgang's tensions were as critical as ever. What good was it, he shouted, that he had a night-club job? He wanted to be a serious musician, to concertize. He needed, for his self-esteem, to walk onstage as a soloist with a great symphony orchestra behind him. There were times, too, when studio work left me high-strung and argumentative. I had overextended myself. No woman for long, without reaching the breaking point, could be co-breadwinner, shopper, short-order cook, laundry collector, ironer, housekeeper, dog walker, bill payer, checkbook keeper—and lover. Our weekly paychecks had banished real poverty but little else. Wolfgang at the time had been accorded recognition as a major artist by Los Angeles *Times* music critic Albert Goldberg, who had heard him accompany Virovai in concert, but he was still an unknown in Hollywood. In order to come in closer contact with the inner circle of professional musicians, he began to play at Evenings on the Roof programs at the home of Peter Yates. In performance, he was as brilliant as at any time in his life. His compositions were striking in their originality and daring. When would Hollywood begin to use my husband? When would he be called upon to write original film music, to take his place alongside Korngold, Waxman, Steiner, Newman, and his good friend Ernst Toch?

Betty Walter, pregnant a second time, appealed to me to accompany her and her small son, Harry, to New York to rejoin Ed Royce. It would involve a railroad coach trip to Detroit, where we would pick up a brand-new car that Ed, habitually strapped for money, had somehow bought.

"I can't do it without you, Meta," Betty pleaded. "I'm not physically up to it. And if I become ill on the trip, who will take care of little Harry?"

The loss of a week or more of work at the studio would put

a dent in my finances. But Betty and I had grown up together; our mothers had been friends; I could not refuse her. Everything had to be done almost overnight. I wrote Bill an airmail, special delivery letter, giving him an approximate date of my arrival in New York. Could he fly up for a few days so that we could see each other? He was to write me in care of Ed Royce, so that I would have his answer at the end of the trip.

The coach ride to Detroit was grindingly long and monotonous. Harry, bewildered by sudden uprooting, ran a high fever that providentially broke when we arrived in Detroit. Betty and I took turns at the wheel of the new car through Canada, arriving without mishap at a run-down building in New York City. Ed Royce, holding his son and embracing his weeping wife, handed me a letter with an Oxford postmark; I opened it with trembling hands.

"I am too poor to afford the price of even a one-way bus ticket," Faulkner had written. "Every penny I get goes to my creditors. I will try not to think of you in New York, so much closer, for if I do I will want to get very drunk."

I found a cheap hotel room, saw Bil and Cora Baird for a few hours, and began the return trip to Los Angeles the next day.

Chloe came into season and began to whine troubledly at the screen door.

"Let's breed her," Wolfgang suggested. "Let's find her a handsome dog of a dog *mit* whom she will make beautiful puppies."

Because I knew that he loved Chloe, although he regarded her as my and Faulkner's dog, not his, I agreed. Wolfgang took her to the kennel where Bill had paid for her and, satisfied with the points of the recommended stud, left her there for the pairing. When her time came, Chloe was unable to whelp and moaned in pain for hours in the clothes closet. Wolfgang rushed her to a veterinarian, who ordered a Caesarean. Our troubles had just begun. Chloe, terrified of the three blind, crawling creatures, ignorant of what they were, fled from them. To keep the puppies alive, we fed them formula milk from dolly milk bottles that I found at the five-and-ten and kept them warm in the oven. The best of the litter was claimed by the owner of the stud; a beautiful black puppy went to Henriette, who no longer had Babka and needed something on which she could bestow her love; and the other, the runt of the litter, a lovely pale gold, became Wolfgang's pet, variously called *Der Perkchen* and *Der Geperkelte*. He loved her inordinately. I wrote Bill that our Chloe had become a dam. Would he tell Jill, if she remembered her visits to Normandie Village and our picnics, about the puppies? I would send photographs of Chloe and Perky. As for myself, I was working on the second unit of a Warner Brothers war film, *Dive Bomber,* with Errol Flynn, Fred MacMurray, Alexis Smith, and Ralph Bellamy. We were shooting aboard the aircraft carriers *Enterprise* and *Saratoga,* and in one sequence there would be a hundred or more Navy planes. Because we were on a government military installation, I had been fingerprinted along with other company members. Hollywood was making more and more war pictures, with Warner Brothers leading in number, but there was strong criticism from isolationists. It seemed to me that with Bill's knowledge of planes and his experience in World War I (I still believed that he had been shot down), Hollywood producers would be clamoring for his services as a screenwriter. I could not understand why his agents, whoever they were now, could not set a deal for him.

Bill himself offered no clue. His letters became briefer, a few lines, no more. He was still over his head in debt, sorry to say. That and the war in Europe made him fumble in his writing. Here it was 1941 and his books still weren't paying him enough to live on. Did I ever run into Howard Hawks? He thought of me at all times. I was his love. I wasn't to forget it.

It was Henriette who found the key for me. "Bill hurt himself in Hollywood the last time," she told me. "Badly."

"How?" All at once I knew the answer but I wanted to be wrong—dead wrong.

"After they dried him out at the hospital, he went back to

the studio. But I guess he was too shaken by your marriage to be any good as a screenwriter. He didn't give a good goddamn. When he wasn't drunk, he was surly and rude. He didn't show up for work and barely finished anything. And you know what happens to drunk writers and actors?"

"The blackball?"

"Right. The old Louis B. Mayer, Adolph Zukor, Darryl F. Zanuck blackball."

"They won't have Bill then."

"Not if the ball's bounced." Henriette shook her head in exasperation. "They all secretly hate one another, but every studio cooperates on the blackball. It's like the smell of blood in the jungle. Word gets passed down the line. Don't hire Joe Blow. Don't give Suzie Glutz the time of day. He's a drunk. She's a screw-up and temperamental to boot. They froze out Luise Rainer that way. You've no idea how many others."

"Poor Bill, he doesn't know."

"Then don't tell him, Meta."

All went well for me on *Dive Bomber* until top brass arrived at the U.S. Naval Base in San Diego. Production was suspended for part of the afternoon because of an air show arranged for visitors. All movie cameras were to be inactivated. Nobody on the base, military personnel, civilians, or visitors, would be allowed to photograph the planes. As the giant bombers roared overhead, I stepped out of the car in which the studio cameras were loaded and watched the air exercises. In the bleachers erected for the show, wives of officers craned their necks to follow flight patterns. Completely forgetting the ban, I put my personal camera to my eye, tracking the planes through the finder just to see if I could keep them in the frame. The air spectacle was impressive. I moved out of the blinding sunlight into the camera car to watch the rest of the show.

Three minutes later, no more, a jeep filled with grim-faced Navy officers crossed the field. I was asked to step out of the camera car. What was my name? What was I doing on the base? I was to get into the jeep, please, but first I was to hand over the camera strapped around my neck.

"Where are you taking me?" I asked, aware now that crew members were not playing a joke on me.

"Back to the hotel, ma'am," a senior officer in his dress whites answered curtly.

"But I'm working on *Dive Bomber*."

No response. Eyes fixed straight ahead.

"What did I do?"

"You broke regulations."

"Regulations?"

"You photographed Navy planes."

My protests, my claims that there was nothing on the film but photographs I had taken of crew members around the hotel swimming pool, fell on stone ears. Panic struck me. I could see headlines: "HOLLYWOOD SCRIPT GIRL ARRESTED AS SPY." My parents in Arizona would go into shock. Faulkner would pick up the Memphis *Commercial Appeal* and read the bold print with sorrowing eyes. Would I face a firing squad at dawn tomorrow?

Warner Brothers dispatched one of its unit production managers from Burbank, a fatherly, imperturbable type, hardened to crisis, to assure me that yes, my employers were behind me, and no, I would not be pink-slipped. The second-unit company would get along without me until the Navy was satisfied that I had not photographed planes.

"Why is it taking so long?" I complained.

"Your camera was disassembled and sent to Navy Intelligence in Washington."

On the third day, I was escorted from the hotel room, where I had been served all my meals, to a hearing on the base. Officers of stern mien regarded me dully as a lieutenant commander began his questioning, with a yeoman recording the proceedings in shorthand. Once the interrogating officer established that my husband was German-born and that I had been in Frankfurt and Berlin in 1937, the examination took on a new ferocity.

Don't let them rattle you, I told myself, as I calmly answered questions calculated to trip me. Boneheads, to think that Wolfi and I are involved with Nazi Germany. My husband is a German Jew, I wanted to shout at them; he has lost everything because of Hitler—relatives, a career, his legacy. Across the room, the studio production manager nodded encouragement.

It was not until my camera and the photographs developed in Washington, D.C., were introduced as exhibits, and a new line of interrogation began, that my composure deserted me. A surreal scenario was being acted and only I among the players did not know my lines and business.

"You did say, didn't you, that you photographed planes on shots number ten and eleven?"

I glared at the officer who had asked it of me as he held a film strip to the light. "No, I didn't say anything of the kind."

Another officer: "Now on shot number seven where you photographed a single plane—"

"I didn't photograph any planes at all," I remonstrated.

They wouldn't give up. With the chief officer leading, there was another half-hour of inquiry in which accusatory questions continued to be asked.

"Mrs. Rebner," an officer comparing film and prints wanted to know at one point, "do you recall what type of plane you photographed on the fourteenth frame?"

"Stop it, stop it!" I screamed, conscious of the disapproval on my studio adviser's face. "You have it all in front of you. There's not one shot of a Navy plane or any other kind of plane on that film and you know it."

A few minutes later, after a whispered conference among the officers, the hearing was ended. The U.S. Navy was sorry to have caused me inconvenience, but in these dangerous times any infraction of rules had to be investigated. It was the hope of all present that I would understand this. A jeep would take me back to the movie company. I swept the inquiry room with a look of contained outrage and left. My fellow crew members were shocked at what had happened, but Wolfgang laughingly dubbed me "Meta Hari."

Second-unit work completed on *Dive Bomber,* I was assigned to training films being made for the armed forces. The Warners were genuinely patriotic; their rah-rah, flag-saluting brand of Americanism spread through the studio; we authorized more payroll deductions for defense bonds, defense stamps, and for all or most of the relief funds for our allies. We gave blood and felt ennobled for a few hours.

I was doing well and would do even better. We moved to a small, pleasant apartment on Alta Vista in Hollywood. Although I did not think of myself as a careerist, others did. Hometown-girl-makes-good articles appeared about me in the Memphis papers. Secretaries I had known years before were impressed that I was now a full-time script clerk. When I visited the Studio Club, I had celebrity status. In Oxford, William Faulkner was being made aware more reassuringly each day of his spreading fame. His pockets were lined with nothing more than lint, but his desk was piled high with requests for interviews, portrait sittings, and autographs. His photograph appeared on a national magazine cover. Only Wolfgang was at a virtual standstill, moving, when he did, at a snail's pace. He had knocked on the right doors, followed the stratagems advised by musician friends, humbled himself before men whose knowledge of music was negligible. The promises crumbled to grit in his hands.

Self-pity began to sap his energy. Wild anger—"They don't want composers. They want hacks. Entertainers. Copyists."—blurred his purpose.

If I suggested that he conform until he had three or four film scores to his credit, he glared at me incredulously.

"I'm not a backslapper or a backside-kisser. I refuse to do anything second rate or derivative."

"Then show them what you can do."

"How can I when they don't want to deal with me? They know that in many respects I'm as good as, BETTER than, the composers they use over and over again. It makes them uncomfortable."

Wolfgang was unable to pull out of a sea of despair. Now there was not only maddening frustration but the knowledge that time was rushing by. He had passed his thirtieth birthday. Four years in America and he was still nowhere. The late hours at the Bar of Music cut into daily practice time at the piano. Another irritant was added; the suspicion of foreigners had become morbid at the movie studios, particularly in the valley area close to North American and Lockheed: Universal, Warner Brothers, Republic, and the Columbia Ranch. Anyone with the faintest of Teutonic intonations might be a saboteur. Over and over, Wolfgang was asked whether he was a citizen. He had not been in the United States for the prescribed time. The explanation drew stares of mistrust. As in New York, there were tirades. Doors were slammed. Plates danced as he pounded the table. Dinners were uneaten. The dogs crept under the bed and trembled there.

"Why am I the unlucky one?" Wolfgang shouted. "Ludwig and Edgar knew when to leave Germany. They got out in time—with their share of the inheritance. They're well-to-do today. But what do I have to show for what was to have been my share of the estate? This immigration has spoiled my chances."

Bitterness and self-castigation drove the love from him. I could have borne the rest of it, but not the absence of love, flowing as a steady current from my husband to me. He looked at me blankly when I said that I no longer felt loved by him. He had to think about his life, his career, where they were going. Of course he loved me. But he didn't, not then.

Our marriage was coming apart again, as if it had been pasted together with flour and water. I was a Southern woman. I needed to be cherished, treasured, truly loved. I could do without emotional reciprocity, since I had learned by now that it was seldom equal. What I no longer received from my husband, I found in Faulkner's letters, all tenderness and affection. Suddenly I needed to see Bill again, to feel the warmth of his skin under his shirt, to meet the heated gaze of the great brown eyes, to hear the voice that could be haunting only to another Southerner. When I reconciled with Wolfgang, I forced New Orleans from my memory, but now I let myself think of my night with Bill in the French Quarter. I wanted him again as a lover. I imagined it was he when Wolfgang reached for me at night. There was an in-burst of terrible guilt that racked me for weeks.

One evening at dinner, Chloe and Perky sitting in their own chairs at the table like well-behaved children, manners impeccable except for excessive chop-licking, I told Wolfgang that I was going to divorce him. Nothing would persuade me to change my mind. We would divide our worldly goods, such as they were, under California law. I would not ask for alimony. I wanted nothing from him at all.

Wolfgang left the apartment the next day for a small back-yard guesthouse on McCadden Street. He returned on Sunday for Perky, his clothes, books and music. We both wiped tears away. We would try to be friends. I filed for a dissolution of our marriage in the Los Angeles courts.

Bill made no comment beyond expressing the hope that I would not let myself be lonely. He was going through a bad time, but it would let up. The draft was taking Oxford boys left and right. There were young faces missing on the court-house square.

Work pressures kept me from despondency. In the fall, I was assigned to my first Warner Brothers feature picture, *The Maltese Falcon,* directed by John Huston, and starring Humphrey Bogart and Mary Astor. In the co-star cast were Peter Lorre, Sydney Greenstreet, Gladys George, Barton MacLane, Lee Patrick, Ward Bond, Jerome Cowan, and Elisha Cook, Jr. The screenplay, credited to Huston (there was an inner-studio-hallways rumor that Dashiell Hammett had actually written the third film version of his book), was lean and brooding. I liked Humphrey Bogart, who had not yet come into legend. Mary Astor, with a hard-edged beauty and an aura of worldliness after the headline stories, was the darling of the crew, an "all-right lady," as they termed her. Peter Lorre was enchanted to find that I had a smattering of German at my command and spoke to me frequently in that

language on the set. The grave and hulking Sydney Greenstreet, a stage actor who had been with the Lunts, projected
unalloyed villainy; offstage, he was mild-mannered and fas-
tidious.

There was a curious foreknowledge among company members and executives that *The Maltese Falcon* would be a
highly successful film, and I felt a part of a going project.

If John Huston was worried at all about a script clerk with
whom he had never worked and whose last first-unit feature
picture credit was in 1937, he gave no sign of any great concern. By the end of the first week, in any case, I had demonstrated that I was a professional in every sense and that he
could rely fully on me. There was about me then, and even
today, though to a lesser degree, a kind of prim, wide-eyed
lady-librarian quality that made certain men want to shock
me. John Huston was one of them. In tandem with Bogart,
he conspired to unhinge me with jests and deceptions. When
I went for the bait, as I did most of the time, he roared with
laughter, Bogart joining in. I was not to meet another director who delighted to see the color rush to my face until I
worked with Mike Nichols. Huston found out that our mutual friend Katherine Strueby (whom we all called Katie)
addressed me as Sandy, the nickname by which I was known
in Memphis as a teen-ager. From that time on, through the
years, I was always Sandy to him.

On *The Maltese Falcon*, Huston introduced a number of
technical innovations, notably an incredible camera set-up.
We rehearsed two days for the twenty-two uninterrupted
moves that Huston and cinematographer Arthur Edeson de-
vised. The camera followed Greenstreet and Bogart from one
room into another, then down a long hallway, and finally
into a living room; there the camera moved up and down in
what is referred to as a boom-up and boom-down shot, then
panned from left to right and back to Bogart's drunken face;
the next pan shot was to Greenstreet's massive stomach from
Bogart's point of view; Greenstreet slowly rose from his chair
and moved to the fireplace to stand facing Bogart as our cam-

era followed him. The choreography of it was exacting and exciting. One miss and we had to begin all over again. But there was the understanding that we were attempting something purely cinematic, never tried before, and everyone—stars, camera operators, and cablemen—worked industriously to bring it off. The rehearsal period stretched over two days. A hushed silence fell over the company as Huston called for a take. After a nerve-racking seven minutes or so, in which actors and camera crew were incredibly coordinated, Huston shouted "Cut" and "PRINT IT!" A shout went up and crew members heartily applauded Bogart, Greenstreet, and Edeson and his camera specialists. Only one close-up was made to cut in to the "one-take" scene: Bogart's face showing greater inebriation as he watched the Fat Man's stomach. The camera had already captured Greenstreet's massive paunch, revolving, pulsating, going in and out of focus during the long master scene.

For the first time, with John Huston, I found myself thoroughly fascinated by the processes of moviemaking. In the final days of filming, Faulkner wrote that something was under way that might bring him back to Hollywood. I was not to count on it (I did, however) , but it appeared that the long drought was over. A movie deal would put some order back into a life made ragged by debt. More important, it would enable us to be together once more.

"Bill has some kind of offer," I told Henriette gleefully. "He didn't say what studio, but something is in the works."

She pressed my hand. "Honey, I'm glad. You're alone too much. You work too hard. You need Bill."

"It seems he hasn't been blackballed."

"He's lucky."

"You still don't think he'll get his deal?"

"Meta, I just don't know. The blackball doesn't *always* hold. A studio can have a special need for a particular actor or writer who's on the list."

"Then please pull for Bill now!"

Henriette nodded vigorously. "I'll pull for myself at the

same time, baby. I've been so damned disorganized. They're on my neck at Fox. I tried to put some kind of order into my writing, but I can't seem to turn out enough work."

Nothing to go on as yet, Bill wrote a few weeks later, but he was hopeful. The letters during this period of high expectancy were unabashedly erotic, the outpourings of a man too long denied carnal love. Bowen, asserting himself, was uncontrollable. At night, Bill found it difficult to sleep; Bowen was trying to take him over completely, and since Bowen couldn't write, though he did what he was designed to do competently enough, that would be unfortunate. "I weigh 129 pounds and I want to put it all on you," he said in one note, "and as much in you as I can can can can must must will will shall."

John Huston went out of his way to commend me as a script clerk on the completion of *The Maltese Falcon*. Directors began to ask for me. A picture would "wrap" on Friday and on Saturday I would be given the screenplay of a new film beginning the following Monday.

"I tell myself that you'll be here any day," I wrote Faulkner. "I've become a workhorse. I need you to rub the harness sores away. When do you think it will be? Let it be soon, please."

The shortest letter I had ever received from him informed me the following month that nothing had come of the Hollywood deal. Nobody seemed to want him—at any price. He was deeply ashamed of the poverty that kept him from me.

Henriette had not been misinformed. There was a blackball going against Faulkner in Hollywood and he must have known it all along. We were right back where we had been in the 1930's. Bill was trapped in Oxford. Without a definite movie assignment that would yield him money immediately, he did not dare come to Hollywood. I resented the slippage into the same pattern of hopes raised, hopes dashed, but there was nothing I could do to change it. The space between Hollywood and Oxford became a terrible black void when I thought of it during the working day or at night when, yearning for Bill, feeling sensual stresses I had not experienced for years, I closed my eyes to invite sleep; ships fell into inky depths of a swirling abyss, sailors drowned by the thousands.

A prize assignment came to me not long after *The Maltese Falcon*. Russia's amazing resistance to Hitler's armies still commanded the admiration of most open-minded Americans. Out of a spirit of patriotism, the Warner men signed the Ballet Russe de Monte Carlo to dance two of its programs, *Capriccio Espagnole,* music by Rimsky-Korsakov, and *Gaîté Parisienne,* set to Offenbach's music, before the cameras. Jean Negulesco, not then a major film director, worked with the great Leonide Massine in transposing both ballets to the screen. A Rumanian-born charmer with a rolling accent, he left the choreography to Massine but called the turns on filming the ballet. He was the ideal director for the project; in addition to his credits on a few feature films and innumerable shorts, he was an imaginative painter and a patron of the arts. His sense of cinematic movement and his stunning visual innovations kept the project from being a mere photographed ballet. Massine was exuberant. It was the beginning of collaboration between the dance and films, he told me; ballet would be available through the motion-picture medium to people who could not otherwise see great dance.

For days the stars and supporting dancers rehearsed on a Spanish marketplace set for *Capriccio Espagnole*. Their excitement at being in front of a camera never lessened and there were times when they were too thunderstruck to hit their marks on the sound-stage floor. Negulesco shot the full ballet, then photographed it schematically, movement by movement, using close and medium shots, with the camera looking down at the dancers, swooping into their midst, rising up from the floor. *Gaîté Parisienne,* the more elaborate of the two filmed ballets, was rechoreographed for the camera by Massine and shot on many sets.

All the great ballet stars of the ensemble whom I had seen with Wolfgang in New York danced in the featurettes:

the great Tamara Toumanova starred with Massine in *Capriccio Espagnole* and Milada Mladova danced the Glove Seller in *Gaîté Parisienne,* with Alexandra Danilova, George Zorich, Frederic Franklin, Igor Youskevitch, André Eglevsky, and, of course, the magnificent Leonide Massine himself.

Almost childlike in their naïveté, the members of the corps de ballet created a problem when filming began by mixing freely in the large dressing rooms assigned to them, the young men helping the young women zip up or unzip, the young women unblinking in the presence of young men applying codpieces. The near-nudity and the absence of self-consciousness shocked studio bluenoses. An edict was issued: No more mingling of the sexes in dressing rooms. For a few days, the Russians grudgingly followed the rules, but long before production had ended they were again all tumbled together like puppies.

Even the great stars, Leonide Massine and Tamara Toumanova, were visibly pleased when the likes of Ann Sheridan, Bette Davis, George Brent, Barbara Stanwyck, Errol Flynn, Olivia de Havilland, Ida Lupino, Ronald Reagan, and James Cagney left their sets to observe the dancers in action. Lesser lights were frustrated by guards stationed at heavy soundstage doors with the legend "Closed Set." Refused entry by a guard who had never heard of him, Monty Woolley, recreating his Broadway role in the film version of *The Man Who Came to Dinner,* flourished a call sheet in his face.

"See where it says composer?" he said icily. "Well, that's who I am—Jacques Offenbach, the composer."

He was admitted with a "Sorry, Mr. Offenbach, but I didn't recognize you."

One day Charlie Chaplin arrived and was almost crushed by the adoring ballet dancers. (He was to make headlines the next year by demanding a second front to relieve the gallant Russians.) It was a full hour before filming could resume.

I'm sure every picture on the lot is behind schedule [I wrote Faulkner]. Big stars stand on the sidelines watching the Russians.

The rank-and-file dancers don't understand how much it costs to film. The assistant director misses them. Massine spreads his hands in bewilderment. Nobody knows where to find the vanished ones. Eventually they are located on other sets watching the very stars who watched them a few hours before.

Toward the end of production, the dancers gave a party at the rented Hollywood house of George Zorich and Alexandra Danilova into which many of them had moved in order to save money. Four or five dancers shared one room. Others slept on pallets in the hallways. They were being paid no more for the films than they received for their stage performances. One by one, the dancers tiptoed to my chair and whispered that I was invited to their party. I was to tell no one else for only I, of the staff and crew, was being asked. It remains the most flattering and privileged invitation I ever received. The party was in progress when I arrived, dancers off their points scurrying about the small house, hastening into the kitchen and out again with paper plates mountained with spaghetti. I was welcomed with screams and embraces and kisses and was borne into the living room, where the company members—with spouses I had not met before—were seated on the floor. Everywhere around me Russian was being spoken, often to me, who nodded as if I understood. Shortly before midnight, with everything in a vodka haze, people singing, others whirling in Russian folk dances, Charlie Chaplin arrived. He was led to a chair and given the homage reserved by the Russians for honored artists of their country. Dancers sat at his feet and sprawled out on the floor as, lights dimmed, Chaplin talked of his travels in Europe, of people in high places whom he had met, of the films he had made. He also told stories, acting out the characters and delighting his audience. All of them had seen his most recent picture, *The Great Dictator,* some of them many times, and all but the youngest remembered some of his earlier films. To the members of the Ballet Russe de Monte Carlo, Chaplin was not only a comedy genius but an accomplished dancer.

They mimicked him delicately devouring a boiled boot in *The Gold Rush,* imitated him as the victim of a feeding machine in *Modern Times,* took turns, men and women, twisting across the floor with an imaginary walking stick and a finger held under the nose as The Tramp. Chaplin threw back his head and laughed until his eyes brimmed with tears. It was four in the morning when he had told his last anecdote and answered the last question put to him. Nothing that came after that in Hollywood—production wrap parties, Academy Awards, charity galas, premieres, sit-down dinners at the homes of movie greats—ever matched that evening in bonhomie and human warmth.

The dancers of the Ballet Russe de Monte Carlo impressed me as the most unaffected of any performers with whom I had worked.

"When you rehearse until your feet blister and bleed," Massine explained to me, "it keeps you from being pompous and pretentious. That's all very well for actors, but not for dancers."

Two days after the Russians resumed their California tour, I was on another film.

It was work as usual at Warner Brothers Studios the day after the surprise Sunday attack on Pearl Harbor by the Japanese. Actors spoke their lines and crew members moved cameras and walls, but everyone's thoughts and hearts were elsewhere.

An assistant director announced that shooting would suspend long enough to allow us to hear President Roosevelt's address to Congress. Arc lights were turned off. Electricians came down from the catwalks. The company formed a circle to listen tensely as FDR asked Congress to declare a state of war between the United States and the Japanese Empire.

Nobody wanted to go to the commissary for lunch. We drank black coffee and conjectured on what war would do to the country. At two-thirty in the afternoon, the call came for quiet on the set and the principal actors took the places of their stand-ins under hot lights to complete a master shot. We had a fixed number of screenplay pages to finish that day and we would be working later than usual to make up for the interruption.

A Christmas card came from Bill—a drawing of Jill and himself.

"Oh, Faulkner," I said yearningly to his photograph on my bedroom dresser, "we've never had a Christmas together."

The war brought a new energy to Hollywood. The boulevard was thronged with enlisted men and officers from Vine to La Brea. "You would not know it," I wrote Faulkner. "It's no longer the street where we walked hand in hand. Everywhere there are uniformed men and young girls, some of them looking so young that I suspect they're from Hollywood High." At the studio, men with critical skills moved into defense work; a backlot shortage developed as male employees, some of them over the age of forty, checked off the lot to report to induction centers; young men on labor gangs whom nobody had noticed before were honored by studio billboards on which their names appeared as heroes serving their country.

Guild officers exhorted us to buy more defense bonds, give more blood, donate to the USO. Hats were passed in theaters for this relief and that. Actors on films to which I was assigned were given time off to entertain aircraft plant workers during the lunch hour.

Nothing was the same as before except the hustle that had started way back when the first crank camera was set up in bright, unquenchable Hollywood sunlight and the deal makers moved in.

Security measures were tightened at studios and memoranda advised employees not to invite outsiders to sets or to the commissary. Everybody had to apply for security cards; overnight the industry was scandalized by the number of noncitizens on studio payrolls. Because powerful lights might guide Japanese bombers, all outdoor shooting was halted for the duration of the war; be they Westerns or jungle epics, all films had to be filmed within blacked-out sound stages.

Boys who had delivered studio mail or worked in film shipping died in foxholes on Bataan and Corregidor. Top male stars were given farewell luncheons as they answered the call to arms, but the talk around the lot was about one of the more dashing movie kings who had received a 4-F classification when it was discovered by his draft board that he was syphilitic. Caught up in war fervor, I allocated a good part of my weekly check to whatever I was asked to support or buy. I also became an air raid warden in my neighborhood and scanned the skies for enemy planes.

A disturbing letter from Bill: He could not sit idly by or even continue writing while other Americans fought to preserve our way of life. He was applying to Washington, D.C., for a commission in the Air Force. It might be that he would even go up to Washington, hat in hand, to speed things up, cut through red tape. I would understand, he knew, why he needed to get into uniform again. He hoped I would not be worried.

Something that would not be drawn up from the well of memory prodded at me for days. My fears for Bill were real enough, but that was another matter. What was it that would not miter together? One day, seeing Howard Hawks stride past without looking my way—he was preparing *Air Force* for Warner Brothers—I remembered: Bill had a silver plate in his head. He had told me so and I believed him. Wouldn't that with his age and his back trouble preclude any serious consideration of him as an officer? Intuition told me that Faulkner was in for another jarring disappointment.

No passably attractive woman attached to a movie company on a distant location need ever lack for dinner invitations from men or for male bed partners. There was always the actor with flawless profile and teeth capped by an expensive Beverly Hills dentist, who would suggest that it would be helpful were I to come up to his hotel suite when the nightly production meeting was over to help him run the next day's lines. More often, it was the quiet member of the technical crew—one knew instantly that he was the father of school-age children—with offers to drive me to the next town where there was, he had heard, an outstanding restaurant or a great roadhouse or a night ball game; as the weeks went by, his desperation to make conquests, at least one in the time left away from his wife, showed in his face like a birthmark. I had no interest in assistant directors, production managers, cinematographers, camera operators, and sound mixers who slipped off their wedding rings on charter planes after takeoff. Bill Faulkner was the only man I wanted as a lover, and if it was not to be, then I would do without love. The want of it would not kill me—not for a while.

"Metachen"—it was Wolfgang on the sound-stage telephone—"I'm sick. I've never been so sick in my life."

"Have you seen a doctor?"

"No."

"Are you at your place?"

"In bed. Chills and fever. Can't you hear my teeth going like Spanish castanets? *Ach, Gott in Himmel.*"

"Stay there. I'll find a doctor for you."

He had pneumonia and needed someone with him around the clock. There was no money that either of us could spare for a registered nurse, so I called Auntie in Phoenix. Wolfgang was seriously ill. Would she, as a great favor to me, come to Hollywood once more and take care of him?

Her answer was unequivocal. If Wolfgang really needed her and it meant that much to me, she would, of course, drop everything and come.

"Besides," she said, "I want to see you."

"I can't ask Mother."

"Dear me, no. It mustn't cross your mind."

"She never approved of Wolfgang."

"I'll wire you my arrival time."

For weeks, Auntie watched over the man whom I was divorcing, washing him, giving him his medicine, cooking for him, scrubbing the walls and floors of the ramshackle guesthouse, and walking Perky.

When Wolfgang was past all danger and regaining his

strength, she moved in with me. Suddenly there were hot dinners at night, vases filled with fresh flowers, everything clean and fragrant, and Chloe brushed until her coat was shining copper. Everyone called her Auntie—it suited her— and all my friends confided in her; her murmurs of "Oh, my" and "Goodness, gracious" and "I declare," along with the tsk-tsk of her tongue, were somehow a powerful antidote against despondency.

"I fixed some lamb stew and took it over to Wolfgang," Auntie informed me one night. "We walked around the block today. Isn't that wonderful?"

"I'll try to see him for a few minutes on Sunday."

"Meta"—she twisted her wedding ring on a long, bony fin-ger—"he wants you to come back to him."

"I know."

"You've thought about it, then?"

"It wouldn't last. He wouldn't let it. I wouldn't let it."

She closed her lips tightly on something that she wanted to say, then found herself unable to hold it back. "I think one reason is that you have never quite put Mr. Faulkner out of your heart."

"I never meant to," I said flatly. "I just thought I could go on to another life without closing him out. It seemed to me altogether possible that one part of me could go on loving him and that with the other part, the everyday me, I could love Wolfi as a wife loves her husband."

"When I was a girl, we called that a divided heart. If I remember, we were warned against it."

"It could have worked," I said, defending myself. "In Ger-many it did work. I'd sit in the sun and try to read Faulkner in German and I'd think about him."

"Really, Meta?"

"Yes. But I still adored Wolfi. It took nothing away from the way I felt about him. Then in New York, after the first year or so, it went wrong. Out here, too. Wolfi was to have been my counterbalance. But the love I needed wasn't there anymore."

"Are you in touch with Mr. Faulkner?"

"We write." Surmise swept over my mind. "Auntie, do Mother and Father know about Bill and me?"

"I can't say for sure where Beulah is concerned. My sister always shuts her eyes to what she doesn't want to see or to any situation she considers improper. But I think your father knows; I think Clark has known almost from the first."

Auntie never mentioned Bill again except as a writer and a Mississippian. But her anxious looks when I read his letters betokened a deep concern for me should I resume the relationship with Faulkner. I had no answer for her and none for myself either. It had not occurred to me that I might not see William Faulkner again. There was Hollywood's punitive response to his excessive drinking and go-to-hell arrogance— bounce, bounce, little blackball. No further succor of Faulkner could be expected from the movie industry. There was also Bill's disinclination, perhaps his inability, to write books that would shower extravagant royalties down upon Rowan Oak. Our geographical distance—the great enemy—tossed in my mind like a special-effects sea in a sound-stage pool. We might never meet again. I had to face that dread likelihood. Would there be only letters from now on? Would they slow as the years went by to a postcard every now and then, a birthday greeting every November? No! I wouldn't let it happen. If Bill couldn't come to me, I'd go to him. Somehow I would get to Oxford. I would present myself to Phil Stone and demand that, willing or unwilling, he act as my confederate. Even as I saw myself registering under an assumed name at the Oxford Hotel—was there an Oxford Hotel?—and waiting in a room overlooking the courthouse square for Bill to arrive, I knew that I could never bring myself to go there. Dear God, I didn't have the money or the hubris for it.

In April I went to work on what was the first of a number of Bette Davis starring vehicles to which I would be assigned —*Now, Voyager*. Irving Rapper, with whom I was also to be associated many times, was the director, and Paul Henreid and Claude Rains were Bette's leading men. In the cast, too, were Ilka Chase, John Loder, and Bonita Granville.

Bette Davis was the first sovereign female movie star with

whom I worked. Mannered, all quick movements, caught up in an emotional torsion that threatened at any moment to spin her wildly around to the starting point like a top, she was cordial in the beginning but hardly friendly. One morning the reserve was gone. She called me Meta and said that I was to please address her not as Miss Davis but as Bette; she was uncomfortable with star deference except when she demanded it—and got it—from cold-blooded studio executives. By questions asked of me, I understood someone had told her that I was married to a concert pianist and that I was something of a musician myself. There was even a strong likelihood that she had also been apprised of my emotional involvement with William Faulkner. On location for *Now, Voyager* at Lake Arrowhead, taking long walks together through the woods and exchanging confidences, we came as close to friendship as the Hollywood caste system would allow. I was a romantic figure to her—I, who was awed by her stature as a great emotional actress, her outspokenness, her royal anger when crossed. It made no difference when I protested that I was not any of the things she saw in me; she would not be dissuaded from her belief that the script clerk on the picture was most extraordinary, as script clerks go. One day I invited her to meet Auntie, who adored her on the screen. Nowhere in the cramped apartment, with its ordinary furniture and working-woman décor, could Bette find mystery or glamour. We remained friendly, but she ceased from that day to mythicize me. Many years later, we came face to face in a production office at another studio and she was stiff in her greeting to me; it was almost as if we had never met.

The Crowns gave a Sunday-afternoon musicale at which John announced that he was joining the University of Southern California as a professor of music. Wolfgang and I arrived separately, but I sat next to him—out of habit and the damnable need of a woman, imposed upon her by society, to be in the company of a male or risk being thought undesirable. Musicians drafted into the armed forces dropped by and mingled in their khakis and blues with other musicians in safe mufti.

Wolfgang, as usual, was penitent. Enough time had passed. I was the best thing that had ever happened to him, best of them all in the universe, and he wanted me back. His life was bleak and meaningless without me. Could we not try once more now that Auntie had returned to Phoenix? We would be four happy creatures—the Wolfichen, the *Tierchen, der* Chloe and *der* Perk. It was his impatience, his selfishness, his tendency to take for granted those who were vital to his happiness that had created the breach in our marriage. Lately he had talked to Ernst Toch, who had made it clear to him that only after the war was over and concert halls of Europe again resounded with great music would those artists now fettered by world events move into their own.

If I would come back to him, warm his icy bed, save him from restaurant heartburn, he would no longer let himself be obsessed with what he had been led to believe was his destiny. He would be satisfied to earn a living in the studio orchestras. Perhaps he would find the recognition and acclaim for which he yearned as a composer. I was to give serious thought to all of this, please.

John's and Sally's happiness over his USC affiliation was not shared by a number of the musicians present that afternoon. John was settling for security, they charged, giving up. They were wrong. John Crown performed brilliantly as a musician for the rest of his life. But he also, as a USC administrator, unofficial dean of the School of Music, and chairman of the piano department, became a major cultural leader and shaper of artistic taste in Los Angeles. He infused new vitality into the School of Music and gave many American composers their first hearing. In the final year of his life, USC bestowed upon him an honorary degree of Doctor of Law. His humanity was a glowing coal that only death could extinguish.

When Faulkner wrote that once again there were negotiations that might bring him to Hollywood, I put the letter away with a sigh of pity for him. My famous, universally lauded Bill, acknowledged as America's greatest novelist, looked only to an uncaring Hollywood to provide him with the money to pay off his debts and to continue his support of those dependent upon him.

On the lot today, someone pointed out Erskine Caldwell [I wrote]. You were never very sure about him as a writer, I remember, never certain that he would hold his place in American literature. He is at the studio to work on the screenplay of *Mission to Moscow*. That's a good sign, isn't it? They're reaching out for novelists again, by-passing the Hollywood hacks (even if they do know form) to get quality screenplays. Oh, Bill, I close my eyes at night and say, to any powers, even dark ones that may be listening, Give Bill his deal so that he can return to Hollywood. This time let it happen.

I did not believe that Bill could overcome the damage he had done to himself. In casting conferences, I had overheard studio executives mutter "Never!" at the suggestion that an actor long idle might be right for a part. Victor Kilian, to whom I listened patiently while he wept in his bourbon over Betty Walter, gave me the names of a score of actors who were unemployable by reason of walking out on films during shooting, quarreling with directors, attempting to change scenes and dialogue, or allowing alcoholism to interfere with their performances; anything that added to production costs was cause for exclusion.

Now Faulkner's letters crackled with an excitement that he rarely permitted himself. With the expectation of Hollywood employment, his declarations of love and passion resumed. There were complications with which he would not bore me. Unnecessary delays. These would be overcome. He had put everything in order and would be able to leave Oxford on a day's notice.

I read the quick pen strokes and closed my eyes wearily. It couldn't happen.

But one Saturday at dusk, I pulled my car up in front of my apartment and there was Bill sitting cross-legged in front of my door, his luggage stacked neatly on the steps.

Chapter 15

Five years had passed since we last walked along Hollywood Boulevard to Musso's. I looked sidelong at Faulkner as he described the lengthy negotiations between his agent and Warner Brothers, not really hearing, letting him move me against the tide of servicemen and young girls. In New Orleans I had been too ill to see it, but he had aged perceptibly, his hair now almost completely gray, his moustache bristly and full, his eyes pouched. The last traces of the young man that I had seen in his face when I first looked at him long and searchingly had vanished; I could see lineaments now of middle age; that old guarded eagle look that would become far more pronounced was already visible in the sharpness of his nose and the furrowing brows.

The major-domo ushered us to our favorite booth against the wall. Bill leaned back and rolled his head against the leather upholstery.

"I thought," he said, "that I'd never make it back here with you to this good ol' place."

We drank to lines that converge because they must and to all that Hollywood money.

"It's not that much, honey love. Not this time."

"Less than your established salary?"

"A heap less."

"You were making about twelve hundred and fifty a week, weren't you?"

Bill nodded glumly. "They're paying me three hundred dollars now."

"That's awful."

"It's all they'd go for. But after so many months, I get raises. Increments of fifty dollars, I think it is."

"I just can't believe any studio would do that to you."

"I took it. I had to."

"Oh, Bill."

"And glad to get it."

"You signed the contract?"

"In Oxford."

"Maybe you can get out of it."

"I won't try, honey, because I've been told that if I behave myself, stay sober, turn out the work, cause 'em not one scintilla of trouble, they'll tear up the contract and give me a new one."

"They didn't put it in writing?"

"No'm. But I expect they're honest people."

The meager weekly check that he would be getting infuriated me. Beginning screenwriters received much more. This was William Faulkner, America's greatest novelist, not a cinema student just out of UCLA or USC. The contract was demeaning and the studio knew it.

"We could live together," I mused, after we had returned to my apartment, testing out the hold of convention upon the woman I had become, wondering if I would ever dare, shutting out from my mind what my neighbors would think, what they were thinking at this moment if they had watched my door and had not seen Faulkner leave.

"I don't think you really want that," Bill said slowly.

I breathed in the clean smell of his bathed body. "Do you?"

"I would like," he said, "to live in an old house with you and hear you moving about as I work. I would like to write my last words for the day and move out of my solitude to you—beautiful and quiet and untroubled."

"What kind of house?"

"One that is ante-bellum and stately. With a good, sound roof on it and white columns, perhaps a Georgian-style porch, and a smokehouse in back."

Was he thinking of Rowan Oak or of an old sagging mansion that he had passed one day on his travels through Mississippi, tarrying for a moment to frame me in the doorway and to put himself inside the musty darkness of it?

"It would be a grievous error," Faulkner said, "for us to live in Hollywood together, dear love."

"Estelle?"

"She couldn't say a word this time."

"Then what, Bill?"

He pondered it for a moment. "My Southern rectitude."

"The author of *Sanctuary?*" I mimicked his chuckle.

"And your Memphis maidenliness."

"What's left of it, suh."

"The mystery of each other, mainly mine for you, if I have any."

"You are not easy to know, Bill Faulkner."

"You'd rail at me. 'Bill, don't put your pipe on the table. Hang up your coat. Don't feed Chloe at the table. Wipe your shoes on the doormat, for heaven's sake.' "

"And you'd see me in all my imperfections," I reminded him.

"Let us be faultless one to the other," Bill said with a grin.

I had almost forgotten until our renewed intimacy Faulkner's curious physical tidiness when he was with me. He was obsessed with keeping from me the grossness of his physical self, running the water in the bathroom to cover the evidence of his animality, bathing each time we made love. Always the sleeved handkerchief was drawn out to suppress a cough or contain a sneeze. Once at Normandie Village, he had become ill from tainted food and I recall his agonizing attempts to muffle the sounds of his violent retching.

It was, of course, another manifestation of the romantic in him, compounded of the Southern gentleman's need to pedestal the female, to spare her the indelicacies and harshnesses.

Around men, on hunting trips, riding, flying, fishing, or in the fields, he must have been as coarse in his maleness as his companions or even the Snopeses of whom he wrote. I would have loved him profane, but he didn't know it and it would have shocked him had he guessed.

The suggestion that we live together had been made out of deepest concern for his financial situation—how would he manage on the mean terms at which he had been bought by the studio?—but I would have retreated in consternation had Bill found it acceptable. Although he, and later Wolfgang, had freed me from my moral hobbles, I still could not run or leap. Sleep with Faulkner I would, but only if by Estelle's death or a miracle I became his wife would I share the same space with him day after day.

There were questions I was burning to ask. What about the war? What about the officer's commission?

"I was turned down flat," Bill admitted. "Then I applied for a desk job in Washington."

"You didn't tell me."

"I was downright embarrassed to. I didn't have the education that was required. They said I was illiterate."

Not for anything would I show curiosity about Estelle—any word must come from him—but I could safely ask about Jill; in fact, he encouraged it.

"Miss Jill," he announced significantly, "is taking piano."

"Oh, that's wonderful, Bill. Do you think she is talented?"

"How would I know, ma'am? What I do know is that she's riding a full-sized horse and that she's damned good." Pride flecked his brown eyes, glittered like a scattering of mica. "Her legs are still a little too short and her seat is bad, but her hands are all right. A little awkward, but they feel the horse."

"That's good."

"I don't mind about the seat." He was dead serious, the model Southern father weighing the aptitudes of his progeny, their chances of finding acceptance. "She can learn that. But either you have hands or you never will."

Bill rented a modest, cheap room with an adjoining terrace on the top floor of the Highland Hotel on Highland Avenue at Franklin. (When I made a sentimental exploration of the building years later, it was inhabited only on the lower levels; as I climbed to a remembered height, past padlocked doors, the floorboards creaked in the dark hallways and there was a pungency of offal.) He had a panoramic view of the Hollywood Hills, Spanish stucco houses covering them like children's blocks. Every morning he was picked up by fellow screenwriters who had formed a car pool—A. I. (Buzz) Bezzerides, Thomas Job, and Stephen Longstreet among them from time to time—and was driven to Warner Brothers Studios. His office was on a lower floor of the Administration Building on the Olive Avenue side, with its twisted conifers, a stand of tall eucalyptus trees, and the studio flagpole. In the evening, there was always a ride for him back to his hotel, where, if he was not meeting me, he would put on his white shorts, remove his shoes and socks, and take a stiff drink of bourbon out onto his cool terrace with its cane chairs; the sun shot its heat down on the hotel roof the day long and by evening the room was hot and oppressive. Sometimes he would work on the terrace at a portable typewriter. On occasion he would wear dark glasses to protect his eyes from the glare and I would tease him about "going Hollywood."

Once, as the lights bloomed on the hillside and cars on the street below pushed their way slowly to the Hollywood Bowl, I told him of an acquaintance on whom all the boils of Job had been inflicted—cancer, the loss of loved ones, business reverses, false accusation, dishonor.

"You have to live," Bill said somberly, "so that you can die."

He was assigned, because of his World War I experience and his knowledge of flying, to war films in development at the studio, and he persevered to merit the new contract that had been hinted. The salary he was receiving, 10 percent of which went to his agent, kept most of his creditors (paid in dribbles) at bay, but there were still enormous bills facing him. More than at any time in Hollywood, however, he appeared to tolerate screenwriting; for one thing, there was no novel in progress to stab at him while he was writing movie dialogue; for another, he liked his fellow scribes in The Ward, as the writers' offices were collectively called.

I was working on *The Adventures of Mark Twain,* produced by Jesse L. Lasky and directed by Irving Rapper, who had asked that I be assigned to the film. Fredric March and Alexis Smith were the stars. The make-up process toward the end of the film as Samuel Clemens grew older took hours of the morning schedule; the nose had to be gradually elongated, made bulbous and turned under, and the eyebrows made shaggy. Watching Freddie work—sometimes his wife, Florence Eldridge, visiting the set, drew her chair close to mine and talked about their way of life, their travels, their steadfast liberalism—I gained a new respect for the mechanics of great acting.

March, Bette Davis, Claude Rains, Karl Malden, and other actors of stature spent every free moment on the set pouring over screenplay pages for resonances and meanings that the writer had not spelled out—could not, in fact, in economical scripts of 110 pages, rarely more than 125. They made meticulous notes on physical movements—when to stand, when to sit, at what point to put on or take off eyeglasses or gloves, and all for dramatic or psychological reasons that would heighten interest and suspense. Before difficult scenes, while sets were being lighted or cameras reloaded or the cinematographer scanned the sky for an elusive sun, they sat quietly in their dressing rooms, building the blocks of quintessence, drawing verisimilitude to themselves concentratedly. There are actors who play off the tops of their heads and do it with style and competence. The great ones, however, are thinking of the day's quota of pages from the moment they leave their homes in the morning; in the theater, they would have the luxury of weeks of out-of-town tryouts in which to build their characterizations; in motion pictures, the shadings must be found in a matter of hours, sometimes minutes, or not at all.

The Marches went out of their way to show their appreciation for whatever help I gave to Freddie on the set. On a number of occasions, I was invited to visit them in their hotel suite (I longed to bring Faulkner, but he was not overfond of actors). When there were crew parties, Florence Eldridge, who knew that I was waiting for my final divorce papers, asked me to go with them.

Even more than at Twentieth Century-Fox, Faulkner and I avoided being seen together. We never sat at the same table during the lunch hour, never visited each other's office, though there were times when Bill would tell me that he had "snuck on your set for a few minutes just to see the back of your pretty head." I sailed past his table in the Green Room at which he often sat with Bezzerides, Job, Furthman, Pagano, and Longstreet, all of whom knew of our romance, without looking his way.

We had resumed our relationship as though no time at all had passed, as though we were both unchanged by the passage of years, but almost at once we realized that it was not the same and could never again be as it was. Too much time had passed. Neither of us was what we had been. I was now my own woman, making my own way in the world, solving my problems; no longer credulous, untutored, capitulatory, I had outgrown gifts of puppy dogs and hair ribbons and rubber ducks for my bath. When I fell in love with Faulkner, I had the reasonable, if simple-hearted, expectation that we would eventually be married. Now I looked for nothing at all, asked for nothing at all, except his love and his emotional support. He was my lover, my rock; it was not enough, but I made it enough.

Faulkner had allowed Hollywood to buy him at a fraction of his worth as a screenwriter, and in the beginning it made no nicks or gouges in his self-esteem. The literary establishments, in New York, London, Paris, Rome, and Tokyo, confirmed his own unshakable assessment of his worth: he was not only the best of America's regional novelists but the best of all American writers, and his books would live. A clipping service, if he had been able to afford one, would have filled a

283

whole room at Rowan Oak with published appraisals of his work.

The tremendous recognition, the unimpeachable evidence that nothing could touch the immortality he was gaining, intensified Bill's remoteness. He was ruder to people who asked personal questions, far more uncivil to those whose manner, opinions, or even appearance repelled him. Many who met him for the first time thought him to be overweening in his smugness.

But that was with others. With me, he was by turns lover, passionate and vigorous; concerned adviser; gentle, staunch friend. The great difference now was that he pretended not to need me as impellingly as he once had for companionship. When I acknowledged it to myself, never thinking that once again it was for my protection and independence, I began to break the night-after-night pattern into which we had again fallen. I would say "I'm exhausted" or "I have letters to write and bills to pay." Freed from obligation to construct his life in Hollywood around me again, he began to accept invitations he would ordinarily have refused.

Not all that comfortable around women, though he liked Henriette Martin, Cora Baird, Sally Crown, and Betty Royce —and I had seen him completely relaxed with Dorothy Parker—he spent whole evenings with male writer friends at bars and restaurants. There were dinner invitations from the Crowns. He kept in touch with Wolfgang, who knew that we were lovers again; it seemed not to diminish their regard for each other. There was time on Sundays for him to fish, hunt, golf, ride at a stable in the Griffith Park area, and fly at a nearby airfield. Now I could attend concerts and dance recitals and plays. Friends from whom I had alienated myself welcomed me back into their circle.

The lines of fatigue disappeared from my face with full nights of sleep. I suddenly realized with a lancing shock that my dependence on Bill was not as great as it had been. I loved him more than ever, but I wanted to see him when I could no longer stay away from him, when I was vital and undrooping, when I had ardor of my own. Sometimes we parted without any agreement on when we would meet again, but neither of us thought it the least bit irregular; the next day we were sure to be in touch.

It was good for Faulkner, better than it had been before, if not as intoxicatingly romantic. Far from Oxford, he was the lover of a self-assured woman in her thirties who still drew appraising glances from other men, who wanted only him and was incapable of keeping it fixed in her mind for very long that he was America's towering writer, who did not lionize him, who made no demands upon him, and with whom he could be himself, no need to impress her. She dressed in the pale pastel colors that he liked best on her—lavenders and oranges and yellows and soft blues—kept herself slender, stayed out of the treacherous Southern California sun, and once again reverted to low heels, which were unfashionable but did not spoil the line of her legs. The guilts that had swarmed around Faulkner's head were gone. Estelle knew that I was back in his life and she let it go. The bill collectors had left her doorstep. Their debts were being whittled down. There was even a little money to spend. Only in Hollywood could her husband earn substantial sums. I was in Hollywood. Nothing could be done about me.

There was a single incongruity. Bill was happier, but he was drinking heavily. At Musso's or (when he had an extra check from a short-story sale) at Preston Sturges' Players on Sunset Boulevard or at LaRue's, he was not ready for dinner until he had downed three or four straight bourbons. There were also bottles in his hotel room and I had been told that he kept a flask in his office. He was never drunk, however, and I chalked it up to my influence.

The Adventures of Mark Twain was in its last days of shooting and I had been unable to see Bill for almost a week. Bezzerides appeared on the set in midafternoon. He was a big, dark bear of a man who had written a novel that Bill liked and had become a topflight screenwriter following the success of *They Drive by Night*. Buzz beckoned to me while Irving Rapper was discussing the décor of a period hallway with the set decorator.

Faulkner, he confided worriedly, had passed out in his own office. He had never seen anyone in the condition that Bill was in. Was there something I could suggest? I told an assistant director that I had an emergency involving a close friend and would return to the set as soon as possible.

Faulkner was at his desk, head down on the blotter. Pages from the screenplay he was working on were scattered over the room and there was a bottle of whiskey, one-third full, tipped over on its side near his typewriter. His ashen skin, when I lifted his head, struck alarm in me. It was as if some terrible dysfunction had hit him with paralyzing force.

"We have to get him out of the studio before Jack Warner hears about it," I said decisively. "If word gets around, it's the end of Bill at the studio."

Buzz nodded. He knew as well as I that this time the black-ball would never stop bouncing.

"There's a bathhouse on Cahuenga at Yucca where they'll dry him out," I remembered.

It had been done in films a hundred times. I stood on one side of Faulkner and Buzz on the other. We lifted him from the chair and supported his weight by hooking our arms under his so that he could shuffle along with us. Bill seemed to know what was happening. He opened his eyes, pupils suspended in them like the yolks of eggs, fixed his mouth in an apologetic smile, and made himself hollow-boned for us. Studio workers who passed us saw a man who was ill or who had injured himself being helped to the parking lot.

Two days later Bill telephoned me from his office. He was back on the job. Would I meet him at the hotel for dinner?

"I won't ask you why," I said as I opened the door of his room. "I promised myself not to. But I'd sure as heck like to know why, Bill."

He sighed and found a memo from the legal department advising him that Warner Brothers had lifted his option and that for the next period of the agreement he would be making only fifty dollars more each week.

"I was counting on a new contract at my rightful salary," Faulkner said. "You know how much I need the money."

"It's shabby of the studio. I'm so sorry."

I moved into his arms and leaned my head against his chest and patted his shoulder in understanding and commiseration.

"You and Buzz saved my job," he said. "They would have had a pink slip on my desk."

"Bill, please don't drink anymore. Not that way—whatever way it is that turns you into someone I don't know."

"I'll try, dear love. I swear I'll try."

He nevertheless went on drinking to excess. I didn't try to stop him so long as he seemed to hold the whiskey. But one night at a restaurant when he had no stomach for food and drank for a solid two hours, I became alarmed. Something was building up in him that I had never sensed before. He ordered a double bourbon, his ninth or tenth.

"Bill, I think that's enough," I said gently.

"I'll just finish this . . ."

"I want you to take me back to your place. I want us to leave right now."

I stayed the night with him, more nurse and priestess than lover to his whiskey-sodden body. He knew what I was doing. Behind the wild lover's face, there was the visage of the drowning man. Slowly I brought him back from the darkness into which he had ventured. He sweat bourbon. Finally he was safe and ready for the day's work at the studio.

I knew what it was that had sent him close to another of his deadly blackouts. It was Hollywood, the indignity of making far less money than Pagano and Bezzerides and Job and all the others in The Ward. It was the itch that never left him to begin a new novel. It was all that and the war news, unrelievedly bad, and the men in uniform, some of them no younger than he, whom he saw almost daily in the corridors of the studio. And he was achingly homesick.

"You miss Jill, don't you?" I said.

"Yes'm, I do. I sure do."

"And your mother and your brother."

"Yes'm."

"All the Faulkners."

"Don't leave out Malcolm and Cho-Cho."

287

"You really are a family man, Faulkner."

"I do what I have to do, no more, no less."

I thought of something else, but I held it back from speech. He didn't sleep with his wife, no guilt attached itself to sexual congress with another woman, but he wasn't cut out for adultery. It was inconsonant with his deep feeling for family and children and Southern respectability. It would not ulcerate. But it was there.

Bill walked me down the stairway to Highland Avenue and my car. The air was sharp and clean. Long Chinese lacquered fingers of light probed the night sky.

"What good deed," he asked, "have I done to deserve you?"

"Or I you?"

"You're my reward for something—in this life or another."

We kissed good night. There was no trace of alcohol in his mouth.

"I'll call you," I said. "Or you call me."

"Yes, ma'am."

The next day a gold locket of unusual design, with an ingenious sliding clasp, was delivered to me. All I could think was that one creditor in Oxford would not get his payment the next week. I miniaturized one of my favorite pictures of Bill and wore the locket for years. I cling to it still.

After that, I made it a point not to let more than a few days go by without seeing him for at least an hour, to read his moods, to look for the danger signs. I could at least put a hand over the edge of a glass as a reminder of my concern. As he began to socialize and when he had come to trust the discretion of his hosts, he wanted me along with him. I had made many new friends as a script clerk, but I was careful not to thrust them at him. Some were people I had known when I was married to Wolfgang; others, readers all, would be overawed by him or ask questions. At a later time, I let down my guard and had cause to regret it. Morris Ankrum, a fine character actor with whom I had worked, heard that Faulkner was my lover.

"Meta," he said, "I'd like to meet William Faulkner. Will you introduce me to him?"

"If it's possible, Morris."

I had no intention of subjecting Bill to actors and promptly forgot my promise.

A few weeks later, Morris sought me out on the sound stage where I was working and pressed his case.

"I'm an incurable Civil War buff," he told me, "and I regard William Faulkner as one of the great authorities on that war. He's particularly well informed on the Confederate generals and on the great battles. I'd like to sit down and talk with him about the Civil War."

"Well, Morris, he's writing at night . . ."

"Would you both have dinner with me?"

I thanked him for my half of the invitation. At the first chance, I'd talk to Bill. Perhaps something could be arranged. Weeks went by. Morris stopped me in the commissary.

"I'm disappointed that I haven't heard from you about the evening I'd hoped to have with you and Mr. Faulkner."

"Oh, Morris, I've been—we've both been—so busy."

"I hear he's a caustic, arrogant sort."

I bristled. "Not at all. He's not the easiest man in the world to approach, but he's not any of those other things you have said." I turned and walked away.

Whether Morris had consciously manipulated me into the dinner that followed, I am not certain. In any event, I stewed over his allegations for days and finally decided that I would show him that Bill was not a monster. I think I also took a perverse pleasure in being the only person in Hollywood who could effect the meeting.

Faulkner growled when I relayed the dinner invitation, then grudgingly agreed to meet the "actor fellow." I had not forced strangers on him in a long time. If I asked now, it must be important to me. (It wasn't, but I couldn't back out.)

"But he will be *our* guest," Faulkner insisted. "I may be

poor, but I don't want anyone picking up checks for me."

Morris extended himself at dinner, joining Bill drink for drink, letting silences come without rushing in to fill them. He had not misrepresented himself. He had read volumes on the War Between the States; names and dates and places came to him easily, but his knowledge was academic compared to Faulkner's sweeping insights into the tragic conflict. Bill's great-grandfather had been a Confederate colonel. As a boy, he had listened to oldsters who had fought in the war. The two men talked of Lee, Jackson, Stuart, Beauregard, and Johnston. Names of battles I had not heard since childhood— the Seven Days, Bull Run, Chancellorsville, Murfreesboro, Chickamauga—led them into discussions of military victories and miscalculations.

As usual, Bill returned to his bourbon after dinner. Morris and I sipped liqueur. Bill was lighting his pipe as Morris said, "Bill, I hear you're into a new book."

Faulkner tensed with the use of his first name by a stranger. The jaw muscles in his face began to work. He hated the instant familiarity that he encountered wherever he went in Hollywood.

"May I read what you've written so far?" Morris asked.

Bill's face went rigid. "No!" He beckoned to a passing waiter. "Check, please."

Struck dumb, Morris watched him scatter bills on the table and rise to allow me to leave the table first. I managed a throttled "Good night, Morris," but Faulkner, seething inside, walked away without a word. Morris was to tell of the incident with William Faulkner for years afterward, and with not too kindly an opinion of his dinner host.

Howard Hawks, never satisfied with the final draft of a screenplay, was worried about a number of key scenes in *Air Force*, which was about to begin principal photography in Tampa, Florida, and asked the studio to put Faulkner on it. Bill was elated. Hawks had requested him, the payday low man, not fellow scripters making ten times what he was being paid. Moreover, *Air Force*, the drama of a B-17 bomber called *Mary-Ann,* was a film project close to Jack L. Warner's heart, one in which he had a personal stake. If Bill could solve the problems in the screenplay, it might galvanize Warner into giving him the new contract.

"I may not be the slickest screenwriter in Hollywood," Bill told me, "but I know how to fix a screenplay. I'm giving Howard what he wants."

His next assignment was with Jack Chertok, who was to produce *The Liberator.* Faulkner liked him immediately. Chertok was from Atlanta. Accustomed to Southerners with peccadilloes, he saw nothing annoyingly idiosyncratic in Bill's behavior during story conferences, and was excited over his ideas and concepts.

I drew *Old Acquaintance,* which teamed Bette Davis and Miriam Hopkins. Henry Blanke was the producer and Vincent Sherman the director. Gig Young, who had zoomed to stardom by stepping into roles vacated by actors in the service and who the following year would himself be called to duty, and John Loder, who was courting Hedy Lamarr, were the leading men.

Miriam had played the title role in *The Story of Temple Drake,* Paramount's screen version of *Sanctuary,* and Faulkner was interested in what I could tell him of the Southern-born actress who had caught Temple's erotic nature in the film. He was also fascinated by my running account of the dissension between the two stars, who had taken an instant dislike to each other.

Although I had found Miriam pleasant enough in the 1930's, she was prone to make enemies among her fellow actors by conscious scene pilferage. Edward G. Robinson grumbled throughout *Barbary Coast* that she would not look him in the eyes and that she walked away from him to draw the audience's attention to herself. Every day during production of *Old Acquaintance,* there were clashes and explosions of temperament that Vincent Sherman was powerless to avert or quell. The crew sided with Bette. She had worked with Olivia de Havilland and with Mary Astor on two films, and there had been no discord whatever. It was that Hopkins dame who was at the bottom of the trouble that beset the film, they decided, and Bette agreed with them.

Sometimes there was dialogue, angry and cutting, that wasn't in my or anyone else's script. Miriam was a formidable adversary with a razored tongue; Bette was no match for her. After a particularly fiery confrontation in which Bette, for the first time, gave as good as she got, Miriam developed laryngitis and we were forced to shoot around her for several days. The crew gave her nasty looks when she reported back to work.

Bill and I could laugh about it at dinner, but the warfare created terrible tensions on the set. When Miriam, directed to stand still during one of Bette's emotional moments, walked away instead, Bette aimed a fusillade of wrath at her. Miriam would do as Vincent Sherman told her, by God! Miriam would listen! Miriam would meet her gaze!

"I'm asking to go home for Christmas," Bill informed me one evening after he had been interviewed and photographed on his private terrace for a leading magazine. "I want to be with Jill if I can. You know what a miserable Christmas it would be for her without her pappy."

"Bill, there's no question. Go home, by all means."

"You won't mind too much?"

I did mind, but he would never know. "Bill, I have my parents. I have my brother and his family. I just might visit them. If the studio will let you leave, you must—for Jill."

"Carpenter, you are my dear love."

"Just tell me one way or another so I can make my own plans."

I held my head a trifle too high in counterfeit bravery. Christmas wasn't going to be a jolly Bing Crosby vocal. The business of picking up my final divorce papers had depressed me. Every day the Bette-Miriam hostilities broke over my head. I had been shattered by the horrible death as a result of burns in Boston's Cocoanut Grove fire of cowboy star Buck Jones, for whose independent company at Universal I had worked before I joined Howard Hawks.

Bill's request was granted. I sent along a small gift for Jill and was sorry for it later; she was nine years old, not a baby-dumpling girl with whom her father could share secrets. Since her pappy was too broke to afford a present for me, he asked that I please not give him one. I returned a humidor to the tobacconist's shop where I had purchased it. Christmas came and went. I spent a Sunday with the Crowns, admiring their two-month-old daughter, Jean. At Bette Davis' urging—"You're pretty and Southern, the boys will like you"—I dragged myself to the Hollywood Canteen when I was done with paper work at night to serve sandwiches, doughnuts, and coffee to enlisted men on furlough or en route to bloody combat in the South Pacific. Boy-faced young men with premonitions of their own deaths asked me to dance with them. Eighteen-year-olds from Alabama, South Carolina, and Tennessee kissed me because I was from "down home." Bette, one of the founders and president, was at the canteen every night.

Bill was back in mid-January with an account of Christmas at Rowan Oak. He was happy and loquacious and didn't mention Estelle. It wasn't only Jill he had gone back to; it was the whole Faulkner clan, including his dead brother's widow and child, and the blacks. He had been lord of the whole damned manor because it was expected of him and because it afforded him pleasure. I forgave him in my heart and loved him the more for it.

On the day that Bette was to seize Miriam by the shoulders, shake her hard, and slap her—it was all in the script—I told Bill to drop by for the tempest. He couldn't make it, but almost everybody else on the Warner Brothers lot tried to crash the act. The two actresses rehearsed the physical action thoroughly. Bette was so gentle that Sherman asked her to put more muscle in it.

Bette did when the camera turned, so violently that Miriam fled to her dressing room in tears. The next day she called in to say that "that woman has left black-and-blue marks all over my body. I'm in terrible pain. I can't possibly come to work."

The studio announced that Miriam had suffered a sinus attack. An executive, flourishing a trade paper, approached Bette and said, "I didn't know your name was sinus." The wags had it that the studio would bill them as "Bette Davis Versus Miriam Hopkins in *Old Acquaintance*."

Air Force was a smash hit. So was Hawks' *Corvette K-225*, which he had produced for Universal. He could have anything he wanted from Jack L. Warner and now he requested Faulkner for the screenplay of *Battle Cry*, not the Leon Uris book, which was to appear in the next decade, but an original drama about the war and its aftermath. It would be road-show length and there would be an all-stellar cast, with every player on the lot in a lead role. Faulkner sat in a projection room day after day to familiarize himself with the personalities of the Warner Brothers contract stars in order to tailor parts for them. He had no doubt this time, with all his options exercised at due date or before, that a new deal was in the offing. He had even talked to Hawks about it.

For months the studio had been preparing an embellished film version of *This Is the Army*. To my surprise, I drew the second unit, directed by LeRoy Prinz, involving all of the musical sequences of the picture. Michael Curtiz was to direct the dramatic episodes connecting the whole. It was a draining show. By midafternoon I sagged. But the spirit of the enlisted men who had worked in the stage presentation for more than a year without a furlough stimulated me. Irving Berlin faced the cameras one day to sing "Oh, How I Hate to Get Up in the Morning," and Kate Smith, out of pure patriotism, refusing any billing at first, reported to the studio to sing "God Bless America." The soldiers were drilled when they weren't before the camera, and once officers flew in from Washington, D.C., to inspect them on the Army installation set up near the studio.

Faulkner took pride in *Battle Cry* until Hawks brought in other scribes to rewrite and polish sections of the ambitious, multilevel script that eventually was to be shelved and forgotten. "Everybody out here rewrites everybody else," Bill said with a shrug. His interest picked up when the first-draft screenplay convinced Hawks of the error of four opposing sensibilities working on a single script; the sutures showed and the connective tissue that Bill had labored to give the script had been eliminated in crucial areas. The screenplay was turned over to Bill and Steve Fisher, who wrote mystery-suspense novels, for a final draft.

"Howard wants us to go with him to June Lake to work on the script," Bill told me irritably one evening when I drove him home from the studio (the pickup point was the drug-store across the street from the studio). "He thinks we can lick it away from The Ward."

"June Lake's beautiful. You'll be in the country."

"He's talking about two weeks."

"That long?"

"I don't want to leave. I don't want to be away from you. There's never enough time as it is—"

"But honey, if he needs you . . ."

"I can tell him I'd rather not."

"Bill, you know, and I know, that's not wise. He's the one film maker in this town who knows what a great writer you are. He's been your friend. I really think you should go. There'll be time for us."

He came back grousing about the separation and the end-less story parleys and writing that began in the morning and went on until midnight. When six o'clock came, he wanted nothing to remind him of screenplays. His nights were for himself. The telescope of his mind was turned to the moon-scape of Yoknapatawpha. Sometimes as we sat on his terrace, he would drift into a serene removal from me and from all traffic sounds, and I could tell by the play of his facial muscles and the blinking of his eyes that new short stories were being generated and that chunks of the novel to come were falling into place and locking. If I told him of an incident on the sound stage or spoke of my hope that there would be an Allied offensive in Europe any week now, he would murmur "Mmmmmmmmm," not breaking the chain of invention and recall, and pat my knee. I could understand when I was being pushed by ragged Snopeses and the personae of his fictional county to the far edges of his consciousness.

It was a good summer for us in the midst of a terrible war. Henriette went from Monogram to RKO to write *Dear Uncle Sam*. Wolfgang, teamed with Bill Hoffman at two pianos, was in Ken Murray's *Blackouts* at the El Capitán, and Faulkner went backstage with me after the final curtain. John Crown concertized in the Western states. I was busy on *Rhapsody in Blue*, the film biography of George Gershwin.

There was a farewell party for the soldier-actors of *This Is the Army* at the Mineral Wells Picnic Grounds in Griffith Park. I dropped Bill off at the riding stables and arranged to pick him up after I had wished the boys "happy furlough." Rumor that they were to be sent into combat in Europe was unfounded. Instead they were formed into new companies to tour the battle zones with the show.

There were new faces at Musso's—Clifford Odets, Arthur Miller, Tess Slesinger, Raymond Chandler, Mary McCarthy. When I heard that Carl Sandburg and Sinclair Lewis were coming out to work on screenplays, I rushed to tell Bill in the belief that it would make him feel better about Hollywood: it didn't. He snorted contemptuously when the newspapers announced that John Steinbeck was working with Alfred Hitchcock on the screenplay of *Lifeboat*.

In December, as I knew he would, Faulkner left to spend the holidays in Oxford once again after getting special permission from the studio. He was a fine screenwriter and they had bought him at a bargain-basement price; the war had created a shortage of good writers, and refuse him they couldn't. "I'll Be Home for Christmas" was being played, amplified from public-address systems, all over Hollywood. I put my hands over my ears and conceived a lasting hatred for it.

Friends gave me gifts and I had modest gifts for them. There were Christmas cards from Betty, the Bairds, Bucky Fuller, Edgar Rebner, my former brother-in-law and his wife, Bette Davis, the Marches, a soldier in the South Pacific whom I had met briefly at the Hollywood Canteen. Nothing from Bill. I had dinner with Wolfgang, who was as forlorn as I.

Suddenly it was 1944. My next picture, I was informed, would be *To Have and Have Not,* based upon the Ernest Hemingway novel. Humphrey Bogart, who had been touring the fighting fronts, would be the star. Howard Hawks would produce and direct.

"Hawks?" I gasped. "Did he ask for me?"

The production manager said no, that it was a routine assignment. "But he knows you're going to be on the show."

I reported to my former employer with mixed feelings—gratitude because he had given me my first chance to become a professional in Hollywood and uneasiness because of how much he knew about me.

"Hello, Howard," I said, as breezy as the archetypal Hawks girl. "I'm going to be with you on *To Have and Have Not.*" I had always called him Mr. Hawks before.

"Hello, Meta," the director said. "I'm glad we'll be working together again." The princely reserve was the same as Faulkner's, as much a part of him as his erect carriage and clipped speech. Hawks remained a master of the art of detachment. For a quick moment, he flicked his eyes over me—what did his good friend William Faulkner see in me that he himself had missed?—then the mask adjusted itself and he was as I remembered him, deliberate, unsmiling.

"How are Athol and the children?" I dared ask.

"Well, thank you."

"I would like to be remembered to Athol."

"Of course."

The new Mrs. Hawks, whom everybody called Slim, had a year before discovered a tearing beauty in a fashion magazine and had persuaded her husband to place eighteen-year-old Betty Bacall, renamed Lauren for marquee lure, under a personal, exclusive contract at a hundred dollars a week. Her salary was to climb to fifteen hundred dollars a week in seven years. There were several other budding actresses whom Hawks had signed to pacts, among them Ella Raines. Now it was time to unveil Betty. I sat at Hawks' side as he directed her in a test with Humphrey Bogart. Once she was secure in her lines, she gazed up at the famous star like a smitten movie fan—odd conduct for a young woman who had attended the American Academy of Dramatic Arts and had made the rounds of Broadway producers. Bogey responded in predictable male fashion, a malleable wad in the hands of the newcomer. There was no question when the test was run that she would play Marie.

Betty's voice was husky from the start. I never believed the publicity department apocrypha that she had, at Hawks' suggestion, achieved the Bacall basso by screaming her throat raw in a rowboat. Everybody else accepted the story.

We were in trouble soon after the Bacall screen test. Jules Furthman had loosely followed the Hemingway novel in his screenplay, but Washington, D.C., voiced strenuous objections to it. A film about an American who smuggled rum and revolutionaries between Havana and Key West, and in which the Cuban flag was raised, would deeply embarrass the government. What official Washington felt was of crucial importance to the Warners and to the executives who surrounded them. The brothers were patriots of the first order. Besides, there were war films on the planning boards for Errol Flynn, Humphrey Bogart and John Garfield that could not be made without the full cooperation of the War Department.

Hawks, pressed for a way out of the quandary, anxious to mollify Washington, asked the front office to assign Faulkner to work on the screenplay. Faulkner had never failed him when he hit a story snag and he would not now, he was confident. We were days away from the start of principal photography.

Rested, clear-eyed, Bill knew what to do straight off. The year before he had worked on an original screenplay about General de Gaulle and now he drew freely from his research. Harry Morgan would still own a boat, as in the Hemingway novel, but it would be berthed at Fort-de-France, the capital of French Martinique. In the course of the story, Morgan, who had been apolitical, would experience a change of heart and join the Free French against the Vichy government. Marie would not be his wife but an American girl stranded in Martinique without money for her passage back to the States.

Howard Hawks and the brothers Warner bought the new story line almost before Bill could finish telling it. New sets were ordered constructed the same day.

Actors who had been signed for Furthman's solo script were paid off and new ones selected. Within days, cameras began to turn as the sets were converted. Every morning Bill arrived at the studio and pounded out pages that would be filmed the following day for Bogey, Bacall, Hoagy Carmichael, Walter Brennan (it was my third picture with him), and assorted villains. *To Have and Have Not* was almost pure Faulkner, superimposed on what was left of the Furthman script. There was simply no time for Hawks to ask his cast how they would say the lines or to call in a third writer. Bill worked slavishly, employing a remarkable discipline in order to stay ahead of Hawks and his cast. He liked hearing his words spoken as written. The film would be his first screen credit in years. Neither of us overlooked the series of odd circumstances that had brought us full circle; we were working for Hawks again and Bill was sharing screen credit with Furthman, as he had with Joel Sayre on *The Road to Glory*.

It was a dangerous way to make a motion picture. In later years, I worked on films in which the script was delivered piecemeal, notably Leo McCarey's *My Son John*, with Helen Hayes and Robert Walker; all were crashing failures. *To Have and Have Not* succeeded mainly because of Faulkner, the screenwriter who was thought by other inhabitants of The Ward to know little or nothing about the screenplay form.

That Humphrey Bogart and Betty Bacall were in love was evident after the first days of shooting. Throughout production, Bogey walked about singing "Mairzy Doats" and "The

Hutsut Song," muttering oaths when he couldn't remember the tongue-twisting lyrics. When he wasn't in his leading lady's dressing room, daily filled with fresh flowers, he would gather crew members around him and tell of his arduous and dangerous tour of the Mediterranean and African theaters of war.

Faulkner often came to the set for conferences with Hawks in the director's portable office. If Hawks was busy, Bill would stand quietly and watch the scene being played. Hoagy Carmichael was his favorite cast member. When Hoagy sang the two songs he had composed for the picture, "Hong Kong Blues" and "Baltimore Oriole," Bill paid special visits to the set to hear him.

To Have and Have Not gave Jack L. Warner no seizures of terrible contrition over the unfair contract to which he had handcuffed Faulkner, but it earned Bill strong respect around the studio. Under circumstances that would have turned most screenwriters into hollow-eyed, pill-gulping wrecks, he had saved an important Warner Brothers feature picture that had the clinking ring of money about it. Bill was inwardly pleased at first, but after a while, the deference of secretaries, waitresses, barbers, and mail-room messengers annoyed him.

"All this head bowin' and foot scrapin'," Bill grumbled. "Nobody looked at me before this, and if it's a flop, none of them will look my way again."

Something now began to weigh on his mind that had nothing to do with studio mores or the work at hand. The anxiety, pressure, worriment—whatever it was, one did not ask him—would not go away. I guessed, wrongly, that he was unhappy over the novels that weren't being written, the short stories that he was too exhausted to complete.

Over late dinner one weekend, Bill found the resolution to tell me what he had not been able to weeks before.

"Carpenter, I'm bringing Estelle and Jill out for the summer." It was said with great deliberation, his eyes fixed intently on my face. "Soon as Jill's school is over."

"For how long?"

"All summer."

"Why, Bill?" Anger stirred within me.

"It can't be helped."

"Is it Estelle?" I asked boldly. "Is she back to drinking herself blind?"

"No more than any other time."

"Then what?"

"Mainly it's that Jill's been begging me to let her come to Hollywood. She misses me, and Lord knows, I miss her."

"I see."

"Then, too, I don't want her to be at home with Estelle all summer long. When she's at school, she doesn't see her mother drinking. But now that school's letting out . . ." He slammed his cup down decisively. "I've already rented a house."

For the first time in our long relationship, I felt myself put upon cruelly, my most personal feelings wholly overlooked. No wonder Faulkner had delayed telling me of his decision. The inequity of it angered me. I wanted to shout at Bill, he to whom I had never raised my voice, that it was unfair, thoughtless, hurtful. Hollywood was my province with him! Estelle and Jill belonged to his life in Oxford! Why was Bill doing this to me—to us? I had the short end of the stick, the sweepings, the leavings. His wife and daughter had everything. Why did they have to intrude on my poor little piece of earth with Bill?

"It doesn't have to make any difference—their being here," Bill said. "We can go on as we have."

"As if nothing had changed?"

"Nothing will have changed."

"Of course it's changed," I let myself go and blazed at him. "Eight years ago, when she was here, Estelle didn't know about me. And Jill was three then, needing me to take care of her when Estelle passed out. Now that she's almost a teenager, it's not the same!"

"Carpenter—"

"And I'm not the same."

"None of us are, dear love."

"Bill, I remember the way it was the last time. I'm not going through that again. Waiting for you to be able to slip away at night. Staring at the telephone as if that would make it ring and you'd be on the line. No, Bill, no."

Lines of puzzlement bit into his forehead. "I just can't see that anything's fundamentally different."

"Can't you?"

"You're putting it on the basis of some arcane kind of female morality."

"It's my morality—with my name engraved on it—and I'm sorry if you think I'm naïve and confused."

"I don't think anything of the kind."

"Maybe I'll feel differently someday, but right now—"

"I don't cohabit with my wife. I don't sleep with her."

"That doesn't make it right for us."

"You're vexed with me, honey. Don't be."

"I can't help it." People were staring at us. I lowered my voice. "You're taking the whole summer away from me. Not just a week, not just a month, a whole summer."

"What do you want me to do? Shall I tell them not to come? Disappoint Jill?"

I turned to him in disbelief. Was he testing me or would he actually, by the nod of my head, change his plans to bring out his wife and daughter?

"It's your decision, not mine," I said. "You know now how I feel. It's up to you."

He was pensive as I drove him to his hotel, hunched down in his seat, hands folded between his legs.

"It's early," he said. "Come up for a while."

"I'd rather not."

"You're really put out with me."

"Good night, Bill."

When I reached my apartment, the telephone was ringing and I made my way to it in the dark, almost stumbling over Chloe.

"Meta, I've been thinking . . ."

I knew what was coming.

"I don't see how I can go back on my promise to my little girl."

"All right, Bill."

"Or how I'll have a minute's peace of mind thinking of what may be going on at Rowan Oak."

"Then that's it."

"Yes, ma'am." I held the receiver away from my ear to make his voice small, distant, benign. "You won't let me make love to you, I know that, but can I just see you—without the other?"

"No, Bill."

"Away from your place. Drinks together. Dinner. Anything."

"Bill, I think it will be much better if we don't see each other again—ever."

"Meta, dear love, what in the world—?"

"This is painful. Please. You just go your way from now on and let me go mine."

I hung up in slow motion, hearing him remonstrate before the receiver clicked into place. For an hour or more, I sat motionless in the dark. Later I moved dazedly around the apartment, directionless, fumbling objects, staring at walls. I couldn't cry anymore. It was over.

The Corn Is Green was about to start. It was a difficult film and there was no place for a woebegone script clerk. I made myself into an automaton, bricking up, for as long as the sand, cement, and water would hold, the terrible sense of betrayal, the feeling that I was inconsequential in Faulkner's life. The commissary was off limits because I might run into him, and I gave the writers' building the widest berth. Henriette had left Hollywood to work on training films for the WAAC and there was no one else to whom I cared to unburden myself. As for the Crowns, a curious change had come over them with marriage and parenthood; neither would allow anything of an unpleasant nature to be discussed, and

John, if there was illness in the family or if one of them was faced with a serious problem, would draw a curtain over it. I loved them both and adapted myself to the new ground rules. Wolfgang telephoned one night to say he had heard I was not seeing Bill anymore.

"Who told you?" I asked, surprised that anyone knew.

"Bill. I saw him at Musso's."

"Was his wife with him?"

"No. He was alone."

"Wolfichen, did Bill ask you to call me?"

"No, *Tierchen*. He just looked like some sad animal out of the sea and seemed to be drinking a lot. He said you'd finished with him."

Work was a safe, dark shell that I could close over myself during the day. After studio hours, I joined with others of my profession, sick of second-class status in the motion-picture industry, to organize the Script Supervisors Guild and to win belated recognition from the Producers Association. When I walked on the set of *The Corn Is Green* the first day, it was as a script supervisor, not a script clerk. The picture was beset by endless problems and I let myself become totally involved with them. Successive films, one after the other, and too much time devoted to the Hollywood Canteen had depleted Bette Davis. Because she was far younger than Ethel Barrymore, who had appeared in the play in Los Angeles the year before, there was concern that a sexual construction might be placed on the relationship between the altruistic schoolteacher and the gifted young Welsh miner, played by John Dall. To counteract it, Bette wore drab shirtwaists and skirts, pinned up her hair, and allowed herself to be matronly bosomed. Every scene was carefully rehearsed and the dailies were projected over and over, at Bette's insistence, for the slightest glance or nuance that might mislead the audience.

The children in the film were noisy and mutinous. They and their ambitious mothers stretched Irving Rapper's patience to its limits. He spent more time than he had planned on scenes of delicate content between Bette and John, and when he called for the juvenile horde, a stern schoolteacher invariably announced that it would be another hour before she was finished with mandatory classroom work.

The picture gave me a new friend: British actress Rosalind Ivan, who had played Watty on the stage with Ethel Barrymore, was an accomplished pianist, and had translated books on music and literature from the Russian. Mildred Dunnock was another cast member whose warmth was steady and enveloping. On Sundays, a stand-in who had once earned a living as a chef prepared astonishing dishes for us at my apartment, and Rosalind and Mildred talked of their stage experiences and travels.

During the summer, I ran into Jo Pagano. He and his wife, he told me, had entertained the Faulkners at dinner, and Bill had stopped by with Jill once or twice on the way to stables in the Griffith Park area where the Paganos lived. It was the first word I had had from anyone who had seen the visitors from Oxford. If Bill had brought Estelle to the Crowns', they charitably avoided letting me know it.

In the early fall, Henriette returned from the East to look for work as a screenwriter. Predictably, she was late for our luncheon appointment and arrived in a winded burst of apologies and explanations.

"I ran into Bill Faulkner this morning," she immediately informed me. "I had no idea that it was all off between you two."

"Was Estelle with him?"

"No, she and Jill are back in Oxford. As a matter of fact, Bill said he was looking for a place to stay and I offered him the room with its own bath and entrance at our place. My sister and her husband won't mind. Neither will Dad. We can use the rent money."

"How does he look?"

"The way some boozers do. Absolutely marvelous. Your average teetotaler should look so good."

After Bill moved to the house on Ridpath, Henriette gave me running reports on him. He was living in the midst of a great-hearted, intellectual Jewish family. Victor Lichtenstein, Henriette's father, had been a member of the violin section of the San Francisco Orchestra as a young man and still played his instrument every day. Nelda was dark-eyed and gentle; her husband, Frank, a non-Jew, was a political fire-brand under his quiet demeanor. Faulkner came and went as he pleased. Never, to Henriette's knowledge, had he brought anyone to his private room. On Sunday mornings, Bill had breakfast with the family, and once he had remained to hear her father play for several hours. The car pool picked him up in the morning and delivered him to his door after work.

"Does he ever ask about me?"

"Always."

"What does he say?"

" 'How is she?' 'Is she well?' " Henriette waited for me to react. She had given me an opening that would allow her, if I was moved by Faulkner's concern, to urge me to make up with him. When I shrugged, in pure bravado, she quickly dropped the role of conciliator.

It was Victor Kilian, now dividing himself as an actor be-tween the New York theater and Hollywood films, who shat-tered my implacable front. He had been telling me about little Richard, the second son born to Betty and Ed Royce.

"Oh." Victor held up his hand, remembering something. "Guess who I saw last night at Musso's? Bill Faulkner. A very drunk Bill Faulkner, let me add."

"I can imagine."

"You know, as long as I've known him," Victor mused, "I don't think he ever spoke more than ten words to me. He always puffed on that pipe of his and looked wiser than Solo-mon. But last night, he leaned over from the next table and actually talked to me."

Victor assumed Faulkner's solemn Mississippi-jurist ex-pression when he was in his cups, tucking in his chin, weav-ing unsteadily.

"Bill said"—it was an actor's concept of Oxfordian speech— " 'Meta doesn't love me anymore, Victor. One day Meta just stopped loving me altogether. Tell me what to do, Victor. Tell me how to get her back.' "

"He was drunk. You said he was."

"Yes, but it was real misery and from deep down."

"Oh, Victor." I gestured for him to stop. I didn't want to hear any more. I couldn't hold out another day. I had to see Bill. It had been a bleak summer. I would go on being dismal without him. He had always said, "We do what we have to do." He had had to bring Estelle and Jill to Hollywood because he was a loving father and a forbearing, long-suffering husband. It did not diminish his love for me. I had made a mistake.

The next morning I drove to Henriette's house and parked on the street. The morning was a great golden blister of sunshine. It would be a hot day. Bill came out and squinted into the light. He was wearing a seersucker suit.

"Carpenter . . ." He stood at the car door, uncertain, looking back toward the house.

"May I give you a lift, dearest one?"

The tightness into which his face was packed gave way. Bones relaxed. He touched his moustache nervously, unable to speak.

"Come on, Bill, get in."

"The studio car pool . . ." He gestured toward Laurel Canyon.

"Nelda and Frank can tell them that you've been picked up by a very forward woman."

He hurried to the house, then returned, a small, handsome, excited man nearing the half-century mark, scrupulously neat, skin shining from after-shave lotion, hair brushed and alive, body taut, belly flat.

"They'll cuss me out for not waiting for them, but I don't give much of a damn."

We gazed at each other in tremulous wonderment, confirming all remembrance, ratifying love, with quick, searching eyes. Faulkner's voice broke as he said my name. We kissed within the narrow confines of my car and he held my free hand as I drove, kissing the knuckles, bringing the palm to his mouth.

"I thought it was over," he muttered. "Done with."

"So did I."

"Lord, I've missed you, m' honey."

At the studio, he walked with me to the sound stage where my company was shooting. We found a dark place against a far wall. Workmen hammered away nearby. Make-up artists dabbed hastily at the faces of extras before a series of mirrors. We clung together. I wept for my pride, for all the molds into which I had been poured as a girl and for those from which I still could not break out. I thought of the lost days that could not be retrieved. My name was called from a distance. Faulkner blotted my tears with his handkerchief. We would see each other tonight. He had an appointment with an old friend who was in town, but he would cancel it. I was all that mattered to him in Hollywood.

And so we resumed, as close for the first few weeks as we had been at the beginning, resentful when night shooting preempted me or when Howard Hawks asked Bill to sit in on after-hours screenplay conferences. On weekends, brooking no interference from the studio, we drove to the beach for fried shrimp in paper cones, corn on the cob, hamburgers, and hot dogs; headed for Santa Barbara when I could obtain extra gasoline; spent time with Henriette, the Crowns, the Paganos, and other friends. Once we went to Sister Aimee Semple McPherson's Angelus Temple; Bill thought Southern evangelists and faith healers more honest. Musso's was hit by food shortages; I brought butter from my own refrigerator and we spread it sparingly on sourdough bread. The menu had become unreliable so the waiter would tell us what was left in the kitchen and we settled on the available. Faulkner laced my fingers in his and held my hand under the table. He was happy to be with me, but sick of Hollywood, screenplays, his paltry salary, the Warner Brothers contract that still had years to go. Southern California weather was too variable for him. He looked at the night sky and asked what kind of sky it was—stars paled out by city lights, sickly, puny!

The Big Sleep went before the cameras in November. Bill had written the screenplay with Leigh Brackett and Jules Furthman, and the studio hoped that it would ride the hard-boiled detective cycle with as much box-office appeal as *Farewell, My Lovely,* another of Raymond Chandler's mystery novels that had been filmed. Once more I was working with Howard Hawks. Bill's touches were recognizable in every scene. Only a Southerner could have created the millionaire who hired Philip Marlowe.

Bill came on the sound stage one morning to discuss story-line changes and a rearrangement of scenes with Hawks. When the meeting was over, he sought me out. It would be some time before the set was lighted and Betty Bacall was out of make-up.

"I've asked the studio for a leave of absence," he said in a tight voice. "I'm sure you're not surprised."

"No." He had been in a bad way for weeks, jumpy, morose, and at times peevish.

"There are worries back home that I need to settle my mind on." He sighed. "Most of all, I have to get back to my own writing. It's been too long."

"A new novel?"

"I'll never get it written in this town. Sometimes I think if I do one more treatment or screenplay, I'll lose whatever power I have as a writer."

"That mustn't happen, Bill."

"It could though."

"Then you're doing the right thing."

He looked at me in gratitude. "I'll never be happy away from you, Carpenter."

"And I'll never be happy with you away."

"The minute I get back to Oxford, I want to be near you again. A month later, I get so unsettled thinking of you, I don't sleep. Still and all, I have to go back."

In a few weeks he was gone. His letters were all I had of him and sometimes there were weeks without one. There were the usual complaints about Estelle. She was tippling; by nightfall, she was drunk. She had become slovenly. Would I go to see his mare for him? (I did.) Work was no longer palliative for me. The shocks of history unhinged me. Roosevelt died and I wept. That was a somber, gloomy day. Hitler was dead, a suicide, and Berlin fell to the Red Army. Germany surrendered and Hollywood Boulevard went wild.

Faulkner came back to Hollywood early that summer. He had been gone six months. For the first time, seeing him walk with that curious tilt of body, hearing the broadened drawl, it hit me that he possessed an acute and affecting sense of place, and that he changed as he moved into new ambiences. The variations in New York, where he quickened his pace and fell into a crisper speech pattern, were different from the alterations that came over him in Hollywood, where his posture was straighter, his dress less haphazard, even on the natty side at times. I could picture him after the first few days in Oxford taking on the gait of townspeople, slowing his speech, falling into vernacularisms, hanging up his city clothes for trousers and jacket that he would wear over and over.

Lying in Faulkner's arms, I thought of how the love-making would be with war wives whose young husbands would return to them now that peace had come to Europe, the bursting relief after the long continence, the miracle of shy response, the self-surprise of initiative and abandon.

"I didn't rightly know how you'd feel about me," he said, "staying away long as I have."

"I said I'd wait."

"Yes'm, I know."

"Was it the studio? Did they put pressure on you to come back?"

"No, honey love. I could have stayed on and handled the Warner lawyers. There's only one reason I'm here. You."

Everything, I promised myself, would be idyllic—until December, when he would again be drawn to Oxford, as if one cycle had ended and another had begun, and I would again, self-abnegating, make no objection. I could count on almost six months with him. The separation had imposed severity upon me, thinned the line of my mouth, dulled my eyes, but now I felt my youth coming back like a lost moon.

Faulkner was immediately put on the screenplay of *Stallion Road* with Stephen Longstreet. He worked diligently, sometimes inspiredly, but he was unable to summon the purpose that had carried him through in Hollywood in past years. He rarely smiled or chuckled. He was downcast. He hated the studio, the system that paired writers on a single project, even though Longstreet was his friend, the obligation to punch a time clock. Hollywood irked him more than ever. Only the Pacific when we drove along the coast highway held any beauty for him. In The Ward, his colleagues finished their screenplays and rewrites and moved on to Twentieth Century-Fox, MGM, Columbia, and Universal, but he was a fixture, he complained, like the dinky buildings on the lot. The contract to which he was tied and the pittance that he was earning as compared to other established screenwriters rankled.

I knew long before he told me that he was not going to stay. I would not have him until the end of the year. The polarities were unequal. The pull to Oxford and the Faulkner way of life was greater than to me. Everything at Rowan Oak, even the wife whose body he did not touch, whose weaknesses bound him to her, drew him away from me.

He finally found the courage to say to me that he was through with Hollywood, finished with screenwriting. He was walking out on the insulting Warner Brothers contract and to hell with the legal consequences of it. What's more, he was taking Jill's mare back to Mississippi with him in a trailer because damned if he'd let any Faulkner mare foal in Hollywood.

The anger came later. At my apartment one night just before he left, I turned an unloving face to him as he drew me close and undressed me. He had promised that when Jill was old enough—she was twelve now—he would move for a divorce. Once I had considered it. Now I would rather die than have Jill take the witness stand to choose between mother and father. I would not do that to her or any child. But Bill had forgotten his promise. I could not forgive him that. When he reached for me in the night, I pushed him away.

In a letter delivered to me in a studio transmittal envelope on Monday, he addressed me as "Honey Love" and asked to be forgiven for not having realized until the next morning that if I had wanted him to stay the night with me, I would have invited him. Newt House had informed him that he would be ready to leave for Oxford the following week with the colt.

"If you agree that this bloke in question really means better than he does, how's for seeing your face before I leave—looking different from what it did when you brought it into the kitchen and it said, 'Good morning, Bill.' "

He was forgiven. My face on our last night together was worshipful. The last thing he touched as he left me to meet the man who would pull the horse trailer was my outstretched hand.

Chapter 16

Wolfgang threw me a lifeline and I held to it with straw fingers, afraid of what would happen if I continued to shut myself from everyone but movie people, into whose shadowless compass I intruded each morning and from which I withdrew, worn and dispirited, when the day's filming was over. A woman who works behind the camera, even today, must have a strong personal life to counteract the mutative process that occurs when she is thrown with a company of men who are, with few exceptions, from producer and director to the man who sweeps the horse dung away on a Western, power-directed, paranoid, insecure, often sadistic, mulish, and coarse. It is not that these lonely women take on the masculine grain but that their womanliness is chipped away in the daily give-and-take with male co-workers whose hostility pours from them like sweat. Her voice unconsciously deepens. Her stride bespeaks efficiency and resolution. Outwardly, she becomes androgynous. The men with whom she works call her by her surname—Jones, Purcell, Lattimer. They tell dirty jokes, ignoring her presence. She has become invisible to them.

"We're both getting older," Wolfgang said gently. "I think we really do love each other. Shouldn't we have another try at it?"

I looked at him obliquely. Marriage? Was he saying that we should marry again? I knew that I was still concerned about him, that I admired and respected him for his bright and quick mind, his extravagant humor, and, above all, his great talent. I also realized that the years were slipping away. Many times, alone, I shuddered to think of the bleak stretch ahead, without love or companionship.

Unaccountably, I had developed a mistrust, almost a fear, of the men who had shown interest in me after Faulkner's flight from Hollywood. The thought of a love affair with anyone other than Bill, married or unmarried, was repellent. I needed love more than at any time in my adult life; only love could restore me, point my bones to heaven, but I did not dare look to strangers for it. Men of whom I knew nothing at all terrified me. I sensed threat and danger. The prefiguration in me of ancestral maiden ladies and mourning widows whispered to cloister myself in dark rooms.

"*Tierchen*," Wolfgang reminded me, "you haven't said anything."

"I know, Wolfi . . . I'm just thinking."

It was a possibility that had crossed my mind once or twice, then had been dismissed as offering no real solution for me. Now I was beginning to think that he might be right. I was thirty-eight; in two years I would be forty. We were bonded by the Nazi fire we had gone through, the poverty, the rejection. Even the violent outbursts, the words that once said we wished we had not said, the accusations, the little sins against each other, were enmeshing. I loved him in many ways. It had nothing to do with Faulkner, who would understand if I remarried Wolfgang. It would all be as it was years ago when Bill would come to New York and see me as a friend. The letters would continue to come, that was the main thing. I would always need and want the emotional connection.

Wolfgang and I were remarried in December, 1945, and honeymooned in Santa Barbara. On New Year's Eve, he left me alone in our hotel room and earned a fee of two hundred dollars playing a program of classical music at a party given by a wealthy couple at their San Ysidro ranch. (His patrons introduced him as their guest, a distinguished pianist, and "prevailed" upon him to give an after-dinner concert—an old

European trick of the wealthy that even Paderewski lent himself to in time of early need.)

Wolfgang had found a place for himself in Hollywood. Now he was in demand in music scoring sessions for motion pictures and often, when working at Warner Brothers, he would visit me on my sets. For a time he was under contract as pianist to Twentieth Century-Fox, where Alfred Newman was the conductor, and again to the Samuel Goldwyn Studios orchestra, also under Newman. One year he earned eighteen thousand dollars, a handsome income in that era. We bought a house on Kling Street, in North Hollywood, where, in a garage converted to a studio, he could practice and rehearse with chamber-music groups—trios, quartets, and quintets—and where his friends from the inner circle of professional musicians could gather to play and discuss new works of contemporary artists.

Hard times had taught my husband very little about money. It slid through his fingers as it had when he was a young man in Germany. There was no time when I could stop working; my earnings at the studio were needed for our community life and partly as a contribution to his concertizing, which seldom yielded a profit. He was a brilliant artist who needed to fulfill himself musically and his chances for recognition were far better now that the war was over. He would say, "Can we spend that kind of money, *Liebchen?*" and I would say, "We'll put off something else." Wolfgang was engaged to play a first performance in Los Angeles of a seldom-performed Mozart concerto with the Harold Byrns Chamber Orchestra at the Wilshire Ebell Theatre. Most of the paid rehearsal time was consumed with orchestral works, leaving only a brief period for Wolfgang to rehearse the concerto with the orchestra.

"The time's up," the steward said. "I'm sorry."

"But," Wolfgang protested, "I haven't even rehearsed the last movement with the musicians. How can I possibly play the concerto for a first performance here without a decent rehearsal?"

The steward raised her shoulders. "I'm very sorry, Mr.

Rebner. Those are union rules. We cannot continue the rehearsal unless we are sure the orchestra will be paid for the extra time."

Wolfgang flashed a look of anguish at me.

"You need a good rehearsal with them," I said firmly. "We'll pay."

Before concert time next evening, we had scraped together seven hundred dollars to compensate the musicians. It was worth every penny. Wolfgang performed with verve and passion. Albert Goldberg, of the Los Angeles *Times,* and other local music critics praised him. But we both knew that no concert artist of any stature had ever been launched in Southern California. Wolfgang needed New York, or Paris, London, Vienna, Berlin, when those great cities of Europe recovered from the war.

It was not the best of marriages; I could not, with my Southern high mettle, be a compliant *Frau* for more than a few minutes at a time, and he could not change his attitude toward women; but it was far from the worst. I was back in the world of music, the proud wife of a concert pianist; the applause and cheers of music lovers when Wolfgang returned to take his bows were my reward for what the marriage lacked. We entertained and were entertained. Childless ourselves, we spent hours with the Crowns and their two daughters; Joan, the youngest, had been born shortly before we had remarried.

I read everything that came my way about Faulkner—book reviews, interviews, evaluations of his body of work, squibs in *Time* magazine. When he wrote that MGM had purchased the movie rights to *Intruder in the Dust,* I rejoiced for him. It was the windfall for which he had been waiting.

In his letters, as before, Faulkner did not always remember or choose to remember that I was Wolfgang's wife. I hid from my husband's chance scrutiny a declaration of love written during the week in which MGM's screen version of his *Intruder in the Dust* was given its world premiere in Oxford. He wanted me to know that he dreamed of me often, even too often, but that now it was not so "grievesome."

". . . I know grief is the inevictable part of it, the thing that makes it cohere; that grief is the only thing you are capable of sustaining, keeping; that what is valuable is what you have lost, since then you never had the chance to wear out and so lose it shabbily, Darby and Joan to the contrary."

In that same letter, he recalled that a character had said in one of his books—I knew the quotation from memory—"Between grief and nothing, I will take grief."

Faulkner's reputation became outsize in the late 1940s, legend attaching itself to him like Spanish moss to Delta live oaks. People who were aware that I had once had a romantic liaison with a Southern writer (that short, glum, unfriendly fellow whose name meant nothing to them, non-readers all, at the time) now looked at me with awakened interest. I protested many times to those who now asked me about him that I had never thought of William Faulkner as a genius, but as a writer down on his luck most of the time, broke, debt-ridden, his books out of print. Actually, it was only when Bill mentioned the possibility of the Nobel Prize that the two figures—Faulkner, my gentle, earnest lover, and Faulkner, a titan of American literature—became a single entity in my mind, and I knew for a certainty that I had loved and been loved by a man for the ages.

Later he wrote that he did not want the Nobel Prize, considering it a gratuitous insult to the trade of letters, but that it was not a thing to refuse. Moreover, he preferred to be compartmentalized with Theodore Dreiser and Sherwood Anderson than with Sinclair Lewis and Pearl Buck, whom he dubbed Mrs. Chinahand Buck.

That letter is burned on my memory, for in it he recalled my hair with that little scrap of a white thing as he called it (the hair ribbon he had bought for me on Hollywood Boulevard), and my eyes that time in New Orleans, and jasmine blooms (the Miramar Hotel).

"This is a rotten letter," Faulkner closed, "but I never could write them. I never had but one thing to say, and three words did that. Goodnight, sweet love. Bill."

When the announcement was made late that year that

Faulkner had indeed been awarded the Nobel, Wolfgang and I were living under the same roof, but our marriage was a twisted wreckage. I sat alone by the radio and listened to the news programs in the hope of hearing Bill's voice, although I should have known he would resist giving a statement to anyone with a microphone in hand. What I wanted, in childish impatience with prohibitions that smothered small pleasures, was to call Faulkner long-distance and say, "Oh, Bill, I'm so glad, so proud," but I had never intruded into his life in Oxford. His friend Bezzerides could call, but I dared not. The lights would be blazing in the Faulkner household, I imagined, upstairs and down. Estelle would rush flutteringly to the telephone to take calls from her husband's publishers, friends and admirers. Bill would pretend to be calm, stoical, but the tobacco bowl would not remain unstuffed and unlit for long this night. The family would gather. There would be embraces and kisses. Jill would have young friends over. I often wondered whether she still called him Pappy.

When he returned from Sweden, Bill wrote that we must contrive to see each other. Did I realize how long it had been? Couldn't I find an assignment with a movie company that would be on location in the South so that we could meet somewhere for a few days? He supposed there was work for him in Hollywood if he wanted it, but he didn't; even if he were brought back, it would be as a Warner Brothers serf, lashed to that old miserable contract. I answered that not only did I not know of a Dixie-bound movie production, but that of late, with fewer pictures being made, I found myself out of work a good part of the time. Then he would have to come to me, he answered. I did not believe that he would, but suddenly a flurry of short notes began to arrive. Howard Hawks wanted him to do a new screenplay. Now there was a new agent representing him. Warner Brothers just might scrap the contract. His agent was powerful, the sort of man who, with one word, could accomplish more than a battery of lawyers. I was to be sure to let him know my right address (at one point I had fled the Kling Street house and found refuge with Henriette for six weeks) in the event that he had to fly to Hollywood on short notice.

A note reached me two days before he arrived:

"Coming out Monday 9:40 P.M. to do a job for Hawks. Will you leave telephone no. or address at Charles Feldman's Agency for me? Bill."

He called me from the airport.

"Meta. This is Bill." A slight pause and, as if to reassure me, "Bill Faulkner."

"Bill. Bill. Really?"

"Yes, dear love—my dear, dear love."

"Oh, Bill, it's really you!"

"Can I see you tonight?"

"Yes. Oh, yes. Of course. Where?"

"The Feldman Agency booked me at the Beverly-Carlton out on Olympic. When I check in and freshen up, I'll call and maybe you'll drive over. All right?"

He looked like the photographs that had been taken in Sweden—august, bonier and more severe of mien, somewhat professorial—but layers under, the face of the man I had loved broke through in the set of his mouth, the crinkling of his eyes. He was five years older than when he had last made love to me, a man in his mid-fifties, and now there was no longer the unbridled passion that I remembered from the years before, but a grave and sweet ardor, and afterward an unwillingness through the night to let me move out of his arms for even a moment.

"Why did we let it happen?" he asked. "I, more than you. This long, agonizing time away from each other. Foolish. Senseless waste. No warrant to it."

In earlier years, Faulkner had seemed to take pleasure in talking to me unrestrainedly about Jill, almost as if I were the one person to whom he could comfortably convey his almost excessive adoration without worrying that it would reveal him as a manifest sentimentalist. There would be a fund of stories about her that he had saved up for me, recollections of small happenings that had touched him, recitations of blurted-out wisdom, accounts of enchanting hours alone with her. Now she was almost eighteen, a young woman, closer to her mother than to him, and he hardly spoke of her. He did, however, make a point of correcting a criticism of Estelle that he remembered having expressed in a letter.

"I've been hard on her in many ways," he said, "some of them, I now realize, without justification."

"Her drinking?" I guessed.

"No'm. That still goes on. But for a time there, I was upset by her slovenliness. I thought her careless about her person, and I rebuked her many a time for dust on the furniture and the general untidiness of the house." He threw away a kitchen match, deciding not to light his pipe. "Now I discover that she was afflicted all the time with cataracts. Her vision has been badly affected and she doesn't see properly."

While I dressed to leave, he opened his suitcase and brought out a copy of a slim, just-published volume, *Notes on a Horsethief,* pre-signed in the front. I watched him as he inscribed the last page, "This is for my beloved," and signed his name once more.

Faulkner was paid a handsome two thousand dollars a week at Twentieth Century-Fox, a sum he should have drawn all along at Warner Brothers, for his work on *The Left Hand of God.* He did not share Hawks' belief in the property as the basis for a successful motion picture, but he said nothing. It was a short assignment for Bill; in a month or so he had completed the screenplay. Until he left for Oxford, we were together almost every night and every weekend. I had learned the value of the smallest moment with him.

"We'll have to see each other again before the year's up," Bill said when his flight was called at the airport. "Promise me."

"I promise."

"No more letting the years go by, m' honey."

"No, Bill. No more."

"Maybe late summer?"

He was gone, hurrying, clutching his leather portfolio in which there was a copy of the script. Now I would put some order into my life again. Bill had given me new direction and purpose. Wolfgang moved out of the Kling Street house with Perky, and Auntie came to live with me. Almost as soon as she arrived, there was a letter raising my hopes that Bill would be returning sooner than either of us expected. Jerry Wald had suggested a week's discussion on a screenwriting deal, and if it jelled, he would see me before he was due to fly to Paris for what he termed "a French govt. literary jubilee." Meanwhile, he was busy farming, training a colt and doing some writing.

The Wald project failed to materialize. For a long time, there was no word from Faulkner, and when I finally wrote, complaining that I had not heard from him since his European trip, he gave me reason to believe, in an immediate response, that I would see him before the year was out. There was work to be done for Howard Hawks on *The Left Hand of God*. His trayful of bangles, he added, now held tokens from "the newspapermen's guild" (Bill's all-lower-case title for the organization), Book of the Year, the Verdun medal, and the degree of Officier in France's Legion of Honor. He also had a London suit of gray flannel. *Requiem for a Nun*, which he had first written as a play, was now a completed novel.

Although Faulkner rarely discussed his books with me, he wrote lengthy letters about the play. It was the only reason he could not come out to Hollywood and spend two or three days ("nights in bed," he parenthesized it). If the play was not well along in rehearsal soon, it would miss the 1951 season. His weekly royalty check could be as much as two thousand dollars.

Requiem for a Nun, more than any novel-in-progress that I had known about, absorbed him completely. For all his struggles to write a well-made play with theatrical thrust and power, it was one of his failures, and the final setbacks to production depressed him.

I sued for divorce the next year and Wolfgang did not oppose the action. He knew as well as I the futility of trying to build again on the junkyard remains of our second marriage.

"Now that you've finally done it," Aunt Ione said, "it's time you let yourself meet other men and marry again. You're still young and, if anything, you're as pretty as you ever were."

"I don't think I ever want to marry again, Auntie."

"You'll wait around for Mr. Faulkner to come back?"

"Well, he stands for everything I've ever wanted in a man."

"And you'd settle for a month this year, a few weeks next year?"

"Yes." I nodded. "I think so."

"Meta, that's very little for the rest of your life."

"Auntie dear, I don't know anymore what's a little or what's a lot."

Disappointed that the year had passed without a meeting and fearful that another great slab of time would go by, Faulkner began to press for a holiday together. The first letter urging a rendezvous came the first of the year. Could we meet somewhere after the first of February—if not Los Angeles, then Memphis or El Paso or any city on the airline route? He would send me the money, of course.

"You are beautiful," he wrote. "I want to sleep with you. I didn't sign your book. I was waiting to be with you to sign it."

Our problem was one of timing. When I was finished with a movie that had tied me up for months, Faulkner was either unable to leave Oxford for unexplained reasons or he was again on his way to Europe. Once I worked out a complicated plan that would take me from a Mexican location to New Orleans for a weekend, but when I joyfully wrote Bill that it was arranged, he replied that he couldn't leave Oxford at that particular time. I didn't realize until a letter from him that summer that in the spring, leading a colt on a rope while riding "her mamma," he had been pulled from the mare's back onto the ground. The result was a painful back condition that had finally been alleviated by a Swedish masseur in Oslo. There being a danger that the vertebra would pop out of place again, he was forbidden to ride horses or lift anything. The difficulty was that he had trouble remembering the prohibitions in time.

I had never known Faulkner to wear jewelry, but on a visit to my parents in Arizona, I came across a beautifully wrought turquoise ring in a strong, masculine setting, made by a Zuni silversmith; the stone was sky blue with a striking matrix. I had his locket, but there was nothing of mine that he had (the napkin with the maiden's imprint was in another lifetime) except my photographs and letters (if he had kept them). Suddenly I wanted him to have that ring—let him explain it to Estelle as he would—and to wear it every day. When he acknowledged that yes, he wanted it, and later informed me that he would not be in Hollywood to accept it from me as he had hoped (*The Left Hand of God* had vanished from Howard Hawks' slate and would be directed by Edward Dmytryk with Humphrey Bogart and Gene Tierney), I sent the ring to him. Bill wrote he would wear it, even though he would have to lie about where it came from. I was proud. It would be a tangible reminder to him of my love and devotion.

In two letters that followed, Faulkner again recounted the details of his accident and his relief at the magical hands of the Swedish masseur, the likes of whom did not exist in Oxford. I had never known him to repeat himself in letters or, for that matter, to tell the same story twice or make the same comment; the calculator built into his mind kept accurate record of every line he wrote and every thought he articulated. The lapse, along with his complaint that he was nervous and depressed, unable to work, alarmed me.

"I wish," he made it known in that tiny, oblique handwriting, "I could spend about two weeks with you, lying on my face with the sun on my back. That would do more good than anything."

It was not until the next year that my fears for the clarity of his mind proved to be well-grounded. Faulkner wrote that he had had three spells of what he termed "almost amnesia," causing him to say things twice, as he had to me, and not to remember things. He would know this week if he had sustained a skull injury and a blood clot not yet absorbed in his fall from the horse.

Again he spoke of wanting to come out, but now matters were reversed; he seemed to be able to earn money only in New York.

"I want to see you," he wrote, and I could almost hear him saying it with that edge of firm intention in his Southern voice. "I have not forgotten any of it, never will, never."

I was to write him, he informed me, care of Saxe Commins at Random House.

Although I should have anticipated it—he had been moody and without his natural verve for months—Wolfgang's quiet announcement over the telephone that he was returning to Germany for good staggered me.

"There's nothing here for me anymore," he said. "Conditions in my field are better in Germany, I hear. At least the Rebner name is still known and may help to open doors for me."

"How long has it been since we were in Frankfurt together?" I asked.

"About fifteen years, *Tierchen*. How time has slipped by. It's almost unbelievable."

He came to dinner at the house we had shared for so long. The dogs scampered about. I looked at my ex-husband's lean face from which all the certitudes and the hubris of youth had been drawn, glanced at his right arm afflicted for some years with a nervous condition or neuritis, and I knew that he had summoned whatever was left of his battered ambition for a final stake on the eminence that had evaded him. There would be one go at it and no more; he had lost the passion and the strength for lunges and tilts and feints. I listened to his plans, detailed with forced cheerfulness. He would stop in New York, where some of his compositions were to be played at a Modern Composers' Forum, and he would see some agents and managers. Didn't I agree that that was a sensible thing to do? Oh, and by the way, would I give him Bill Faulkner's address in New York?

He wouldn't let himself be talked into staying in this country. Too many younger artists against whom he would have to pit his talents, all of them children when he and I had lived over Horn & Hardart's and he had split the skin of his knuckles on doors that failed to open. No, his best chance was in Germany. Concert halls were reopening. Chamber music always had an audience. Also, he was now making a serious effort in the field of composing. What, I thought to myself, if he is too old now even for the country of his birth? What if he doesn't make it this last time in any field of endeavor? What will it do to him? In Hollywood, he could tell himself that he was a displaced artist. How would he find support in Germany and from whom?

"I'm taking Perkchen with me," Wolfi said.

"Of course you are. She'd die without you."

"She's my only perquisite." He took my hand and held it to his cheek. "I'll write to you. It's odd, isn't it, that twice we could not find our way together, yet you are closer to me than my next of kin." His eyes became grave and concerned. "What are you going to do with your life?"

"My life?"

"You seem to have retreated from it. Except for Bill, you have no love, no one I know of."

"No. No one at all."

"And you'll go on this way?"

"I haven't made any vows."

"I feel . . ." He opened his arms in a gesture of compassion and hopelessness.

"Bill will be back," I said with confidence. "My life won't be empty."

The day Wolfgang was to leave Hollywood, I called him from the studio.

"If you see Bill in New York, don't say anything to make him feel guilty about me," I begged. *"Bitte,* Wolfichen."

He promised.

325

Bill's letters were piercingly sad, full of his own rue. E. (Estelle) had hemorrhaged and he had had to rush back to Oxford with Jill. After nine transfusions and two weeks of hospitalization, she was improved enough to be taken to Memphis for an examination. The doctor found that Estelle's liver was in bad shape from drinking and might have refused the blood load, causing the esophagus to explode.

He was adapting one of his books into a movie script for Julie Harris and he had seen Wolfi the past month.

"Change in people," he deplored, "saddest of all, division, separation, all left is the remembering, the dream, until you almost believe that anything beautiful is nothing else but dream."

I had worked continuously at Warner Brothers through the 1940's, but there had never been a contract guaranteeing steady employment. Now movie production was at a low ebb and the day of going from one picture to another for even the most creative script supervisor was over. That summer I had no assignment at all and I was compelled to draw on my savings, hoping to be called back to the studio before the balance was at zero. Overnight the film that I had been promised was postponed indefinitely. For the first time in years, I was flat broke.

Early in our romance, when we were both abjectly poor, Bill, over my protests, had taken thirty dollars out of two of his paychecks so that I might have a Catalina vacation.

"I want you to have everything," he had written in a note in which the first fifteen dollars was enclosed. "I wish it were my privilege and in my power to give it to you."

It was the only time in our relationship that he had offered money to me and that I had accepted it. Now I wrote to Faulkner asking for a loan until the next picture—if he could spare it.

His answer was immediate. How much did I want? The hundred and fifty dollars that I figured would keep me afloat was dispatched through Western Union and I was able to breathe again. When I returned to work, I sent Faulkner a check for seventy-five dollars, promising the balance with my next pay check. I had heard at the studio that Howard Hawks wanted him for a multimillion-dollar spectacle. Did that mean we would be seeing each other soon, perhaps working together?

He answered that the picture, *The Land of the Pharaohs,* was to be made in Europe, not Hollywood, and that he would be abroad on it from December until March.

"Am just finishing what I think is the best work of my life and maybe of my time, a book, novel, fable. Here is your check. [He had torn it into pieces.] You can't possibly owe me anything like money. I remember too much."

As a child, I had seen a movie of which I recall only the desperate search for each other through the streets of New York of two lovers who became separated upon arriving in the city. Faulkner rarely wrote without mentioning the possibility that he might be brought to the West Coast or urging me to meet him if ever my work brought me eastward.

But life conspired against us, shuffled us about. When I went to Europe on a film, stopping in Frankfurt to sign documents that returned Grossmutter's mansion and property to Wolfgang and his brothers, Bill had already completed work on *The Land of the Pharaohs* and was back in Oxford. He was in South America when I was able to spend a weekend in Memphis. When I was briefly in New Orleans on a film starring Teresa Wright and Joseph Cotten, Bill was appearing before the Delta Council in Cleveland, Mississippi, along with Governor James F. Byrnes of South Carolina. One morning, I opened the New Orleans *Item* to find my photograph on the front page with the two Hollywood stars, and Bill's likeness with an excerpt from his speech on the reverse side:

"We have lost that one thing, lacking which, freedom and liberty and independence cannot even exist. That thing is the responsibility, not only the desire and the will to be responsible, but the remembrance from the old fathers of the need to be responsible."

327

The company returned to Hollywood before Bill could join me.

It was 1955 and we were still turning corners and missing each other in a movie script of our own. Faulkner wrote matter-of-factly that he had accepted an invitation from the State Department to visit Japan. The irony of it was not lost on me. His country had refused to give him an officer's commission in World War II and Washington had scornfully rejected his plea to assign him a desk job; now he was one of America's most illustrious envoys to the world. Japan! He would fly from Los Angeles to San Francisco! At last we would see each other again! A night together—I would settle for that! My banners were hurled down by Bill's next letter, in which he informed me that he did not think he would be allowed to stop in Los Angeles. Moreover the State Department, which was paying him a salary and expenses, was thinking of sending him somewhere else after his three weeks in Japan; he didn't know for certain, but it might be India or the Middle East, and after that he might have some choice in where he was to go.

After three bad years, Bill noted, he was having a good crop year. He was training another filly, but his back didn't allow him to do much of it at a time. In August, when it was published, he would send me a copy of his new book of hunting stories.

There was a reference to Estelle:

"Just took E. for her semiannual boiling out at a drying joint Sunday. She says she is going to try Alcoholics Anonymous. Maybe she will; she has used up everything else, from Christian Science up and down."

One New Year's Eve, alone with Chloe, lifting a glass of champagne to the television coverage of Times Square, cheering crowds and revelers wearing paper hats, I suddenly knew, as though the rest of my life had been laid out for me and I was seeing it from a great height, that Bill and I would never meet again. The waiting would go on until one of us died. His letters left no doubt that he was still a passionate man, but he was past the time of the blood's violent flood, the terrible hormonal ambush of the groin. It was not Bowen as much as memory, I guessed, that tormented him in the still hours of the night. Men of Faulkner's age did not go tearing around the country to snatch whatever time allowed of wintry love. Face it, he was not going to rearrange his comfortable, stainless life; he had no real inclination to chop and hack away at the obstacles that kept us apart. I swallowed the last of the champagne. There would be letters. I could not count on anything else.

The next morning, I looked out of the window and there were many small, dark, hopping birds in the yard. The leaves of Hollywood trees had dropped limply to the ground. The Southern California sun shone like a massive movie studio arc light, but if I looked closely, I told myself, I would see the hoarfrost that killed everything.

I knew that morning that I must get out of Hollywood. I asked for distant locations, where the heat was pure African and the cold drove into one like spikes. Hardships kept me from remembering that I had no husband, no children, no home that meant anything. Great expanses of desert and walls of craggy rock shut out memories of Bill, but on the streets and sound stages from which I had fled, I encountered him everywhere, an alien ghost trapped in the confines of a studio that he hated. His letters reached me wherever I was sent and I read them in open fields, unshaded and boiling hot, and on mountaintops, shivering in icy winds.

Once he wrote:

Dear Meta: As soon as I touched that envelope, I knew who it was from. I dreamed about you that night and had to get up and change pajamas.

The setting for Bill had changed. So had his lifestyle. I found it almost impossible to visualize the master of Rowan Oak against the background of Charlottesville, Virginia.

Neither did I like to think of him fox hunting on a hunter whose very size, strength and fearlessness, as he described them, made me worry for his safety. Could I send him a snapshot? Under his signature, he wrote: "Somehow it was like it was only yesterday."

On location in Connecticut, I debated whether to let Bill know that I was on the East Coast. How many times before had I been only a few hours away from him and he had written that he was unable to leave Oxford—no explanation, no anger? Why hadn't he come to me? What held him back? I remember thinking, more than once, that perhaps he was afraid of where his emotions at that time of his life might lead him. Jill was married. Estelle was Estelle, with only familiarity's hold on him. Other men at his age had left wives of many years in a last breakout of passion for another woman. Might not Faulkner be tempted to throw over everything else, face scandal, criticism, in order to live with me? I wrote him after a few days and told him I could meet him in New York; even as I posted the letter, I knew he would not come.

He had retired from literature, he answered, and although it was impossible for him to come East, perhaps he could reestablish contacts and come to California. Horses and bird shooting and fox hunting were his life now; he had broken two ribs and one collarbone, but "nothing shows with my shirt on. . . . Love to Sally and John and to you, dear love."

The sun broke through the clouds early on the morning of Friday, July 6, 1962, in Jackson Hole, Wyoming, where I was working on *Spencer's Mountain,* enabling Delmer Daves to get his first shot of the day before nine o'clock. I was out early, about eight, I think, and lined up with other crew members at the catering truck for coffee and Danish breakfast rolls. Harry Mines, the unit publicist, approached me.

"Meta," he said, no inkling of what his words would do to me, "do you know that William Faulkner died last night?"

I let the paper cup of coffee drop from my hand and looked at him in total disbelief.

"It's over the wires and in all the papers," Harry said, puzzled by my stricken face.

I turned and moved quickly away. The single thought in my mind was that I must not be near people. I couldn't speak. I couldn't answer the questions that would be asked of me. I walked deep into the woods that made a dense green wall at the clearing where we were shooting and tried to control the sobs that shook my body.

Faulkner was not my husband, but as I sank under the giant trees, I felt that I was his widow, bereft, cut off, struck down, I who had believed for almost thirty years that with Faulkner in the world, nothing would hurt or harm me, and that I would have the courage to face anything and that he would always be proud of me for it. I will never know how, an hour later, I was able to make my appearance on the set and continue with the day's work. At the end of the day, when my chair was folded, I walked with Delmer Daves back to the car that would take us to Jackson Hole. As I was going to my room in the motel where we were all staying, I encountered Hayden Rorke, who had a role in *Spencer's Mountain* and had been a close friend since *This Is the Army*. He stared at me incredulously. Weeks later, he told me that it was because I seemed almost an old woman under my shielding sunbonnet.

A telegram from Henriette was in my box. "In his own words: 'The artist is of no importance. Only what he creates is important, since there is nothing new to be said.' Comfort of a sort, at least. Have sent a letter to your home. Will try to contact you Wednesday before going away until following Monday. Love. Henriette."

When I dazedly entered my room, I saw the copy I had brought to location of Bill's last book, *The Reivers*, the marker at Chapter IX. I held it in my hands, close to my heart, as though it possessed substance from him that would support me, help me to understand what had happened. Unable to eat after our nightly production meeting, I went to the motel bar for a strong drink of whiskey. Sleep was torturous. Over and over, I awakened to a feeling of emptiness, desolation, and wrenching loss that was not to leave me for years.

I determined not to allow myself to become one of those "tetched ladies," as we called them in Memphis, those Miss Emilys, who are unable to cease mourning for the departed ones and who in their unending grief whiten, lose flesh, and retreat from life. There was a small sheaf of favorite love letters that I had carried with me to location over the years; at night, when loneliness came at me, I had read them over and over. Now I tied them with a string and placed them in a trunk with other letters, the poems, the photographs, the clippings, the magazines. They would yellow with age, but I could not keep them at hand; they drew me into the past that I had crossed and recrossed for far too long.

When I had worked at Warner Brothers on the screen version of William Inge's *The Dark at the Top of the Stairs,* I had become friendly with Harriet Frank and her husband, Irving Ravetch, the co-writers of the screenplay. The Ravetches had previously written the script of *The Sound and the Fury* and *Sanctuary* (the second version), and their belief in Faulkner as one of the great writers of our time was deeply affecting. During filming, my beloved Aunt Ione died. Harriet, who knew of my friendship with Faulkner, went out of her way to comfort me. Sooner or later, she and Irving would adapt another Faulkner novel to the screen and I would work with them again during filming.

Eight years later, as good as their word, they recommended me through the offices of the production manager of the film, and I was assigned as script supervisor on *The Reivers.* By that time, I had begun my association with Mike Nichols on *Who's Afraid of Virginia Woolf?* and *The Graduate,* and had agreed to do *Catch-22.* The producers knew of the commitment, but still permitted me to work through half of the filming of *The Reivers.* It would be photographed in Greenwood and Carrollton, Mississippi, with Mark Rydell directing. Steve McQueen would star as Boon Hogganbeck; Rupert Crosse, who was later to die tragically, would play

Ned McCaslin; and the cast included Will Geer, Sharon Farrell, and Diane Ladd. The Ravetches were associate producers.

I stepped out of the chartered plane onto Faulkner country —his Jefferson, his Yoknapatawpha County—and walked with my head tilted down to see the look of that earth with its scattering of rock and overlay of light dust and stubborn weeds. Pieces of memory were breaking off, swimming around in my head like flecks in the *Goldwasser* that Grossmutter set on the table in Frankfurt. The sun was warm on the back of my neck. I smiled at Harriet Frank, who had directed a look of sisterly concern my way.

The land pulled at me, for it was earth of which I was a part. Through the window of the car speeding to the production headquarters, I looked in wonder at the familiar live oaks and magnolias and the old barns, their sides painted with advertisements for snuff and chewing tobacco and fertilizer. Everywhere there were emblems of long-staple cotton production. I was back home. The rain a few days later was one-hundred-proof Mississippi rain as I remembered it.

On my final Sunday in Mississippi, I made the journey for which I had come South. The unit still man, Mel Traxel, a brilliant photographer with whom I had worked on *Who's Afraid of Virginia Woolf?* and many other pictures, rented a car and together we drove over rich farmland, past great cotton plantations, to Oxford. My heart raced as we approached the modest outskirts of the town. I had come here once before when I was thirteen, tremulous, all young gooseflesh, to visit with my cousin and to attend the Grand Ball at Eastertime at "Ole Miss," my first big, formal party. Oxford had seemed large and overpowering to a child from Tunica, the courthouse mysterious and forbidding. The square that now looked smaller than the small-town set on the Warner Brothers backlot had seemed alive with commerce then. Mel took photographs of the statue of the Confederate soldier, indifferent to us, still keeping his vigil.

I asked directions to the cemetery from a courteous filling-station attendant.

"And could you tell me how to get to the house of my cousin Lottie Vernon White?"

The red-faced man brushed a finger against his nose vigorously. "Miss Lottie's dead," he said. "She died 'bout five years ago, I reckon. You'll find her buried in the older part of the cemetery."

Estelle Faulkner was in Charlottesville; there was no possibility that I would chance on her. Mel and I found William Faulkner's grave at the back part of the cemetery on a small, rolling hill. It was more grandiose than seemed right for Bill, with an elaborate gravestone set inside an area lined in granite. Mel started taking photographs as we had planned. I could hear the clicking of his camera through the roaring in my mind. Then he moved away and left me in solitude.

Late-afternoon sunlight drifted through the leaves of great-trunked guardian trees, throwing soft shadows over the gravestone. The past, so far back in the thicket of time, yet so immediate to me, bubbled gently from the wells of memory. Ghosts of old pain, of forgotten rancor and complaint, stirred briefly, then settled into oblivion. It had all been as it was meant to have been. It had gone the only way it could have gone, like a river confined to its channel. I had been transfigured by his love. Life had singled me out. I was blessed.

For years I had not been fully able to accept the fact that Bill was no longer alive. I would catch myself shuffling through letters for that envelope with his curious scrawl. Turning the corner to my apartment, I sometimes thought I saw him sitting on my steps. Showering, climbing a hill, reading a book, dozing in a chair at night, I would hear his voice calling "Meta," and my skin would jump. Now all that was over. After all these years, I had finally buried my dead. I was released. I could embrace and savor life again; find love once more. My friends and Bill's would die one by one—Henriette, Sally, John, Betty—and our puppy would expire of old age, but I had drawn life from Faulkner's grave and I would live and he would live, a million, shifting images of him, within me.